The Phenomenology of Religious Life

Studies in Continental Thought

Martin Heidegger

The Phenomenology of Religious Life

1. INTRODUCTION TO THE PHENOMENOLOGY OF RELIGION

2. AUGUSTINE AND NEO-PLATONISM

3. THE PHILOSOPHICAL FOUNDATIONS OF MEDIEVAL MYSTICISM

Translated by
Matthias Fritsch
and
Jennifer Anna Gosetti-Ferencei

Indiana University Press
Bloomington and Indianapolis

7/15/10
WW
#24.95

Publication of this book is made possible in part with the assistance of a Challenge Grant from the National Endowment for the Humanities, a federal agency that supports research, education, and public programming in the humanities.

This book is a publication of

Indiana University Press
601 North Morton Street
Bloomington, Indiana 47404-3797 USA

www.iupress.indiana.edu

Telephone orders 800-842-6796
Fax orders 812-855-7931
Orders by e-mail iuporder@indiana.edu

Published in German as Martin Heidegger, *Gesamtausgabe,* volume 60: *Phänomenologie des religiösen Lebens,* edited by Matthias Jung, Thomas Regehly, and Claudius Strube

First paperback edition 2010 by Indiana University Press
© 1995 by Vittorio Klostermann, Frankfurt am Main
© 2004 by Indiana University Press
All rights reserved

♾ The paper used in this publication meets the minimum requirements of the American National Standard for Information Sciences—Permanence of Paper for Printed Library Materials, ANSI Z39.48-1992.

Manufactured in the United States of America

The Library of Congress has cataloged the hardcover edition as follows:

Heidegger, Martin, 1889–1976.
[Phänomenologie des religiösen Lebens. English]
The phenomenology of religious life / Martin Heidegger ; translated by Matthias Fritsch and Jennifer Anna Gosetti-Ferencei.
p. cm. — (Studies in Continental thought)
ISBN 0-253-34248-1 (cloth : alk. paper)
1. Religion—Philosophy. 2. Phenomenology. I. Title. II. Series.
B3279.H46 2004
200—dc22
2003015581

ISBN 978-0-253-34248-5 (cl.)
ISBN 978-0-253-22189-6 (pbk.)

3 4 5 6   15 14 13 12 11 10

Contents

INTRODUCTION TO THE PHENOMENOLOGY OF RELIGION
Winter Semester 1920–21

PART ONE
Methodological Introduction
Philosophy, Factual Life Experience,
and the Phenomenology of Religion

Chapter One
The Formation of Philosophical Concepts and Factual Life Experience

Chapter Two
Current Tendencies of the Philosophy of Religion

Chapter Three
The Phenomenon of the Historical

Chapter Four
Formalization and Formal Indication

PART TWO
Phenomenological Explication of
Concrete Religious Phenomena in
Connection with the Letters of Paul

Chapter One
Phenomenological Interpretation of the Letters to the Galatians

Chapter Two
Task and Object of the Philosophy of Religion

Chapter Three
Phenomenological Explication of the First Letter to the Thessalonians

AUGUSTINE AND NEO-PLATONISM
Summer Semester 1921

INTRODUCTORY PART
Interpretations of Augustine

MAIN PART
Phenomenological Interpretation of *Confessions;* Book X

APPENDIX I

Notes and Sketches for the Lecture Course

APPENDIX II

Supplements from the Notes of Oskar Becker

THE PHILOSOPHICAL FOUNDATIONS OF MEDIEVAL MYSTICISM

[Outlines and Sketches for a Lecture, Not Held, 1918–1919]

***

Translators' Foreword

These lecture courses present particular difficulties for the translators, given that they were compiled from Heidegger's notes and the notes of students in his lecture courses, rather than from material Heidegger prepared for publication. Details on the text sources and compilation are provided in the editors' afterwords, included at the end of this volume. When the abbreviated or truncated character of the notes, particularly in the appendices, was retained by the editors of the German edition, we, too, have retained this insofar as it was still possible to provide a sensible and readable translation into English.

We have also endeavored to maintain, whenever possible, consistency regarding our translation of terms from the several lecture courses and appendices; we have provided for the reader a glossary which will indicate the terms we have employed to render the more or less technical terms of Heidegger's German. Some German terms (such as "*Zusammenhang*"), however, cannot be reliably translated by a single English word, and the glossary will also help to guide the reader here. In a few cases, additional words have been inserted in brackets in order to render a grammatically acceptable English translation. (Unfortunately, these will not always be distinguishable from the editors' insertions.) Occasionally, Heidegger capitalizes important terms like "How" and "When," in effect rendering them nouns, which in German would then be capitalized; but he does not always do so. We have capitalized the terms when it was so in the German text; otherwise, we have put them into single quotation marks or, when appropriate, italics.

The Greek terms in the volume have, as in the German, been left without transliteration. Heidegger seems to have assumed that his audience knew Latin (in the second lecture on Augustine and Neo-Platonism there is much), but not Greek. Thus, while he rarely gives translations of the Latin, in many cases he paraphrases the Greek terms or sentences. However, he does not always do so. Wherever he does not do so, we have provided English translations on the basis of the New Revised Standard Version of the New Testament. In cases where Heidegger does not give a translation and the Greek terms are not clearly referenced to the Bible, we have supplied our own translation, often on the basis of the standard Liddell and Scott dictionary.

Such translation problems are a bit more convoluted in the Latin that appears in the second lecture course, largely because we could not rely upon existing English translations of Augustine in most cases. As with St. Paul's Greek, the translators faced the difficulty of remaining faithful to Augustine's as well as to Heidegger's text in translating the frequent Augustine passages.

However, some of the Augustine texts Heidegger used, to our knowledge, have never been translated into English at all. In addition, at times Heidegger himself composed (without translating) Latin sentences or sentence fragments by taking his starting point from Augustine's text. Furthermore, as indicated, Heidegger rarely translated Augustine's Latin, and when he did, these translations aim at integration into Heidegger's close interpretation of particular phenomena and thus do not require the terminological consistency of full, existing translations of the text. Despite the need to translate all the Latin afresh, in the case of Augustine's *Confessions*, H. Chadwick's recent translation (Oxford: Oxford University Press, 1998) and W. Watt's older translation (Loeb Classical Library, Harvard University Press, 1912) have been consulted occasionally.

With regard to the translations, we decided not to use three different kinds of parentheses, but to restrict ourselves to two. As Heidegger rarely translates Augustine's Latin except for parenthetical explanations or interpretations, particular care is required in reading the symbols. All round brackets of the German original remain round brackets here. Within Latin and Greek citations, round brackets indicate Heidegger's explanatory or interpretive inserts. Latin and Greek citations that Heidegger did not translate at all are followed by our translation in square brackets. Within these, round brackets repeat Heidegger's inserts in the citations. In rare cases, round brackets in translations of citations indicate inserts we regarded as necessary for rendering the apparently intended meaning. Whenever we encountered particular translation difficulties or the special significance of words or phrases, we gave the German original in square brackets. As noted, some square brackets have also been used by the editors of the German manuscripts, largely to indicate undeciphered passages in the original manuscript or to complete a sentence (cf. editors' afterwords).

Some of our choices of terms ("foreconception" for the German "*Vorgriff*," for example, or our use of "Dasein") reflect an attempt to remain within the range of terms used by translators into English of other works of Heidegger from this period. In choosing English words for some of Heidegger's translations from the Latin, we consulted translations of later works by Heidegger in which the same German originals have been used. For instance, we decided to translate Heidegger's "*Verfall*," "*Abfall*," and their derivatives—themselves based, as these lecture courses make clear, on Augustine's "*cadere*"—as "falling." At times, however, closeness in meaning may be misleading in regard to the German words used in the original. While Augustine's "*cura*" may have inspired the notion of "care" ("*Sorge*") in *Being and Time,* Heidegger translates "*cura*" here as "*Bekümmerung,*" which we render as "concern."

We would like to thank Professor John D. Caputo for his comments on the translation and for serving as a reader. The translators would also like to thank

Nicholas Robertson and Alex Livingston for assistance in preparing the copy of the manuscript. The translators are grateful to Professor Angela Pitts of Mary Washington College for checking translations from the Latin and Greek copy.

Matthias Fritsch
Jennifer Anna Gosetti-Ferencei
Berlin and Essen, June 2002

INTRODUCTION TO THE PHENOMENOLOGY OF RELIGION

Winter Semester 1920–21

PART ONE

Methodological Introduction
Philosophy, Factical Life Experience,
and the Phenomenology of Religion

Chapter One

The Formation of Philosophical Concepts
and Factical Life Experience

The Peculiarity of Philosophical Concepts

It is necessary to determine the meaning of words of the lecture's announcement preliminarily. This necessity is grounded in the peculiarity of philosophical concepts. In the specific scientific disciplines, concepts are determined through their integration into a material complex; and the more familiar this context is, the more exactly its concepts can be fixed. Philosophical concepts, on the contrary, are vacillating, vague, manifold, and fluctuating, as is shown in the alteration of philosophical standpoints. This uncertainty of philosophical concepts is not, however, exclusively founded upon this alteration of standpoints. It belongs, rather, to the sense of philosophical concepts themselves that they always remain uncertain. The possibility of access to philosophical concepts is fundamentally different from the possibility of access to scientific concepts. Philosophy does not have at its disposal an objectively and thoroughly formed material context into which concepts can be integrated in order to receive their determination. There is thus a difference in principle between science and philosophy. This provisional thesis will prove itself in the course of these observations. (It is due to the necessity of linguistic formulation alone that this is a thesis, a proposition, at all.)

We can, however, take a more efficient route in order to realize that a preliminary understanding of the title's concepts is necessary. We speak of philosophical and scientific "concepts," of "introductions" to the sciences and to phenomenology. This shows a certain commonality despite the difference in principle between them. From where stems that commonality? Philosophy, one might think, is just as much a rational, cognitive comportment as science is. This results in the idea of the "proposition in general," of the "concept in general," etc. But this conception is not free from the prejudice of philosophy as a science. The idea of scientific knowledge and concepts is not to be carried over into philosophy on the basis of an extension of the concept of the scientific proposition to the proposition in general, as if the rational contexts of science and philosophy were identical. Nonetheless, there is a "leveled-off" understanding of philosophical and scientific "concepts" and "propositions." In "factical life," these concepts and propositions encounter each other in the sphere of linguistic presentation and communication as "meanings" which are being "understood." Initially, they are not at all marked off from one another. Since we have to realize that the comprehension of philosophical concepts is different from that of scientific concepts, we must find out how this leveled-off understanding of such concepts and propositions arises.

Is this entire consideration not a perpetual treatment of preliminary questions? Apparently, one hesitates evasively at the introductory stage; one makes necessity—the incapacity for positive creations—into a virtue. Philosophy can be reproached for turning perpetually upon preliminary questions only if one borrows the measure of its evaluation from the idea of the sciences, and if one expects from philosophy the solution of concrete problems and demands of it the construction of a world-view. I wish to increase and keep awake philosophy's need to be ever turning upon preliminary questions, so much so that it will indeed become a virtue. About what is proper to philosophy itself, I have nothing to say to you. I will deliver nothing that is materially interesting or that moves the heart. Our task is much more limited.

§ 2. On the Title of the Lecture Course

The title of this lecture course reads: "Introduction to the Phenomenology of Religion." This title can be given a thrice-nuanced meaning, depending on the noun one emphasizes. We must reach a provisional understanding of the three concepts "introduction," "phenomenology"—which for us will have the same meaning as "philosophy"—and "religion." In the midst of these efforts, we will soon encounter a peculiar core phenomenon, the problem of the historical. This problem will lead to limitations upon our present aspiration.

We will begin with the clarification of the meaning of words, but we will refer immediately to the connections among objects indicated in these meanings such that these connections will be put into question.

1. What does "introduction" mean?

An "introduction" to a science is usually comprised of three aspects:

a) the delimitation of the material domain [*Sachgebiet*];

b) the doctrine of the methodological treatment of the material domain (a and b can be taken together: determination (*Feststellung*) of the concept, the goal and the task of the science);

c) the historical consideration of the previous attempts to pose and resolve the scientific tasks.

Can one introduce philosophy in the same way? An introduction to the sciences presents the domain of the subject matter, and the methodological treatment of that domain (its goal and task), and a historical overview of the various attempts at solutions. If the sciences and philosophy are different, and if the philosopher wishes to give what is properly philosophical its due, then it is questionable whether he can simply adopt this schema of an introduction. One recognizes a philosopher by looking at his introduction to philosophy. An introduction according to the usual schema obscures the philosophical connections. With regard to their subject matter [*sachhaltig*], an introduction to biology, to chemistry, and to the history of literature are very different in kind, but they possess a great formal similarity: they proceed according to the same schema. The idea of *science*—not taken logically and abstractly, but concretely as the *enactment* of science, understood as actual research and collaboration, and not, for instance, as a pure rational system—motivates, understandably, the sense [*Sinn*] of the schema of an introduction. Historically, of course, the sciences, even with respect to their *sense,* originate from philosophy. "Originating" is meant in a very specific sense in this context. One usually takes this to mean that specific particular disciplines split off from a universal science, that is, that they autonomized themselves. In this context, origination means the determination, with an independent method, of a specific domain of a subject matter that previously had been worked upon by philosophy. Thus, one presupposes that philosophy itself is a science, too. This conception of the origination of the sciences from philosophy as the "cognitive dealing with the world," in which the sciences are already embryonically present, is a prejudice on the part of current philosophy that is projected back into history. *Only a particular, formative modification of a moment already potentially present in philosophy*—a moment, however, found in philosophy in its original, unmodified form—*turns the sciences, in their origination from philosophy and according to the specific character of this origination, into sciences.* The sciences are thus not to be found in philosophy. This leads us to the question: 2. What is called *philosophy?*

The introductory questions never interest the scientist as much as the proper, concrete scientific problems. And the introduction, especially where it encounters what is philosophical, reveals a certain well-grounded insecurity. We will not let ourselves be disconcerted by such judgments. Perhaps in philosophy the "introduction" has such an important meaning that it has to be considered alongside every step into philosophy. The introduction is not merely technique. The question of the essence of philosophy appears unfruitful and "academic." But this, too, is only the consequence of the common conception of philosophy as a science. For instance, a philologist is not interested in the "essence" of philology. But the philosopher occupies himself seriously with the essence of philosophy before he turns to positive work. The fact that philosophy *constantly* has to attain clarity about its essence is a deficiency only if the idea of science is cited as the norm. The history of philosophy can be understood philosophically only if there is a difference in principle between philosophy and science; for only then can the great philosophical systems be considered, with this problem as the guiding thread, according to the following aspects:

1. What is the original motive of the philosophy under consideration?

2. What are the conceptual, cognitive means to the realization of this motive?

3. Did these means originally arise from the motive of the philosophy under consideration, so that they were not adopted from other ideals, particularly scientific ones?

4. Do certain points of rupture, at which philosophy opens out into scientific channels, manifest themselves, as in all previous philosophies?

5. Is the motive of the philosophy under consideration itself original or is it adopted from other motives of life and from other ideals?

It is in this respect that we will consider the history of philosophy. If the history of philosophy is considered otherwise, it becomes either merely beautiful talk or a classifying occupation.

How do we arrive at the self-understanding of philosophy? This can be attained only by philosophizing itself, not by way of scientific proofs and definitions, that is, not by philosophy's integration into a universal, objectively formed material complex [*Sachzusammenhang*]. That this is so lies in the concept of "self-understanding." What philosophy itself is can never be rendered evident scientifically but can only be made clear in philosophizing itself. One cannot define philosophy in the usual way; one cannot characterize it through an integration into a material complex, according to the manner in which, as it is said, chemistry is a science and painting is an art. The integration of philosophy into a conceptual system has also been attempted by claiming that philosophy deals with a specific object in a specific manner. But even here the scientific conception of philosophy comes into play. In these attempts, the principles of thought and cognition remain unclarified. One can, nevertheless, speak in this manner of painting, despite its not being a science. One can say, for example, that it is an art. In fact, this is, in a *very formal* sense, justified even with regard to philosophy, wherein this kind of formality is still to be clarified.

The problem of the self-understanding of philosophy has always been taken too lightly. If one grasps this problem radically, one finds that philosophy arises from factical life experience. And within factical life experience philosophy returns back into factical life experience. The concept of factical life experience is fundamental. The designation of philosophy as cognitive, rational comportment says nothing at all; with this designation, one falls prey to the ideal of science, thus obscuring precisely the main difficulty.

§ 3. Factical Life Experience as the Point of Departure

What is called "factical life experience?" "Experience" designates: (1) the experiencing activity, (2) that which is experienced through this activity. However, we use the word intentionally in its double sense, because it is precisely the fact that the experiencing self and what is experienced are not torn apart like things that expresses what is essential in factical life experience. "Experiencing" does not mean "taking-cognizance-of" but a confrontation-with, the self-assertion of the forms of what is experienced. It has both a passive and an active sense. "Factical" does not mean naturally real or causally determined, nor does it mean real in the sense of a thing. The concept "factical" may not be interpreted from certain epistemological presuppositions, but can be made intelligible only from the concept of the "historical." At the same time, however, "factical life experience" is a danger zone for independent philosophy since the ambitions of the sciences already validate themselves in this zone.

The idea that philosophy and science are objective formations of sense, separated propositions, and propositional complexes must be eliminated. When the sciences in general are taken to be philosophically problematic, they are investigated *according to a theory of science* as to their extricated propositional truth complex. One has to grasp the concrete sciences themselves in their *enactment,* and the scientific process must be laid out in its foundations as historical. This is what contemporary philosophy not only overlooks but intentionally rejects; [this historicality] is allowed no role. We defend the thesis that science is different in principle from philosophy. This must be considered.

All great philosophers have wished to elevate philosophy to the rank of a science, which implies the admission of a deficiency of the respective philosophy—namely, that it is not yet science. One therefore orients oneself toward a rigorous scientific philosophy. *Is rigor a super-scientific concept?* Originally, the concept and sense of *rigor* is philosophical and *not* scientific; originally, only philosophy is rigorous; it possesses a rigor in the face of which the rigor of science is merely derivative.

Philosophy's constant effort to determine its own concept belongs to its authentic motive. For a scientific philosophy, on the contrary, it is never possible to reject the reproach of ever tarrying with the "epistemological," preliminary considerations. Philosophy is to be liberated from its "secularization" to a science, or to a scientific doctrine of world-views. The derivation of science from philosophy is to be determined positively. Today, one usually assumes a standpoint of compromise: in its particularity, philosophy is said to be science, but its general tendency is to present a world-view. In this, however, the concepts "science" and "world-view" remain vague and unclarified. How can one reach the self-understanding of philosophy? Apparently, the path of scientific deduction is cut off in advance through our thesis. This self-understanding cannot, further, be reached through reference to the "object" of philosophy; philosophy does not, perhaps, deal with an object at all. Perhaps one may not even ask for its object. Through mystical intuitions we would cut off the problem in advance.

The point of departure of the path to philosophy is *factical life experience.* It seems, however, as if philosophy is leading us out of factical life experience. In fact, that path leads us, as it were, only *near* philosophy, not *up* to it. Philosophy itself can only be reached through a turning around of that path, but not through a simple turning which would orient cognition merely toward different objects but, more radically, through an authentic *transformation.* Neo-Kantianism (Natorp) simply reverses the process of "objectification" (of the cognition of objects) and thus arrives at the "subjectification" (which is supposed to represent the philosophical, psychological process). In this, the object is merely drawn from the object into the subject, whereas cognition qua cognition remains the same unclarified phenomenon.

Factical life experience is very peculiar; in it, the path to philosophy is made possible and the turning around which leads to philosophy is enacted. This difficulty is to be understood through a preliminary characterization of the phenomenon of factical life experience. Life experience is more than mere experience which takes cognizance of. It designates the whole active and passive pose of the human being toward the world: If we view factical life experience only in regard to the experienced content, we designate what is experienced—what is lived as experience [*das Erlebte*]—as the "world," not the "object." "World" is that in which one can *live* (one cannot live in an object). The world can be formally articulated as *surrounding world* (milieu), as that which we encounter, and to which belong not only material things but also ideal objectivities, the sciences, art, etc. Within this surrounding world is also the *communal world,* that is, other human beings in a very specific, factical characterization: as a student, a lecturer, as a relative, superior, etc., and *not* as specimen of the natural-scientific species *homo sapiens,* and the like. Finally, the *"I"-self,* the *self-world,* is also found within factical life experience. Insofar as it is possible that I am absorbed by the arts and sciences such that I live entirely in them, the arts and sciences are to be designated as *genuine life-worlds.* But even they are experienced in the manner of a surrounding world. One cannot, however, abruptly demarcate the phenomena of these worlds from each other, consider them as isolated formations, ask about their mutual relationships, divide them into genera and species, etc. That would already be a deforming, a sliding into epistemology. An epistemologically performed layering and ranking of these three worlds would already be a violation. Nothing is said here about the relation of the life-worlds; the primary point is that they become *accessible* to factical life experience. One can only characterize the manner, the *how,* of the experiencing of those worlds; that is, one can ask about the *relational sense* of factical life experience. It is questionable whether the *how*—the relation—determines that *which* is experienced—the content—and how the content is characterized. We will isolate, furthermore, the *taking-cognizance-of* or the *cognitive experiencing,* since philosophy is supposed to be cognitive behavior. First, however, the meaning of this taking-cognizance-of must be understood from the motive of experiencing itself.

The peculiarity of factical life experience consists in the fact that "how I stand with regard to things," the manner of experiencing, is *not* co-experienced. What belongs to cognition according to its own meaning must be phenomenologically isolated prior to all decrees that philosophy is cognition. Factical life experience puts all its weight on its *content;* the *how* of factical life experience at most merges into its content. All alteration of life takes place in the content. During the course of a factically experienced day, I deal with quite different things; but in the factical course of life, I do not become aware of the different *hows* of my reactions to those different things. Instead, I encounter them at most in the content I experience itself: factical life experience manifests an *indifference* with regard to the manner of experiencing. It does not even occur to factical life experience that something might not become accessible to it. This factical experience engages, as it were, all concerns of life. The differences and changes of emphasis are found entirely in the content itself. The *self-sufficiency* of factical life experience is, therefore, grounded upon this indifference, an indifference which extends itself to everything; it decides even the highest matters within this self-sufficiency. Thus, if we pay attention to the peculiar indifference of factical experience to all factical life, a specific, constant sense of the surrounding world, the communal world, and the self-world becomes clear to us: everything that is experienced in factical life experience, as well as all of its content, bears the character of *significance.* But with this, no epistemological decision has been made, either in the sense of some kind of realism or in the sense of some kind of idealism. All of my factical life situations are experienced in the manner of significance which determines the content of experience itself. This becomes clear if I ask myself how I experience *myself* in factical life experience:—no theories!

Generally, one analyzes only theoretically and thoroughly formed concepts of the soul, but the self is not problematized. Concepts like "soul," "connection among acts," "transcendental consciousness," problems like that of the "connection between body and soul"—none of this plays a role for us. I experience myself in factical life neither as a complex of lived experiences nor as a conglomeration of acts and processes, not even as some ego-object in a demarcated sense, but rather in *that which* I perform, suffer, what I encounter, in my conditions of depression and elevation, and the like. I myself *experience not even my ego in separateness,* but I am as such always attached to the surrounding world. This experiencing-oneself is no theoretical "reflection," no "inner perception," or the like, but is self-worldly experience, because experience itself has a worldly character and emphasizes significance in such a way that one's own experienced self-world no longer stands out from the surrounding world. This self-experience is the only possible point of departure for a philosophical psychology, if one can be posited at all. The wish to return from preconceived psychological theories to the factical is an erroneous undertaking, since these theories are not philosophically motivated in the first place. One could object that I experience myself—*how I* feel—nonetheless factically, without special reflection; I know that right now, *I* acted clumsily, and so forth. But this *how,* too, is no thoroughly formed manner of relating to something but a significance factically tethered to the surrounding world. The factical of which cognizance is taken does not have an objective character but a character of significance which can develop into an objective context.

By no means can we hope that all of this is immediately comprehensible, but only that all these things become accessible in a continuous process of philosophizing, one perpetually developing anew. Here we are concerned only with attaining the starting point for the understanding of philosophy itself.

§ 4. Taking-Cognizance-of

Let us now consider factical cognition, the taking-cognizance-of. What is cognized therein does not have the character of an object but is experienced as significance. A relating, a grouping-together, manifests itself now; therein, a connectedness of objects that bears a specific logic, a material logic, a structure peculiar to the specific material states of affairs, is formed. In a specific situation, I can factically listen to scientific lectures and, in the course of this, then talk about quotidian matters. The situation is essentially the same, except that the content has changed; and yet I do not become conscious of a specific change of attitude. Scientific objects, too, are always first of all cognized with the character of factical life experience. One can, however, push the relating tendency to the extreme and orient oneself toward the ultimate structural complexes of objecthood in general (Husserl's idea of an a priori logic of objects).

Insofar as philosophizing transcends factical experience, it is characterized by the fact that it deals with higher objects and the highest of them, with the "first and ultimate things." Moreover, in philosophy everything is related to the human being and to what concerns him (tendency toward world-views). In grasping the subject, the style remains the same, too: the subject is considered as an object. Admittedly, in this way philosophy, too, through its scientific relation to objects, would have to be designated a science in the sense of a formed-out cognizing.

Our considerations here have thus only increased the difficulty of the self-understanding of philosophy. How is a mode of cognition other than taking-cognizance-of to be motivated? Factical life experience itself, through its indifference and self-sufficiency, always covers up again the philosophical tendency that might surface. In its self-sufficient concern, factical life experience constantly falls into significance. It constantly strives for an articulation in science and ultimately for a "scientific culture." Apart from these strivings, however, factical life experience contains motives of a purely philosophical posture which can be isolated only through a peculiar turning around of philosophical comportment. The difference between philosophy and science consists not only in their objects and methods, but is in principle of a more radical nature. A self-understanding of philosophy is required even if one does not assume the derivation of science from philosophy. Heretofore, philosophers made an effort to degrade precisely factical life experience as a matter of secondary importance that could be taken for granted, despite that philosophy arises precisely from factical life experience and springs back into it in a reversal that is entirely essential.

If this thesis is justified, every compromise vanishes and with it vanishes every assimilation of philosophy into science, through whose assistance philosophy maintained its meager existence for centuries. Philosophy's departure as well as its goal is factical life experience. If factical life experience is the point of departure for philosophy, and if we see factically a difference in principle between philosophical and scientific cognition, then factical life experience must be not only the point of departure for philosophizing but precisely that which essentially hinders philosophizing itself.

I would claim that all of you, with only a few exceptions, constantly misunderstand all of the concepts and determinations which I have set forth. It has to be that way, and it does not do any harm initially. This misunderstanding, in fact, accomplishes for our progress the indication, if misunderstood, of certain phenomenal connections, which will be indicated, and the meaning of which will become intelligible only later.

Factical life experience is the "attitudinal, falling, relationally indifferent, self-sufficient concern for significance." Let us first of all consider the relational sense of factical life experience. What shows itself here is that the course of this experience is characterized by a constant indifference, that the differences of what I experience play themselves out entirely in the content. That I am in a different mood at a concert than in a trivial conversation constitutes a difference which I experience merely from the content. I become conscious of the diversity of experiences only in the experienced content. Thus, the manner of participation within and of being taken along by the world of the "I" is an indifferent one; indeed, it is so indifferent that it engages everything, and accomplishes all its tasks without hesitation. This manner of apprehension, however, tends to fall into significance.

Significance seems, then, to be the same as value; but value is already the product of a theorization and, like all theorizations, has to disappear from philosophy. The pure taking-cognizance-of does not take cognizance of formed-out objects but only of connections of significance. But these connections tend toward an autonomization which can be presented in a downright "logic of objects," of the connections and relations of objects. The experience that takes cognizance of plays, in an unnoticed way, a decisive role. In the falling tendency of life experience, a connectedness of objects increasingly forms and increasingly stabilizes itself. In this way one arrives at a *logic of the surrounding world* insofar as significance plays a role in the connectedness of objects. Going beyond this, all science makes an effort to thoroughly develop an increasingly more rigorous order of objects, i.e., a *material logic,* a material complex, a logic found in the things themselves (e.g., for art history a different one than for biology, etc.). Scientific philosophy is nothing but an even more rigorous forming-out of an object-domain. Object-domains are formed there which "transcend sensible experience" (Plato's world of ideas). But the attitude to the objects, the *relational sense,* remains identically the same in scientific philosophy as in the particular sciences. Only a different dimension of objects appears, insofar as these objects are capable of explaining a context more thoroughly.

More recent philosophy moves consciousness into the center (Kant). Especially in Fichte's treatment of this material problem, the "subject" is a new form of objecthood [*Gegenständlichkeit*] vis-à-vis other "objects." Nonetheless, we find here too, in Fichte's departure from Kant's practical philosophy and his utilization of Kantian anticipations, a basically attitudinal tendency. Judging from its history, philosophy is thus always a forming of connections among objects, as rigorously as possible—although German idealism saw the peculiar difficulty of the cognition of the subject.

At this point we no longer understand how a radical difference between philosophy and science can exist at all. The falling tendency of factical life experience, constantly tending toward the significant connections of the factically experienced world, its gravity, as it were, conditions a tendency of factically lived life toward the attitudinal determination and regulation of objects. The sense of factical life experience thus contradicts the sense of our thesis. We have to look around in factical life experience in order to obtain a motive for its turning around. It is, to be sure, possible to find this motive, but it is very difficult. For this reason, we will choose a more convenient route, since we possess knowledge of past and contemporary philosophy. The factical existence of the history of philosophy is, in itself, certainly no motivation to philosophize. Nevertheless, as a cultural possession, one can take it as a starting point and, with its help, clarify for oneself motivations to philosophize. In order to understand it in as lively a way as possible and to follow the sense of factical life experience rigorously, we will look around in the present and its philosophical tendencies—not in order to understand it philosophically but merely in the sense of the factical taking-cognizance-of. For the sake of brevity, we will consider concrete tendencies of the philosophy of religion in their most typical representatives.

Chapter Two

Current Tendencies of the Philosophy of Religion

§ 5. *Troeltsch's Philosophy of Religion*

The interest in the philosophy of religion is currently increasing. Even women write philosophies of religion and philosophers who wish to be taken seriously welcome them as the most important appearances in decades! One only has to compare, for example, the two essays published in the "Presentations of the Kant Society, No. 24": 1. Radbruch, "On the Philosophy of Religion of Law" and 2. Tillich, "On the Idea of a Theology of Culture."[1] Both are influenced by Troeltsch. In what follows, we wish to characterize Troeltsch's religious-philosophical position, since he is the most significant representative of the current philosophy of religion. Otherwise, things are taking place dependently in theology. Troeltsch possesses a great knowledge of concrete religious-philosophical material and also of the historical development of the religious-philosophical problem. He is coming from theology. The presentation of his views is rendered difficult through the frequent change of his basic philosophical standpoint, throughout which, however, his religious-philosophical position is maintained quite remarkably. As a theologian from the school of Ritschl, his philosophical standpoint was initially determined by Kant, Schleiermacher, and Lotze. In terms of his philosophy of history, he is dependent upon Dilthey. In the 1890s, Troeltsch turned to Windelband-Rickertian "value-philosophy." In more recent years, he switched finally to the Bergson-Simmelian position. He understood Hegel from Bergson and Simmel and in the end oriented his philosophy of history toward Hegel. What goals does Troeltsch posit for the philosophy of religion? His goal is the working out of a scientifically valid, essential determination of religion.

a) Psychology

Initially, a *description* ("positivism") of the religious phenomena is required: immediately, free of theories, the phenomena in themselves (cf. the similar demand by Max Weber for sociology).[2] Religious phenomena are to be ob-

---

1. Both essays may be found in *Religionsphilosophie der Kultur. Zwei Entwürfe von Gustav Radbruch und Paul Tillich.* (Philosophische Vorträge der Kant-Gesellschaft Nr. 24) Berlin, 1919.

2. Cf. Martin Heidegger, *Grundprobleme der Phänomenologie. Frühe Freiburger Vorlesung Wintersemester 1919/20.* Gesamtausgabe, vol. 58, ed. Hans-Helmuth Gander, Frankfurt a. M., 1993, pp. 189–196.

served naïvely, as not yet hackneyed (the prayers, cults, liturgies, in the deeds of great religious figures, preachers, reformers), and then to be characterized in their transcendental, primal conditions. Troeltsch distinguishes between central and marginal religious phenomena. The central phenomenon is the belief in the attainment of God's presence which in principle co-grants as well the ethical command. Marginal forms are the sociology and business ethic of religion—that is, its factical expression in the historical world (as Max Weber, for instance, studied them). In order to attain this goal, the philosophy of religion has to utilize the method of individual psychology and the psychology of peoples, and, further, psychopathology, prehistoric studies, ethnology, and the American method of surveys and statistics. According to Troeltsch, the best description of religious phenomena so far has been undertaken by William James.[3] (Here Troeltsch is influenced by Jamesian and Diltheyian descriptive psychology.) Thus, Troeltsch took up into his own work all basic psychological tendencies.

b) Epistemology

This psychological description is followed, as a second task, by the *epistemology* of religion and *the element of validity contained in the psychic processes*. (Troeltsch, "Psychologie und Erkenntnistheorie" ["Psychology und Epistemology"]. Lecture presented at the American Congress for the Philosophy of Religion, 1904.)[4] The point is here to investigate the rational lawfulness of the religious formations of ideas. In these, specific *a priori* lawfulnesses are always operative, ones which are at the foundations of religious phenomena. The universal *epistemology* has already determined the problem of the a priori in general. (Here, Troeltsch relies upon the Windelband-Rickertian epistemology.) There is a synthetic a priori of what is religious, similar to a logical, ethical, or aesthetic a priori. This isolation of the religious a priori signifies the fixation of religious "truth" in general, of the *rational* element in what is religious. Particularly in his later work, Troeltsch does not mean "rational" in the sense of what is theoretically rationalistic, but rather "rational" means only what is universally valid or rationally necessary. Troeltsch determined it earlier as a rational a priori, but later he moved away from this view and claimed, without any determination of the content, that it is not a rational but an irrational a priori. He claims that it is crucial to connect the logical, ethical, and aesthetic a priori to the religious a priori and to see

3. William James, *The Varieties of Religious Experience: A Study in Human Nature.* New York, 1902 (in German: *Die religiöse Erfahrung in ihrer Mannigfaltigkeit. Materialien und Studien zu einer Psychologie und Pathologie des religiösen Lebens. Übersetzt von Georg Wobbermin.* Leipzig, 1907).

4. Cf. Ernst Troeltsch, *Psychologie und Erkenntnistheorie in der Religionswissenschaft. Eine Untersuchung über die bedeutung der Kantischen Religionslehre für die heutige Religionswissenschaft.* Tübingen, 1905, p. 18.

how the former receive their consolidation from the religious a priori. The work of the epistemology of religion is *critical:* it wishes to separate what is factical and psychological from what is valid a priori.

In this context, factical life experience does *not* fulfill the function of a domain or area in which objects exist. It has nothing to do with a monism of experience or a theory of monism; *here,* nothing is being "explained." In taking up and clarifying given connections of meaning, current phenomenology does not rigorously enough question the right to validity of what is factically given. But factical life experience is what is priorly given, on the basis of which, however, nothing is to be "explained." Phenomenology is not a preliminary science of philosophy but philosophy itself.

Current work in the philosophy of religion takes place primarily in theology, chiefly in Protestant theology; Catholic theology takes on philosophical problems with respect to the specifically Catholic understanding of Christianity. Protestant theology is essentially dependent upon the main respective philosophical trends to which it attaches itself. It is a prejudice of philosophers of religion to think that they are able to settle the problem of theology with a quick sweep of the hand. Apart from these works, we have to consider the work of the *psychology* of religion, about whose contribution we must decide later. Insofar as the religious-philosophical problem is tackled within philosophy, it is without doubt to be supposed that the approximation of Fichte and Hegel, which is constantly increasing at present, will lead to a renewal of religious-philosophical speculation.[5] The application of these principles forces the taking up of the religious-philosophical problem in a certain direction which we will later critically reject. In any case, this speculative tendency has a special meaning for the increase in religious-philosophical work which, no doubt, will take place. That literati of today have appropriated the philosophy of religion is probably well known to all of you, but this should not concern you here.

c) Philosophy of History

Only on the basis of the separation of the psychological from the a priori can one trace the *historical* necessity of what is religious. The history of religion considers the realization of the religious a priori in the factical course of spiritual history—not only the mere facts but the *laws* according to which

---

5. [Insertion in Helene Weiß's transcript: cf. Überweg IV. § 43: Following Kant, modern theology recognized the unprovability of Christian dogmas and therefore constructed its dogmatism upon the personal certainty of religious lived experience while renouncing scientific proof. In this way (similar to Schleiermacher's doctrine of faith), mere psychological self-observation of Christian faith emerges whereby, in Lotze's sense, the high value of Christianity and, in the sense of pragmatism, its "practical value of life," are validated as the guarantee of truth.]

religion develops historically. Hegel first envisaged this goal, but his constructive method is to be rejected. To be sure, this task will not succeed without metaphysics, but only an "inductive" metaphysics can be admitted. The philosophy of the history of religion, further, has to comprehend the present and predetermine the future development of religion. It has to decide whether a universal religion of reason will come about, one which would syncretistically emerge out of the present world religions (a *Protestant Catholicism,* according to Söderblom), or whether in the future one of the positive religions (Christianity, Buddhism, Islam) will reign alone.

d) Metaphysics

This is a metaphysics of the idea of God on the basis of all of our experiences of the world. Critical epistemology, too (Kant, etc.), can amount to such a metaphysics. For one arrives from the teleological context of (transcendental) consciousness to one last meaning, which demands the existence of God.

Troeltsch actually steered the philosophy of religion out of theology. He focused the philosophy of religion around the problem of a unification of religious history and systematics (cf. Albrecht Ritschl 1822–89). For he attempted, in the wake of Rickert's "consciousness in general," a reworking and rational critique of the religious-historical material. The failure of this attempt drove him to a break with theology. He wanted to ground the newer philosophy of religion in a "preliminary phenomenology," that is, a preliminary doctrine of types of historical religions. He names this specification the psychology of religion. The central phenomenon is the belief in the experience-ability of the presence of God; peripheral are mythology, ethos, sociology of religion. Psychopathology and ethnology show that the original phenomenon of all religions is mysticism, the experiences of unity in God. Wherever religion is spiritually actualized, a priori foundations are necessary which mark even the individual psychic processes as religious. The epistemology of religion is to work out, analogically to the theoretical a priori, a religious a priori, which means a fixing of the truth-content, which constitutes the "rational moment" of religion through which religion first becomes possible (cf. Rickert). *Ratio* means, later in Troeltsch, an accordance with the norm not only in the logical, but also in the ethical [sense], etc. The reunification of the thus found and emphasized a priori with the psychic modes of appearance of religion belongs to religious metaphysics. For Troeltsch, the religious a priori stands opposite a higher mental world [*Geisteswelt*], the experience of which is the fundamental religious phenomenon. Religious metaphysics is in principle different in Troeltsch as in philosophical metaphysics, just as religious a priori differs from theoretical a priori. Therefore, there can be a historical representation on the basis of a teleological principle of development won by the history of philosophy. Thereby metaphysics becomes co-effective, but not a constructive-dialectical metaphysic such as Hegel's, but rather an inductive metaphysics of religion. Moreover, the philosophy of religion should transform the further development of religion and, for instance, solve or discuss the question of a religion of pure reason or syncretism or a privileged form of one of the great religions (cf. Söderblom), etc. The metaphysics of religion must integrate the reality of God into the context of the world. Even within an epistemological philosophy, the theological basis and the meaning of facticity of consciousness will lead to a faith in God.

We have then four religious-philosophical disciplines: (1) psychology, (2) epistemology, (3) philosophy of history—these three taken together make up the science of religion—and (4) metaphysics, which is the authentic philosophy of religion. The science of religion is a philosophical discipline like logic, ethics, aesthetics; metaphysics is founded upon these as a final region. Troeltsch himself maintained above all, alongside specific investigations ("Die Soziallehren der christlichen Kirchen und Gruppen" ["Social Doctrines of Christianity"],[6] etc.), the philosophy of history. In its principle foundations, he altered [his view]. Earlier, he understood history teleologically, as progressive development. Of late he affords each religious-historical epoch its own meaning; it is not merely to be viewed as a point of passage. From the provocations of life arise ever-new, no longer rationally graspable motives for the following epoch. Religions arise from rational moments and spontaneous forces of life; they have their own meaning which renders them independent; they thus become an impulse for development. A logical-dialectical connection cannot be determined; a logical schema of development is a violation (cf. Simmel and Bergson). Troeltsch poses the problem of a "historical dialectic" (cf. his essay in the *Historische Zeitschrift*[7]). With that he departs from Rickert's philosophy of history and arrives at Dilthey (cf. the latter's "Aufbau der geschichtlichen Welt in den Geisteswissenschaften" ["Construction of the Historical World in the Humanities"][8]). His fundamental concepts are "individual totality" and "continuity of becoming," rather than "development" (cf. Dilthey's "effective complex" [*Wirkungszusammenhang*]). The modification, which follows therefrom, of his a priori conceptuality has not yet been developed by Troeltsch. Whether he now, following Rickert (cf. Simmel), holds fast to the concept of the religious a priori is doubtful. (Cf. his critique of the book of Otto, *Das Heilige* [The Holy] in *Kantstudien* 1917.)[9]

6. Ernst Troeltsch, *Die Soziallehren der christlichen Kirchen und Gruppen.* Tübingen, 1912.
7. Ernst Troeltsch, "Über den Begriff einer historischen Dialektik: I./II. Windelband, Rickert, und Hegel. III. Der Marxismus," in *Historische Zeitschrift* 119 and 120 (1919) and 120 (1919).
8. Wilhelm Dilthey, "Der Aufbau der geschichtlichen Welt in den Geisteswissenschaften. Erste Hälfte," in *Abhandlungen der Königlich-Preussischen Akademie der Wissenschaften,* 1910. Phil.-hist. Kl.
9. Ernst Troeltsch, "Zur Religionsphilosophie (aus Anlaß des Buches von R. Otto über das Heilige," 1917), in *Kantstudien* 23 (1918).

§ 6. Critical Observations

We do not want to criticize Troeltsch's view, but rather more precisely understand his basic position. At issue is to validly determine the essence of religion scientifically. Troeltsch has a fourfold concept of the essence of religion:

1. The *psychological* essence of religion; the genera of its particularity of form.

2. The *epistemological* essence of religion; the apriori of religious reason.

3. The *historical* essence of religion, understood as general typology; the actualization of (1) and (2) in history.

4. The *metaphysical* essence of religion; the religious as principle of everything apriori. (Position of religion in the entire complex of reason.)

Only all four of these concepts give a total picture of the philosophy of religion. We must now understand in what way this philosophy of religion refers to religion, whether it grows from out of the meaning of religion, or whether religion is not as much as grasped *in the manner of an object* and forced into philosophical disciplines—that is to say, integrated into *material* complexes that already exist in themselves before religion. There is also a psychology, epistemology, philosophy of history, metaphysics of science and of art. These religious-philosophical disciplines thus arise not from religion itself qua religion. From the outside religion is observed and integrated as an *object*. The philosophy of religion itself is the science of religion. The entire problematic is thus thrown back onto the view of philosophy itself. The concept of religion becomes secondary. One could just as easily think out a sociology or an aesthetics of religion.

A driving motto of Troeltsch's philosophy of religion is found in his *view of the Reformation.* He sees nothing new in the Reformation; rather he thinks that it progressed from within the sense-structure of the Middle Ages. What is new is thought to arrive, then, in the eighteenth century and in German Idealism. Troeltsch took up many medieval and Catholic elements in this manner in his philosophy of religion. One rightfully accuses that he, similarly to Dilthey, had no understanding of Luther. Lastly, for Troeltsch it depends on the *metaphysics of religion,* on the *proof of God.* But the proof of God is not originally Christian, but rather depends upon the connection between Christianity and Greek philosophy. This metaphysical view also determines Troeltsch's philosophy of religion.

We do not want to establish a critique on the basis of content. We want to see how religion and philosophy comport themselves, how religion becomes an object for philosophy. In Troeltsch religion is placed into four religious-philosophical disciplines in a finished material complex. Insofar as the philosophical observation of the world moves in different regions, religion is placed into these regions, and it is seen how religion expresses itself in them.

The four concepts of the essence of religion arise with this. The four regions are not only methodological; [they are] rather also divided according to their material character. The psychic reality is, in its structure and in its character of being, something other than the a priori region of rational lawfulness; and this is again something else than the reality of history, in particular the universal history; and this is something other than the last metaphysical reality, in which God is thought. How the regions link together is not treated. Thus the philosophy of religion is determined here not according to religion itself, but according to a particular concept of philosophy, and indeed a scientific one. One would like to see something new here offered in Troeltsch's metaphysics, that here religion is no longer studied as an object, insofar as the primal phenomenon—*faith* in the existence of God—is treated. After all, the existence of God would then be gained in a non-cognitive manner. But Troeltsch says, despite this, that the "object" of faith must be studied as a real object in connection with other real objects, insofar as reason is thought as a unity. In a last universal study of objects, the entire human experience is to be brought to the level of concepts, and thus also God must be studied as a real object. Here it also becomes clear how Troeltsch could maintain his position on the philosophy of religion unchanged by altering in principle his philosophical views. Religion is for him an external object and can as such be integrated into different material complexes (as appropriate to different philosophical "systems"). As such the possibility of constant transformation in Troeltsch is the strongest sign that he posits religion as an object.

The connection between religion and science is, according to Troeltsch, not a forced one. Insofar as religion finds itself in a cultural context, it must contend with science: defensively and negatively in its apologetics; but also positively, the science of religion, through prediction of future religious development, can achieve something in the further development of religion. Science, indeed, does not make religion, yet it represents a fruitful factor in its further development. According to Troeltsch, the history of Christianity shows this; through its alliance with ancient philosophy it has achieved its strong historical position. However, presently, the possibilities of religious-philosophical products are exhausted. At issue is only an emphasis upon the right possibility.

What have we now profited, for our purposes, from this study of Troeltsch? Above all, a concrete representation of the philosophy of religion. Then four determinations one can attribute to religion: the psychological, the rational-apriori, the historical, and the metaphysical. Finally, that philosophy, in its comportment, recognizes religion as an object of cognition. Thus we have argued against our thesis of the radical difference between philosophy and science. For since philosophy has to turn religion into an object of its cognition, it cannot be understood how philosophy is to occupy itself with religion, if between philosophy and science (that is, cognition of objects) is held to exist a fundamental difference of relational sense. Will not the "phenomena" become an object of study in the "phenomenology of religion," just as, for instance, in the phenomenology of aesthetic pleasure? Initially, after all, it is necessary to examine religion in its factuality, before one addresses to it a particular philosophical study.

Chapter Three

The Phenomenon of the Historical

§ 7. The Historical as Core Phenomenon

We want now to attempt to set forth a *core phenomenon* that reigns through the connections of meaning of the three words in the title ("Introduction to the Phenomenology of Religion"). This core phenomenon is the "historical." Insofar as we then intend to view the historical as core phenomenon of what is meant by the title, we will immediately find out how far the phenomena which occupy us can be characterized as historical. To what degree are "Introduction," "Philosophy," "Religion" *historical* phenomena? It goes without saying that the introduction to a science is historical. Science is a complex of timelessly valid principles. The process of introduction proceeds, on the contrary, in time, is dependent upon the particular, factical-historical situation of science, etc. The same holds for philosophy and religion. They are also subordinate to historical development. But is the historical not precisely a matter of indifference for philosophy, which seeks the eternally valid? Moreover, does not the characterization as "historical" fit any phenomenon one likes? Yet if we now assert that the philosophical problematic is motivated on principle from the historical, so is this possible only insofar as the concept of the historical is polysemous. In any case, the necessity arises of grasping the problem of the historical principally, and not to content oneself with the considerations of a sound common sense.

We have characterized philosophy and religion by subsuming it under the historical: "Philosophy and religion are historical phenomena." (Just as: "The Feldberg and the Kandel are mountains," or "The university, the cathedral, and the train station are buildings.") How such a characterization of philosophy is possible is a problem; philosophy subsists, at any rate, in factical life experience. General concepts are handled like objects, so that one moves in a circle with characterizations through general concepts, and never leaves the realm of objects. Now the question is whether the possibility exists of discovering another sense of "historical" altogether, one which cannot be predicated of objects in this way. Perhaps today's concept of the historical is only a derivation of this original concept. To this aim, we must inspect more carefully in which sense the characterization "historical," which we have just performed, is to be understood. Historical means here becoming, emergence, proceeding in time, a characterization that befits a reality. Insofar as one remains within the cognitive consideration of the connections among objects, each characterization or use of the sense of "historical" is always determined through this *foreconception of the object*. The *object* is historical; it has the particularity of proceeding in time, of changing.

We proceed not from the usual philosophy of history, which has the task *ex professo* of dealing with the historical. We mean the historical in the way we encounter it in life; not in the science of history. "Historical" means not only proceeding in time—that is to say, it is not only a characterization which befits a complex of objects. But in factical life experience and in the straight-forward, attitudinal [*einstellungshaften*] evolution of philosophy, the historical, in accordance with this view, obtains the character of a quality of an object changing in time. In a much broader sense than the historical facts existing in the brain of a logician—which results only from a theory of science which empties out the living phenomena—the historical is immediate vivacity.

a) "Historical Thinking"

"Historical consciousness" is said to distinguish our present culture from oth-ers. Historical thinking indeed determines our culture; it disturbs our culture: firstly, in that it provokes, excites, stimulates; secondly, in that it hinders. This means (1) a fulfillment; life gains its foothold in the diversity of the historical; (2) a burden. Thus the historical is a power, against which life seeks to assert itself. One would have to consider the development of historical consciousness in the living cultural history. I refer you to Dilthey, who, I am convinced, has not grasped the core of the problem. What Troeltsch says about this—and also about the Reformation—is essentially influenced by Dilthey and, in terms of content, only determines it more closely.

1. The worldization [*Verweltlichung*] and the self-sufficiency of factical life—that one wants to secure one's own life by worldly means—lead to a tolerance of alien views, through which one wants to gain a new security. From there stems today's fury to understand cultural forms, the fury of clas-sifying life-forms and cultural epochs—a typologization that goes all the way to the belief that it has reached the last frontier. Contenting oneself with this, one enjoys the diversity of life and its forms. Historical consciousness of the present is most sharply expressed in this panarchy of the understanding. In this sense, (present) life is filled with the historical. But what presents itself as the logic and methodology of history has no feeling for this living histor-icality which, as it were, has eaten into our existence [*Dasein*].

2. The opposed, hindering direction lies in that the historical withdraws the view from the present, and that it ruins and paralyzes the naïveté of creating. From there arises the assault of genuine activism against the historical.

b) The Concept of the Historical

The historical is the phenomenon that for us should open up an access to the self-understanding of philosophy. The phenomenological question of method is not a question of a methodical system, but rather a question of access that leads through factical life experience. Attendance to the methodological complex is important for understanding our study. It is a methodological complex in the sense of an access to the problems themselves. We will see that this access to the problems plays a decisive role in philosophizing. It is crucial to find motives in factical life experience for the self-understanding of philosophizing. From this self-understanding, the entire task of a phenomenology of religion first arises for us, one dominated throughout by the problem of the historical. When one hears the problem-word "the historical" immediately and factically, insofar as one wishes to philosophize about it, one seems to have already solved half the task by no more than reference to the philosophy of history, believing this to be a solidly circumscribed discipline.

But we cannot gain the phenomenon of the historical from the philosophy of history, since we reject the entire partitioning of philosophy into disciplines. With this the historical has become homeless, as it were, since it has lost its systematic place. We must therefore derive the historical from factical life. One never says: "Something *is* historical," something, an object, has the quality of being historical. With that the historical shifts into a complex of objects. Philosophy and religion are likewise obviously historical phenomena. However, with such a characterization, nothing exceptional is said, for art and science are also historical in this sense. Particularly in the case of philosophy, this characterization seems secondary, since it depends exactly on what philosophy is in its *meaning,* irrespective of how it is historically actualized. Only if one problematizes the validity of scientific principles, the historical plays a certain (albeit negative) role. One says that the validity of these principles is independent of the historical, is extra-temporal; considering the historical serves then only to demonstrate this. But this would be a more secondary role for the historical; here the meaning of philosophy and validity is already presupposed.

But we assert the importance of the historical for the sense of philosophizing *per se, before* all questions of validity. This assertion is grounded in the concept of the historical as polysemous; and we have not yet grasped the authentic sense of the historical. We must clarify the sense of the historical phenomenologically. What is meant when one says that some occurrence or other, some undertaking, etc. is "historical"? What is meant is that every happening in time and space has the quality of standing in a temporal context, a context of becoming. The quality of being historical is then predicated of an object.

Object [*Objekt*] and thing [*Gegenstand*] are not the same. All objects are things, but not the other way around; all things are not objects. A danger ensues of holding determinates of objects for determinates of things. Conversely, one is seduced into holding some thingly determinates immediately for determinates of objects and into applying formal points of view to specific observations of things. Since Plato, the blurring of these differences has been disastrous. Now, a phenomenon is neither object nor thing. However, a phenomenon, formally speaking, is also a thing—that is to say, a something at all. But saying that says nothing essential about the phenomenon; one has only shifted it into a sphere into which it does not belong. That makes phenomenology so extraordinarily difficult. Objects, things, and phenomena cannot be placed alongside each other as on a chessboard; rather, this systematization of things also is inappropriate for phenomena, and from the point of view of phenomenology, a doctrine of categories or a philosophical system becomes senseless.

For the time being, only the difference between object and thing is important for us. It befits an object to be temporally determined; as such, it is historical. A more general concept of the historical than this seems not to be found. The historical actuality will, in each case, modify itself according to the character of the object; and yet in principle the historical remains the same. The application of the historical to human reality, too, will be a determination of the object-historical. The human being itself is, in its actuality, an object in becoming, standing within time. To be historical is simply one of its characteristics. This view of the historical runs entirely within the bounds of sound common sense. But philosophy is nothing else than a struggle against common sense! In this way, the problem of the historical is not to be settled. Indeed it is difficult to gain a different view today.

If today's philosophy of history were our point of departure, and if we let that philosophy stipulate the problems, we would never escape this object-conception of the historical. Therefore, we want to proceed from factical life. In this [consideration], philosophy of history is regarded only as a factical view of the historical problem. We are not, however, accepting its terms, participating in it; rather we are only trying to understand what the real motives are, in each case, for the viewpoint of the philosophy of history. To aim for a deep-rooted understanding, one would have to feel one's way into the entire present-day constitution of mind. Here we can emphasize only a few fundamental currents.

c) The Historical in Factical Life Experience

The historical plays a role in present-day factical life experience in *two* major directions. 1. *Positively* speaking, the diversity of historical forms provides life with a *fulfillment* and allows it to rest in the diversity of historical formations. 2. *Negatively* speaking, the historical is for us a *burden,* a hindrance.

In both respects, the historical is disturbing; against it, life seeks to assert and secure itself. But it remains in question whether that against which factical life asserts itself is still really the historical. Dilthey's investigations are important here: "Einleitung in die Geisteswissenschaften" ["Introduction to the Humanities"],[1] "Die Aufklärung und die geschichtliche Welt" ["The Enlightenment and the Historical World"] (*Deutsche Rundschau*),[2] "Analyse und Auffassung des Menschen im 15. und 16. Jahrhundert" ["Analysis and View of the Human Being in the 15th and 16th Centuries"] (*Gesammelte Werke* II).[3]

The expression of historical consciousness is, at first, polysemous. The science of history exists because the historical plays a role in our present-day life, not the other way around. "Historical thinking" can have many meanings: In the face of the historical object I do not need at all to think historically; and yet I can think historically without having a historical object before me. The problem of the historical takes its meaning in this, that the historical, through the distancing from a particular, present, world-orienting standpoint, opens the eyes to other life-forms and cultural ages. Now *either* one glimpses the highest itself—which our time, gifted with enormous capacity of feeling, has to offer—in the all-encompassing understanding of this rise of accessibility and openness; *or* one lays out the different types that surface in history, and, in comparing, chooses and decides among them.

Still more, the historical is felt today as a burden. It inhibits our naïveté in creating. Historical consciousness incessantly accompanies, like a shadow, each attempt at a new creation. Immediately, consciousness of transitoriness stirs and takes from us enthusiasm for the absolute. Insofar as a new spiritual culture is insisted upon, historical consciousness, in this sense of being a burden, must be eradicated, and thus the self-assertion against the historical is a more or less open struggle against history.

§ 8. The Struggle of Life against the Historical

We can differentiate three ways of attempting to assert oneself against history. Perhaps this is a somewhat violent differentiation, also because spiritual life today is no longer clearly conscious that it incessantly confronts history:

1. Wilhelm Dilthey, *Einleitung in die Geisteswissenschaften. Versuch einer Grundlegung für das Studium der Gesellschaft und der Geschichte,* vol. I, Leipzig, 1883.
2. [The correct title reads:] "Das achtzehnte Jahrhundert und die geschichtliche Welt," in *Deutsche Rundschau* 108 (1901).
3. [The correct title reads:] "Auffassung und Analyse des Menschen im 15. und 16. Jahrhundert," in *Weltanschauung und Analyse des Menschen seit Renaissance und Reformation* (*Gesammelte Schriften* vol.II). Leipzig and Berlin, 1914.

The *Platonic* way: the historical is something with which a *break* must be made. Self-assertion is itself a break with the historical.

The way of *radical self-extradition* to the historical (Spengler).

The way of compromise between the two extremes (a) and (b). (Dilthey, "Einleitung in die Geisteswissenschaften" ["Introduction to the Humanities"], Simmel, "Die Probleme der Geschichtsphilosophie" ["Problems of the Philosophy of History"][4], and the entire philosophy of history of Rickert and Windelband.)

We attempt to understand these modes of liberation from the disturbance of the historical entirely schematically, in order to understand the sense of the historical itself, as well as the sense of these tendencies of liberation.

a) The Platonic Way

The Platonic way is the most accessible, and, in present-day spiritual life, determined in its essence by Greek philosophy, the most readily given and most popular. Historical reality is not the only reality, not the fundamental reality at all; rather it is only to be understood by reference to the realm of ideas, in whatever way one may grasp them: as substances, as values, as norms or principles of reason. One should keep in mind that the motive in Plato, and also still today, for this discovery of the extra-temporal realm, is laid forth in the territory of theoretical knowledge, of logic; in such a realm, one opposes, in the struggle against skepticism (Protagoras), the content of knowledge to temporally proceeding operations thereof, and thus comes to a concept of truth which is grasped as the validity in itself of theoretical principles. Insofar as this theoretical thinking plays a foundational role in the Greeks, insofar as everything is only as it is known, given the dominating role of the theoretical, the moral act, artistic and practical creation are likewise referred to an ideal reality of norms and values. The primacy of the logical (theoretical) is to be found in Plato's relation to Socrates, in the explication of the principle "Virtue is knowledge." Following Plato, a virtuous life is possible only through knowledge.

Now the connection between ideas and the sensible world arises as a difficulty to which this philosophy has never properly attended. Here, in modern Platonism, there is a great scope of possibilities. Some say that reality is only the occasion for the appearance of ideas, of *anamnesis*. Others want to grasp the historical as a fusion into reality itself [*Einformung in die Wirklichkeit selbst*]. The theories about the connection of the two worlds are various, and need concern us in no greater detail. In any case, the historical has become something secondary.

---

4. Georg Simmel, *Die Probleme der Geschichtsphilosophie. Eine erkenntnistheoretische Studie*, Leipzig, 1892.

b) Radical Self-Extradition

Alternatively, the second way is a complete radicalization in an opposing sense; nevertheless, in principle, it proceeds in the same manner, so that today, in the struggle between absolutism and skepticism, both parties move in the same direction and fight over something they have not yet made clear to themselves. The second and third ways are grounded essentially epistemolog-ically. This *epistemological* foundation [*Fundierung*] must be made clear. *Platonism,* too, has received such an epistemological foundation, but the *ontological* is its genuine uniqueness, that of a meta-real lawfulness. Simmel worked out an epistemological foundation of the second or, for example, third way, in his *Die Probleme der Geschichtsphilosophie. Eine erkenntnistheore-tische Studie* (first edition 1892, second edition 1905, third edition 1907). His view is not original. Dilthey gave the first radical conception of the problem in the *Einleitung.* The philosophy of history of Windelband and Rickert is only an emptied-out, formal study of the points of view that Dilthey had already presented. Today one begins to return beyond this logic of history, to Dilthey, and, after fifty years, gradually to understand him.

If one wants to grasp the problem of the historical philosophically, it is not admissible to proceed from the philosophy of history, because this represents only a forming—out of a historical consciousness—in reference to which we question whether it itself arose from an originally historical motivation. It is telling that the task of turning against the historical falls to *philosophy.* Characterization of three ways: the mode of relation, the relational sense of the tendency-to-secure, and the sense of the conception of history itself.

Simmel asks: How does the "stuff" of immediate reality become the the-oretical formation that we call "history"? The stuff undergoes a process of *formation.* There are two great categories for dividing reality, the natural-scientific and the historical. Similarly Rickert—only in that he (in his *Gren-zen*[5]) supplies a logic of conceptual representation—whereas Simmel asks more in terms of a *psychology of knowledge.* He gives himself the task of investigating the process of formation in which history emerges. The result is that the human being, as known, is the product of nature and of history; yet the human being which knows makes nature and history. The free human personality holds history in its hand; history is a product of free, forming subjectivity. How does this peculiar process of formation occur? Each image of history, because it receives its structure from formative subjectivity, is de-pendent upon a present that views history. Each historical image is thus, in its view of its tendency of development, oriented toward the present. How

---

5. Heinrich Rickert, *Die Grenzen der naturwissenschaftlichen Begriffsbildung,* 2nd ed., Tü-bingen, 1913.

does a historical image, a historical objectivity, arise? How is it that reality is grasped once according to the natural sciences, at other times historically?

It has been said that the historical is that which is effective; if an occurrence shows a certain amount of effects which another does not have, it thus receives historical meaning.[6] However, according to Simmel, the sum of occurrences and of their effects does not equal the historical meaning, but rather brings it about. This is because a sum of occurrences can only be grasped as effective if an *interest* is there, against which the effect is seen as effective. Something becomes historical when the stuff of the immediately experienced releases in us a certain effect of feeling; when we are touched by it. Historical interest has two fundamental directions, which must always go together, so that something like history can emerge at all. On the one hand, historical interest is an interest in the content as such, irrespective of whether the story told is authentic, of whether it is truthfully recounted or not. This interest is enjoyment and pleasure taken in the contest between fate and personal energy, attention to the rhythm of profits and losses, etc. But this interest does not suffice. Then follows, on the other hand, an interest in whether or not the content is real. But a reality in itself is not yet historical; it must also awaken interest in the first sense, that is to say interest in the content. Only when both interests (in the content and in its reality) come together does *historical* interest exist.

What is decisive is that history loses its disturbing character, that in the epistemological analysis its structure is recognized as nothing other than a product of freely formative subjectivity. This tendency is radicalized in the second way. It is pre-formed in Spengler's philosophy of history ("Der Untergang des Abendlandes I"[7]). Spengler has the tendency to present the science of history as such as reliable. In a certain sense, his tendency is new, and one must wonder that the science of history has not welcomed and taken up this tendency in the way it actually deserves. Since Spengler wants to raise history to a science, he thereby supports interests that in the nineteenth century turn against the exclusive rule of the natural sciences. Exactly in that which Simmel emphasized—that history is always formed from a particular standpoint—Spengler sees the deficiency of the science of history. It would be crucial to render the science of history independent of the historical conditionality of the present. One must carry out a Copernican act. How can that happen? In that the present, which drives history and recognizes history, is not absolutized, but is rather placed within the objective process of historical happening.

---

6. [Cf. Eduard Meyer, *Zur Theorie und Methodik der Geschichte,* Halle, 1902, p. 36.]

7. Oswald Spengler, *Der Untergang des Abendlandes, vol. I: Gestalt und Wirklichkeit,* Vienna and Leipzig, 1918. [On April 14, 1920, Heidegger spoke in Wiesbaden on "Oswald Spengler und sein Werk 'Der Untergang des Abendlandes' " ("Oswald Spengler and his work 'the Fall of the West' "). (Cf. Martin Heidegger, Karl Jaspers, *Briefwechsel 1920–1963,* ed. Walter Biemel, Hans Saner. Frankfurt and Munich/Zurich, 1990, p. 15.)]

And this placing-within can only be achieved on the basis of an epistemological conviction. To this Spengler attaches a wild metaphysics, one which resembles Simmel's: History is the expression of a soul ("soul of culture"). History is not contrasted to an extra-temporal reality; rather, the security of the present against history is reached in that the present itself is seen as historical. The reality and uncertainty of the present are experienced in such a way that they themselves are drawn into the objective process of historical becoming, which is nothing else but an ebb and flow of the becoming of "Being which rests in its midst."

c) Compromise between the Two Positions

The third way attempts to combine the first two. Both are fighting fiercely, as the reaction against Spengler's skepticism shows. It directs itself against the extreme position of the *second,* with whose epistemological foundations it begins. For the formation of history as objectivity in knowledge assumes the standard of the value of *truth.* History is a permanent actualization of *values,* which, however, can never be *fully* actualized. Rather, in the historical—here comes the dependence on Spengler—values are given only in a relative form, one through which, as it were, the absolute shines; in the confrontation with history, it is thus crucial not to wipe away, as it were, the historical reality, but rather, in a universal consideration, to form the future by oneself, from the entire treasure of the past, in a process which, according to its own nature, strives to actualize the generally human, the humane.

In all three modes, the tendency to *typologize* plays a role, but in each case the typologization has a different significance. The *first* mode requires the typology in order to refer the historical to the absolutely valid world (ideas)—history is "ideographical" (ἴδιονε γράφειν) (Windelband), it works with "ideal types" (Max Weber). In the second mode (in Spengler) typologization plays a still greater role. Insofar as history is the last reality, it is crucial to follow the different formations of this forming-out. The morphological study of types represents the peculiar vehicle of this kind of knowledge in the science of history. The fundamental reality itself is here a morphological concept; the morphological formation of types is the real vehicle of historical knowledge. For the third mode it is crucial to demarcate the present in its type sharply against the past, in order to determine the future by means of a universal-historical orientation (which is also only possible through the historical formation of types).

§ 9. Tendencies-to-Secure

The attempt to grasp the sense of the morphological-typologizing formation of concepts has never yet been made. The concept of typologizing is important for the sense of the securing that is striven for in the three [aforementioned] ways. We will consider, within the framework of our problem at large: a) the relation of the tendency-to-secure to history; b) the sense of the historical itself which follows from this; and c) the question whether the securing succeeds—namely, whether it actually hits upon that which, in the historical, genuinely disturbs us.

a) The Relation of the Tendency-to-Secure

The *Platonic* way consists not only in the juxtaposition of idea and reality; rather it is comprehensible only through the *relation* of temporal Being to extra-temporal Being. This relation is still today expressed in the characteristic Platonic concepts. The relation should be clarified by *four limit-concepts* or images: temporal Being is an *"imitation"* (μίμησις) of the extra-temporal; the extra-temporal is the *"paradigm"* (παράδειγμα), while the temporal is the after-copy (εἴδωλον); the temporal *"participates"* (μετέχει) in the extra-temporal (μέθεξις); presence (παρουσία) of the extra-temporal in temporal beings. These images signify an *objective* connection of Being between the two worlds of the temporal and the extra-temporal. Here we cannot go into a discussion of these concepts and of the way in which they are epistemologically bent and employed. We are concerned only that the temporal and the extra-temporal are here seen *objectively.* The mode, the sense of securing fulfills itself through the development of a theory about the sense of reality of the temporal. In recognizing what kind of sense of reality the temporal has, it ceases to disturb me, because I recognize it as a forming-out of the extra-temporal.

The *second* way shows the same type of securing. As much as the skepticism of the second way opposes absolute validity of Platonism, the mode of securing against history is the same in both. For in Spengler, the historical world is the foundational reality, the *single* reality; we know *only* cultures, that is to say, the process of becoming of world destiny. My recognizing as a foundational reality the historical in which I myself stand and which disturbs me results in my having to enter into the historical reality, since I cannot resist it. For us today, a conscious participation in the declining occidental culture ensues. Thus also in Spengler the interpretation of the reality of the historical has a liberating effect.

It is now entirely clear that the *third* way is merely a compromise of the first two. On the basis of a theory of historical reality, it seeks to fulfill the tendency toward securing. A "historical dialectic" is designated as the task of the philosophy of history; the oppositions of the temporal and the extra-temporal are to be pursued in their tension and suspension [*Aufhebung*], so that from this the dialectical lawfulness of the historical can be won. On the one hand, I am within history; on the other, I am oriented toward the ideas; I actualize the extra-temporal by entering into the temporal. This beautiful and touching sentimentality of culture has been recited for so long that I do not wish to bore you with it. One sees therein a deep dialectic and thinks with that to have solved the problems of history—while in fact this way represents the most extreme degeneration of the entire problem, already because it is, as a compromise, incapable of grasping originally the motives of the first two ways; rather, it merely takes them up and makes them accessible to the cultural needs of the present. For us the question is whether these tendencies-to-secure correspond at all to the disturbing motive itself. It is thus necessary that we, initially, attempt to understand, on the basis of the ways characterized above, why they actually defend themselves against history. And it is now characteristic of the three ways, and of the entire problem of the historical, that this question is a secondary one, that the disturbance is taken for granted. In the entire consideration, history as the science of history plays no role initially. The theory of the science of history is an entirely secondary problem within the problem of the historical itself.

The present-day confrontation with history testifies, in essence, to the struggle against skepticism and relativism. With this, history appears in a more popular sense, and the basic point of its argumentation is that every skepticism cancels itself out. But logical deduction is no match for historical forces, and the question of skepticism is in this way not to be done away with—for this argumentation was already used by the ancient Greeks. The struggle against history—indirectly and unconsciously—is a struggle for a new culture.

All three ways are fundamentally dominated throughout by the Platonic view, even Spengler, who absolutizes historical reality only *in opposition* to it. The *first* way posits the absolute norm as a higher reality against the historical. The *second* way renounces norms; it sees the reality in the historical itself, in the "cultures." The *third* way recognizes a minimum of absolute values, but ones given only in relative forms in the historical. The orientation of a universal history should further develop in a productive synthesis of all past cultures. The historical reality is, in all three ways, posited as an *objective Being*. The way is that of knowledge [*des Erkennens*], of study of the material. Along with this goes a tendency to typologize, to understand by forming types. This tendency is important because it characterizes the fundamental character of the theoretical attitude in its relation to history. Therein the attitudinal character of the *relation* to history is shown.

"Attitude" has here an entirely particular sense. We use "relation" [*Bezug*] in the general meaning of the word. Not every "relation" is an "attitude," but each "attitude" has the character of a "relation." "Attitude" is a relation to objects in which the conduct [*Verhalten*] is absorbed in the *material complex*. I direct myself only to the *matter,* I focus away from *myself* toward the *matter.* With this "attitude" [*Einstellung*] the *living* relation to the object of knowledge has "ceased" [*"eingestellt"*] (in the sense of "it will cease," for instance, as one says, "The struggle has ceased"). We have then a double meaning in the word "attitude": first an attitude toward a realm of the matter, secondly a ceasing of the entire human relation to the material complex. In this sense we indicate the relation to history in the three ways as "attitudinal" [*einstellungsmäßig*]. History is here *the material* [*Sache*], the *object* toward which I take a cognitive attitude. Spengler too shows in the course of his study that that which disturbs us is the same as that which is disturbed: both are expressions of one soul of culture. His relation is attitudinally cognitive. The morphological study of types is nothing other than the solidification and foundation of the complex of the matter from out of itself; it executes the material complex in the logical sense: the typologization "executes" [*erledigt*] history. If one says that the conduct of system-building is an understanding, an *attitudinal understanding* is meant; but this has nothing to do with *phenomenological understanding.*

b) The Sense of the Historical Itself

What is it then that is disturbed? From out of what is the disturbance motivated? We can now go only so far as it is presented in the three ways, as they grasp it in concepts. It is peculiar of the three ways that that which seeks securing is not at all regarded as a problem. That which seeks securing and which disturbs us goes without saying. Where the phenomenon of disturbance is observed, it is already seen from within the Platonic schema.

(1) The *Platonism of today* is modified from its original through the inclusion of Kantian philosophy. From that standpoint, neo-Kantianism (of the Cohen and Windelband schools), too, seeks to interpret Plato anew. Platonism becomes "transcendental," in the sense of having to do with consciousness [*bewußtseinsmäßig gewendet*]; between the temporal (historical) and the extratemporal (world of ideas), a third, mediating realm appears, the realm of *meaning* (Marburg school, Rickert). In what sense does subjectivity form the mediation? The acts of consciousness, the abilities and activities of consciousness occur, proceed, run a "psychic" course; but they have a sense above and beyond that. Through this they are related to objects [*Gegenstände*] and this relation is determined through norms. But the difficulties of Platonism return in a refined form.

(2) Spengler: The decisive thing is: that which is true reality, the act-context of historical existence [*Dasein*], the human-historical reality, the achieving

life and existence [*Dasein*], desires a *security*, and from this arises concern [*Bekümmerung*]. Spengler and others have the name "culture" for this achieving and creative historical actuality.

(3) Along the third way, what is meant by being in need of security is clearly shown, while the discontent itself remains unproblematized: existence [*Dasein*] is something that goes without saying, something which no longer needs to be attended to; only securing it is much more important. The third way is called the "philosophy of life." Simmel grasps life more biologically, Dilthey more spiritually, Spengler links, in a peculiar way, the first and third ways. "Life" is the fundamental reality and secures itself through the "Turn to Ideas";[8] ideas are the "Dominators of Life" (Simmel).

Thus life tends to secure itself either *against* history (*first* way) or *with* history (*second* way) or *from* history (*third* way). The concept of life is a polysemous one; and, from this entirely general, formal point of view, the critique of present-day philosophy of life would make some sense. Such a critique is justified only when one succeeds in grasping this concept positively in an original sense; but in another sense not so, lest it misjudge the actual motives of the philosophy of life and pull it back into the rigid Platonism. In Rickert it becomes clear that, in the Platonic way, the human-historical reality is not understood from out of itself, but only with regard to an a priori complex of values. Rickert says that the human individual is, in his singularity, nothing other than what he achieved for the values of culture. With this, the concept of the individual is grasped purely Platonically.

c) Does the Securing Suffice?

Does the securing suffice for that which drives forth the disturbance? That which is disturbed, the reality of life, the human existence in its concern about its own security, is not taken in itself; rather it is regarded as object and as object it is placed within the historical objective reality. The worry is not answered, but rather is immediately objectified. Spengler is the clearest on this point and drives the tendencies subsumed with contemporary philosophy to the end. He wants to secure the *science* of history. Through this view, having supposedly first made history into a science, he has *destroyed* history, he has *mathematized* world history such that the types stand next to one another like houses. And the formal, aesthetic study of soul and expression is imposed on history from without. Thus: an aesthetic and a mathematical tendency. The life concerned for itself is set up in a historical context, but the actual tendency to concern is not attended to.

8. Georg Simmel, *Lebensanschauung. Vier metaphysische Kapitel,* Munich and Leipzig, 1918, p. 28.

From where does it arise that, despite this, the three ways are recognized by life as securings? This is grounded in the fact that concern is already touched upon by the *foreconception* of the study. The concern is re-interpreted attitudinally. That comes from the tendency of factical life to fall away attitudinally. Thus the concern itself becomes the attitudinal foreconception of an object.

Here lies the actual fracture-point of the entire problem of the historical. The meaning of history, which is predelineated within the concern itself, cannot become clear in this way. The possibility is offered here to endure the attitudinality [*das Einstellungsmässige*] of the study of the historical, in order to uncover the true distress. We must avoid taking the phenomenon of the historical from the *science* of history. The positing of the logic of history as the fundamental discipline of the philosophy of history already sets the problem up in the wrong context. The attitudinal meaning of history which appears here is a *derivative one.* Mostly, one falsely derives from it all other historical phenomena. We must then attempt to catch sight of the phenomenon of concern *unhidden* in *factical* Dasein.

§ 10. The Concern of Factical Dasein

What effect does concern have in factical life? The relation between factical Dasein and worry is taken, in the three ways, as a *relation of order.* The concerned Dasein is placed within an objective context. But how does the concerned Dasein himself stand with respect to the historical in the three ways? The concerned Dasein is only an object-segment from a great whole object (from the entire objective historical happening). The distressed Dasein turns a) against [the] change; against the happening of existence [*das geschehnishafte Dasein*]. Expressed in terms of transcendental philosophy: Consciousness is more than a course of acts. The acts have a meaning; b) the own, present Dasein demands not only a *meaning at all,* but also a *concrete* meaning: namely, a meaning *other* than past cultures had, a *new* meaning that exceeds the one of earlier life. It wants to be a new creation, be it an entirely original one, a "great synthesis," "away from the barbaric," or however one names these tendencies.

We are asking not for the content and justification; rather we attempt to go back from these expressions of concerned Dasein to Dasein itself. With that we apparently return to the beginning. We attempt to understand the concerned Dasein out of our own life experience. How does the own living Dasein conduct itself as distressed by history, to history itself? How does factical life stand *from out of itself* to history? Theories remain completely peripheral, even as the view that the historical reality is the reality of happening proceeding in time. We attempt only to determine the meaning of history out of factical experience. The difficulties of the problem are those with which philosophy must struggle anew at each step and with each problem. Despite this, the guiding thread for our study will be the old concept of the historical.

In order to understand how this is possible, we must first present a main part of the phenomenological method. The confrontation with history is today so peculiar that one can say they fight with weapons that they themselves do not understand and which belong exactly to that which they are fighting against. The tendencies-to-secure against history have the same character as the grasped history itself, so that the problem moves perpetually in a circle and one theory of history replaces another. It is, of course, not meant that one day a philosophy of history would be given that would stand for all time—that is an entirely unphilosophical ideal; rather, at issue is a confrontation with history which arises from the sense of factical Dasein.

In the three considered ways, the distressed Dasein is considered as an object within history itself. What is genuinely (originally) distressed disappears in this view, and the solution of the distress becomes very simple. But we ask: What *genuinely* wants to secure itself against history? In all three ways life, the human historical reality, elevates itself as that which is supposed to have a meaning. This sphere is not problematized in today's philosophy, or at least is only grasped according to the conceptual schema of the respective philosophy. One does not pose the question, whether it is perhaps impossible to grasp the sense of factical Dasein with today's philosophical means. One does not ask how factical Dasein is to be explicated originally, that is to say, philosophically. Apparently, then, a gap in today's philosophical system of categories is to be filled. Yet we will see that, through the explication of factical Dasein, the entire traditional system of categories will be blown up—so radically new will the *categories of factical Dasein* be.

Factical Dasein, as an objectively proceeding occurrence, cannot be simply a blind one; rather it must carry a sense within itself and thereby require for itself a particular lawfulness. But not only a lawfulness per se is desired; rather the present wants to build itself further into the future, in a new creation of the own Dasein and in an own, new culture. Through this tendency, factical Dasein experiences a particular elevation [*Abhebung*]; all effort points to it.

We leave aside the view of history we discussed above. We ask: How does the historical stand with regard to factical life existence [*Lebensdasein*] itself? Which sense does the historical have in factical life existence? A difficulty is what is actually meant here by "historical." I use already in the *question* a particular sense of "historical." I already have in sight a particular meaning, according to which I decide in which sense the historical exists in factical life experience. Is a particular, perhaps disarranging sense of "historical" already introduced with the posing of the question? But the question cannot be gotten hold of otherwise, if I want to grasp the historical in factical life existence. This is a difficulty that appears in all of phenomenology and easily leads to hasty generalizations.

Chapter Four

Formalization and Formal Indication

§ 11. The General Sense of "Historical"

We will name the methodical use of a sense that becomes a guiding one for phenomenological explication, a "formal indication." The phenomena will be examined according to what the formally indicative sense carries within itself. Through the methodological consideration, it must become clear how it can be that the formal indication, although guiding the consideration, nevertheless brings no preconceived opinion into the problems. One must become clear about the meaning of the formal indication, or else one falls either into an attitudinal consideration or into regional demarcations which one views as absolute. The problem of the *"formal indication"* belongs to the "theory" of the phenomenological method itself, in the broad sense, to the problem of the *theoretical,* of the theoretical act, the phenomenon of *differentiating.* Later the entire problem will occupy us. Preliminarily, we are seeking the difficulty only in the concrete case.

The usual sense of the historical says it is the temporally-becoming, and as such, past. Factical life experience is consequently viewed as to what extent something temporal—to what extent something becoming, and something conscious as past—appears in it. This sense of "historical" is so general (so it seems initially) that nothing would be lost if it were applied, without further qualification, to factical life experience. For factical life experience is, after all, a certain domain of reality; the historical as becoming *per se* is not limited to such. This sense seems then the most general; all other senses, it seems, could only be a determination thereof. But it is problematical to what extent this sense of "historical" is general, and whether this kind of generality can be a philosophic principle. Two questions thus arise here: 1. To what extent can this general sense of historical be addressed as a philosophic principle? 2. If this claim is *not* justified, and yet the meaning is, despite this, a "general" one and merits consideration in the explication, to what extent does it not prejudice—although it, not being original, nevertheless should guide original consideration?

In philosophy for centuries, generality, from the side of the object, is considered a characteristic of the object of philosophy. And exactly our general sense of "historical" can seem appropriate to demarcate a particular realm within the totality of all beings, and, with this demarcation, achieve a final philosophical work, insofar as it belongs to philosophy to partition the totality of beings and assign different sciences to the different regions. Already Aristotle says in his metaphysics: τὸ ὂν πολλαχῶς λέγεται[1] (beings are multiply said). However, Aristotle meant nothing more than what one had theretofore seen. For Aristotle, at issue is not only an ontological consideration; rather an entirely other, implicit consideration hovers therein. Aristotle's metaphysics is perhaps already more advanced than we ourselves are today in philosophy.

One can view this classification of beings as an ontological study. Now insofar as the beings *are* only *for a consciousness,* the ontological classification corresponds to one *related to consciousness* [*eine bewußtseinsmäßige*], in which questions are asked about the connections between "modes of consciousness," modes in which the beings "constitute themselves"—that is to say, become conscious. This problem was posed by Kant; but phenomenology (Husserl's) first had the means to carry out this study concretely. From the ontological aspect, philosophy thus had to do with beings; from the aspect of consciousness, with the original laws of constitution belonging to consciousness. Each thing [*jedes Gegenständliche*] stands under the form of this constitution. In Husserl's phenomenology, consciousness itself becomes a region, and is subordinate to a regional consideration; its lawfulness is not only in principle original, but also the most general. It expresses itself generally and originally in transcendental phenomenology.

§ 12. Generalization and Formalization

The general becomes accessible through generalizing [*Verallgemeinerung*]. The meaning of "generalization" is controversial in philosophy heretofore, and before Husserl's phenomenology was never seriously considered. Husserl first differentiated "formalization" from "generalization" (*Logische Untersuchungen* [*Logical Investigations*], *Volume I.,* final chapter,[2] "Ideen zu einer reinen Phänomenologie" ["Ideas for a Pure Phenomenology"] § 13[3]). This difference had been known implicitly for a long time in mathematics (already since Leibniz), but Husserl first carried out its logical explication. He sees the meaning of the difference, above all, in terms of formal ontology and in the grounding of a pure logic of objects [*Gegenstandslogik*] (*mathesis universalis*). We want to attempt to further this differentiation and, in this furtherance, explain the meaning of the formal indication.

1. cf. *Metaphysics* 1003 a33.

2. Edmund Husserl, *Logical Investigations, Volume I, Prolegomena to Pure Logic,* 2nd revised edition, Tübingen, 1913.

3. Edmund Husserl, "Ideen zu einer reinen Phänomenologie und phänomenologischen Philosophie," in *Jahrbuch für Philosophie und phänomenologischen Forschung,* vol. I, Tübingen, 1913.

"Generalization" ["*Generalisierung*"] means generalizing [*Verallgemeine-rung*] according to genus. For example, red is a color, color is sensuous qual-ity. Or joy is an affect, affect is experience. One can, so it seems, drive this further: qualities as such, things [*Dinge*] as such are essences [*Wesen*]. Red, color, sensual quality, experience, genus, species, essence, are things [*Gegen-stände*]. But the question arises: Is the generalizing transition from "red" to "color," or from "color" to "sensuous quality" the same as that from "sensuous quality" to "essence" and from "essence" to "thing"? Evidently *not*! There is a break here: the transition from "red" to "color" and from "color" to "sen-suous quality" is a *generalization;* that from "sensuous quality" to "essence" is a *formalization.* One can ask whether the determination "sensuous quality" determines "color" in the same sense as the formal determination "thing" [*Gegenstand*] does any thing you like. Evidently *not*. Nevertheless, the dif-ference between generalization and formalization is not yet entirely clear.

The *generalization* is bound in its enactment to a certain material domain. The order of stages of "generalities" (genus and species) is determined ac-cording to the matter at issue [*sachhaltig bestimmt*]. The measuring to [*An-messung an*] the material context is essential. Otherwise for the *formalization:* for example, "The stone is an object." There the attitude [*Einstellung*] is not bound to the materiality of things (to the region of the material things and such), but is free in terms of its material contents. It is also free from any order of stages: I need run through no lower generalities in order to ascend to the "highest generality" "thing as such." The formal predication is not bound in terms of its material contents, yet it must be somehow motivated. How is it motivated? It arises from the sense of attitudinal relation itself [*Einstellungsbezug*]. I see the determination of its "what" [*Wasbestimmtheit*] not from out of the object; rather I read the determination "off" the object. I must see away from the what-content [*Wasgehalt*] and attend only to the fact that the object is a given, attitudinally grasped one. Thus the formalization arises out of the relational meaning of the pure attitudinal relation itself, not out of the "what-content as such."

From here the relational determinations of the attitudes can first be seen. The pure attitudinal relation must itself still be viewed as an enactment, in order to understand the origin of the theoretical. But philosophizing—as we will see later—must be viewed in its original attitudinal *enactment* [*Einstel-lungsvollzug*]; the relation of phenomenological explication and the conduct of thought is also thus illuminated. The origin of the formal lies thus in the relational meaning. That diversity of relational meaning that is expressed in formal-ontological categories circumscribes the inauthentic theoretical attitude in its *relational* meaning, if not likewise in its original *enactment*. In talk of the "formal indication," does the word "formal" have the meaning of the formalized, or does it gain another meaning? What is common to formalization and generalization is that they stand within the meaning of "general," whereas the formal indication has nothing to do with generality. The meaning of "formal" in the "formal indication" is *more original.* For one means by "formal ontology" already something materially formed out. The "formal *region*" is in a *broader* sense also a "material *domain*" [*Sachgebiet*]; also is material [*sachhaltig*]. There exist, for example, certain differences within the formalized. We have:

1. Something is an object (can be said of anything and everything)
2. Experience as such, thing as such, are essences (cannot be said of each object)

These differences go together with the meaning of "general." Contrarily, the *formal indication* has *nothing* to do with this. It falls outside of the attitudinally theoretical.

Philosophy is ever again given the task of classifying the whole of Being into regions. Philosophy has long been moved in this ontological direction. Only late did the opposing consideration arise: How is the experienced experienced in the manner of consciousness [*bewußtseinsmäßig*]? If one now grasps this correlative consideration as a principal task, then the realm of consciousness itself becomes a region, and in turn the task arises of determining it itself more ontologically exactly. Insofar as one describes consciousness, in some sense or other, as activity, one can describe the side of consciousness as an original, active one, because that which is original of consciousness becomes identical to the constitutive-original. From there arises the tendency to see in constitution the genuine task of philosophy. This task was carried out resolutely by Hegel, today most prominently in the Marburg school.

We posed to ourselves the question: To what extent may the general be posited as the last philosophical determination? In what sense is generalization [*Generalisierung*] a generalizing [*Verallgemeinerung*]? In what sense is formalization a generalizing [*Verallgemeinerung*]? Projected back onto our question, the question arises, how far and under what conditions may the general be posited as the last object of philosophical determination; and if that is not the case, to what extent does the formal indication, despite this, not prejudice a phenomenological consideration?

Generalization [*Generalisierung*] can be described as a *way of ordering.* In it an integration of particular individuations into an encompassing material complex results. It is possible that this context itself can be integrated into a still more general, encompassing complex. Therefore the generalization always takes place in a material [*sachhaltigen*] sphere. Its direction is determined through the right approach to the material [*des Sachhaltigen*]. With that the generalizing [*Verallgemeinerung*] has meaning only in an attitude, for the material complex must be free, must have a free hand, in order to entirely order itself according to its materiality [*Sachlichkeit*]. The generalization [*Generalisierung*] is a particular order of stages, and indeed a materially immanent order of stages of determinatenesses, which stand among each other in the relation of mutual concernability [*Betreffbarkeit*], so that the most general determination refers all the way to the very last, most subordinate. Generalizing determinations are always determinations of an object according to its materiality from another [viewpoint], and indeed such that what determines, for its part, itself belongs within the material domain in which the determining 'what' lies. Generalization is thus ordering; it is determination from another, such that this other belongs, as *encompassing,* to the same material region [*Sachregion*] as that to be determined. Generalization is thus an integration into the material complex of another.

Is *formalization* also order? In generalization, I remain in a material region. It can draw out different directions of generalization; once one is chosen, it must be maintained, [for] a leaping over from one direction to the other is not possible. Formalization is not bound to the particular 'what' of the object to be determined. The determination turns away from the materiality of the object, it observes the object according to the aspect in which it is given; it is determined as *that which is grasped;* as that to which the cognizing relation refers. An "object as such" means only the "to which" of the theoretical attitudinal relation. This attitudinal relation contains a plurality of meanings that can be explicated—and indeed such that this explication can be considered as determination according to the sphere of objects. But the relational meaning is not an order, not a region, or rather only indirectly, insofar as it is *formed out* into a formal object-category to which a "region" corresponds. The formalization is primarily only an order through this forming-out. Thus we have to understand under formalization several things: determination of a something as object, assignment to a formally objective category, which is however for its part not original, but rather represents only the forming-out of a relation. Task of forming-out the diversity of the relational meaning. Theory of the formal-ontological (*mathesis universalis*) from the meaning of the relational possibility itself.

§ 13. The "Formal Indication"

Thus we have:

1. Formalization. In this forming-out, a special task arises: the theory of the formal-logical and formal-ontological. Through their forming-out from the

relational meaning, the formal categories make possible the performance of mathematical operations.

2. Theory of the formal-ontological (*mathesis universalis*), through which a theoretical region is posited as separate.

3. Phenomenology of the formal (original consideration of the formal itself and explication of the relational meaning within its enactment).

If such a formal-ontological determination is posited [*angesetzt wird*] as "generality," does this prejudice philosophy? Insofar as the formal-ontological determinations are formal, they do not prejudice. Thus it is fitting to lead philosophy back to them. If we ask whether the formal-ontological prejudices philosophy, this question makes sense only if one accepts the thesis that philosophy is *not* an attitude. In the background is for us the thesis: that philosophy is not theoretical science, thus also the formal-ontological study can be the final one, determining the constitutive-phenomenological. For under this presupposition, the accepted formal-ontological grasp of the object is prejudicing.

What is phenomenology? What is phenomenon? Here this can be itself indicated only formally. Each experience—as experi*encing,* and what is ex-peri*enced*—can "be taken in the phenomenon," that is to say, one can ask:

1. After the original "*what,*" that is experienced therein (*content*).

2. After the original "*how,*" in which it is experienced (*relation*).

3. After the original "*how,*" in which the relational meaning is *enacted* (*enactment*).

But these three directions of sense (content-, relational-, enactment-sense) do not simply coexist. "Phenomenon" is the totality of sense in these three directions. "Phenomenology" is explication of this totality of sense; it gives the "λόγος" of the phenomena, "λόγος" in the sense of "*verbum internum*" (not in the sense of logicalization).

Now does the formal-ontological determination prejudice this task of phenomenology? One could say that a formal-ontological determinateness says nothing about the 'what' of that which it determines, and thus does not prejudice anything. But exactly because the formal determination is entirely indifferent as to content, it is fatal for the relational- and enactment-aspect of the phenomenon—because it prescribes, or at least contributes to prescribing, a theoretical relational meaning. It hides the *enactment*-character [*das* Voll-zugs*mäßige*]—which is possibly still more fatal—and turns one-sidedly to the *content.* A glance at the history of philosophy shows that formal determination of the objective entirely dominates philosophy. How can this prejudice, this pre-judgment, be prevented? This is just what the *formal indication* achieves. It belongs to the phenomenological explication itself as a methodical moment. Why is it called "formal"? The formal is something relational. The indication should indicate beforehand the relation of the phenomenon—in the negative sense, however, the same as if to warn! A phenomenon must be so stipulated, such that its relational meaning is held in abeyance. One must prevent oneself from taking it for granted that its relational meaning is originally theoretical. The relation and performance of the phenomenon is *not* preliminarily determined, but is held in abeyance. That is a stance which is opposed to science in the highest degree. There is no insertion into a material domain, but rather the opposite: the formal indication is a defense [*Abwehr*], a preliminary *securing,* so that the enactment-character still remains free. The necessity of this precautionary measure arises from the falling tendency of factical life experience, which constantly threatens to slip into the objective, and out of which we must still retrieve the phenomena.

Formalization and generalization are thus attitudinally or theoretically motivated. Ordering occurs in their enactment: directly in generalization, indirectly in formalization. To the contrary, the "formal indication" does not concern an order. In the formal indication one stays away from any classification; everything is precisely kept open. The formal indication has meaning only in relation to the phenomenological explication. The question is, whether the posited task of philosophy, as the general determination of the objective, can be maintained in principle—whether this setting of the task arises from the original motive of philosophizing. In order to decide that, we must allow ourselves to be driven into a new situation; we must become clear about the way of phenomenological consideration. This is accomplished by the formal indication. It means a *positing* of the *phenomenological explication.*

We apply the results won to the problem of the historical. If the historical is taken as the formally indicated, it is not thereby asserted that the most general determination of "historical" as a "becoming in time" delineates a final sense. This formally indicating determination of the sense of historical is neither to be regarded as one which determines the objective historical world in its historical structural character, nor as one which describes the most general sense of the historical itself. "Temporal" is, preliminarily, still taken in an entirely undetermined sense: one does not know at all which time is being spoken of. So long as the sense of "temporal" is undetermined, one could understand it as [something] not prejudicing; one could mean: insofar as each objecthood constitutes itself in consciousness, it is temporal, and with that one has won the fundamental schema of the temporal. But this "general-formal" determination of time is no foundation; rather it is a falsification of the problem. For with that a *framework* for the time-phenomenon has been predelineated from out of the *theoretical.* Rather, the problem of time must be grasped in the way we originally experience temporality in factical experience—entirely irrespective of all pure consciousness and all pure time. The way is thus reversed. We must ask, rather, what is temporality originally in factical experience? What do past, present, and future mean in factical experience? Our way takes its point of departure from factical life, from which the meaning of time is won. The problem of the historical is thus characterized.

Philosophy, as I understand it, is in a difficulty. The listener in other lectures is assured, from the beginning on: in art history lectures he can see pictures; in others he gets his money's worth for his exams. In philosophy, it is otherwise, and I cannot change that, for I did not invent philosophy. I would, however, like to save myself from this calamity and thus break off these so abstract considerations, and lecture to you, beginning in the next session, on history; and indeed I will, without further consideration for the starting-point and method, take a particular concrete phenomenon as the point of departure, however for me under the presupposition that you will misunderstand the entire study from beginning to end.

PART TWO

Phenomenological Explication of Concrete Religious
Phenomena in Connection with the Letters of Paul

Chapter One

Phenomenological Interpretation of the Letters to the Galatians

§14. Introduction

In the following, we do not intend to give a dogmatic or theological-exegetical interpretation, nor a historical study or a religious meditation, but only guidance for phenomenological understanding. Characteristic of the phenomenological-religious understanding is gaining an advance understanding for an original way of access. One must work the religious-historical method into it, and indeed in such a way that one examines it critically. The theological method falls out of the framework of our study. Only with phenomenological understanding, a new way for theology is opened up. The formal indication renounces the last understanding that can only be given in genuine religious experience; it intends only to open an access to the New Testament.

Initially, we will interpret the letter of Paul to the Galatians. The letter to the Galatians was significant for the young Luther; along with the letter to the Romans, it became a dogmatic fundament. Luther and Paul are, religiously speaking, the most radical opposites. There is a commentary by Luther on the letter to the Galatians.[1] Yet we must free ourselves from Luther's standpoint. Luther sees Paul from out of Augustine. Despite this, there are real connections of Protestantism with Paul.

The letter to the Galatians contains a historical report from Paul himself about the story of his conversion. It is the original document for his religious development and, *historically,* reports the passionate excitation of Paul himself. Correlatively, only the story of the apostles is to be invoked. To begin with, it suffices to seek a general understanding of the letter to the Galatians in order to penetrate therewith into the grounding phenomena of primordial Christian life.

---

1. *In epistolam Pauli ad Galatas commentarius* (1519) in *D. Martin Luthers Werke. Kritische Gesamtausgabe,* 2 volumes, Weimar, 1884, pp. 436–618.

The original Greek text is the only one to be used as a basis; an actual understanding presupposes a penetration into the spirit of New Testament Greek. Eberhard Nestle offers the best Greek edition: *Novum Testamentum Graecum.*[2] If one wants to use the aid of a translation, Luther's shouldn't be chosen, for it is all too dependent upon Luther's own theological standpoint. The translation of Weizsäcker (Verlag v. Mohr, Tübingen) or that of Eberhard Nestle is recommended.[3]

In the letters to the Galatians, Paul is struggling with the Jews and the Jewish Christians. Thus we find the phenomenological situation of religious struggle and of struggle itself. Paul must be seen in struggle with his religious passion in his existence as an apostle, the struggle between "law" and "faith." This opposition is not a final one; it is rather a preliminary one. Faith and law are both special modes of the path of salvation. The aim is "salvation" (ἡ σωτηρία), finally "life" (ἡ ζωή). The fundamental comportment of Christian consciousness is to be understood out of this, according to the sense of its content, relation, and enactment. Reading modern positions into it is to be avoided. All concepts are to be understood from out of the context of Christian consciousness. In this respect the historical research of theologians has been of service, as questionable as it may be for theology itself.

The letter to the Galatians can be divided in three main parts: 1. Demonstration of the uniqueness of the apostolic mission of Paul and his vocation through Christ; 2. Conflict between law and faith (at first theoretical, and then applied to life); 3. Christian life as a whole, its motives and its tendencies in terms of content.

§ 15. Some Remarks on the Text

1:5: αἰών, "world." The present time has already reached its end and a new αἰών has begun since the death of Christ. The present world is opposed to the world of eternity. ᾧ ἡ δόξα [to whom be the glory] has a particular meaning.

1:8–9: The struggle for the "right evangelism." Intended is not a saving of the Galatians; rather the original Christianity should be grounded from out of itself, without regard for pre-given forms of religion, such as the Jewish-pharasetical. Paul's own religious position is to be constituted.

1:10: Significant! Complete break with the earlier past, with every non-Christian view of life.

---

2. *Novum Testamentum Graece cum apparatu critico ex editionibus et libris mau scriptis collecto curavit Eberhard Nestle. Editio quinta recognita.* Stuttgart, 1904.

3. *Das Neue Testamen. Neu bearbeitet, mit Fundorten und Randstellen.* Translated by Karl Weizsäcker. 10th edition, Verlag von J.C.B. Mohr, Freiburg and Tübingen, 1918.

Novum Testamentum Graece et Germanice. Das neue Testament griechisch und deutsch. Edited by Eberhard Nestle. Privilegierte Württembergische Bibelanstalt, Stuttgart, 1898.

1:12: Paul wants to say further that he has come to Christianity not through a historical tradition, but through an original experience. A theory that is controversial in Protestant theology connects with this: [it is asserted that] Paul had no historical consciousness of Jesus of Nazareth. Rather he has grounded a new Christian religion, a new primordial Christianity which dominates the future: the Pauline religion, not the religion of Jesus. One thus does not need to refer back to a historical Jesus. The life of Jesus is entirely indifferent. Of course that may not be read out of a single passage.

1:13: Important passage for what is characteristic of Paul. ἀναστροφή [conduct-manner of life]: conducting of life, posture of life to which I am turned.

1:14: ζηλωτής: "zealot." Paul's passionateness maintains itself also after his conversion.

1:16: τοῖς ἔθνεσιν (among the Gentiles): One does not know whether this became clear to him already with the calling or only gradually.

1:17: Arabia = East Jordan; perhaps ascetic life, perhaps already missionizing.

1:18: ἱστορῆσαι (ἱστορεῖν): to get to know, therefore, "history" ["*Historie*"]

2:2: Emphasizing the τρέχειν, "running." Paul is hurried, because the end of time has already come.

2:16: δικαιοῦται, "speaking justly," stems from the Jewish religion. The life of the individual is a trial-process before God, against which Jesus turns ethically in the Sermon on the Mount ("conviction"). The δικαιοσύνη (νόμος Χριστοῦ) [the law of Christ] later has a new Christian meaning. Paul's argumentation is here rabbinical-Jewish-theological. His own original position is to be differentiated from this view. The argumentation from out of the Old Testament is characteristically rabbinical.

2:17: This conclusion *ab absurdum* is found often in Paul.

2:19: Very important! Concentrated form of the entire Pauline dogmatic. ἀπέθανεν νόμῳ διὰ νόμου [Through the law I died to the law] merely ethical. Since Christ is identical with the law, the law died with him (as does Paul, too).

2:20: Decisive for Pauline "mysticism." Reitzenstein points to the connection of the terminology with Hellenism.[4] However, one may not interpret exclusively philologically (hermetic writings).

3:2: ἐξ ἀκοῆς πίστεως [by believing what you heard]: from the hearing in faith. Cf. Rom. 10:11 ff.

4:3: ὑπὸ τὰ στοιχεῖα τοῦ κόσμου [to the elemental spirits of the world]: under the elements of the world. In the Stoics στοιχεῖον indicates element, as already in Empedocles. Philo Judas (at the same time as Paul) designates the pagans

---

4. Cf. Richard Reitzenstein, *Die hellenistische Mysterienreligion nach ihren Grundgedanken und Wirkungen* (1910). 2nd revised edition, Leipzig and Berlin, 1920, p. 48.

as τὰ στοιχεῖα τιμῶντες [elemental spirits]. Compare with 4:9 and 10: stars count as world-elements, the feast-times were arranged according to the stars.

4:8: φύσει μὴ οὖσιν θεοῖς [by nature are not gods]. The στοιχεῖα are divine beings. Compare with V. 1: The stages [?] under [?] the guardians are compared to the stage of the star-priests.

4:9: γιγνώσκειν [to know] in the sense of love (as in the first verse). The love of God to human beings is what is fundamental, not theoretical knowledge.

4:14: "You took no offense to my sickness." (Sickness often grasped as lecherousness.)

4:24: ἀλληγορούμενα [allegory]: the allegorical textual interpretation was then practiced by Philo. Ἀγάρ ("Hagar") means in Arabic "mountain," or, that is what the mountain is called in Arabic.

4:26: ἡ ἄνω Ἰερουσαλήμ [the Jerusalem above]: The final state of redemption is described in the Apocalypse Baruch.

5:5: Connection of πίστις [faith] and ἐλπίς [hope] (cf. Cor.) is important. The bliss is not completed here, but is moved to the higher αἰών [world]. Compare to the "unwavering running toward the aim."

5:11: τὸ σκάνδαλον τοῦ σταυροῦ [the offense of the cross]: That is the real fundamental part of Christianity, against which there is only faith or non-faith.

§ 16. The Fundamental Posture of Paul

Paul finds himself in a struggle. He is pressured to assert the Christian life experience against the surrounding world. To this end he uses the insufficient means of rabbinical teaching available to him. From this his explication of Christian life experience has its peculiar structure. Still, it is an original explication from the sense of the religious life itself. It can be further formed out in the primary religious experience. Theoretical contexts remain far [from this]; an explicational context is won, one that presents itself similarly to a theoretical explication. At issue is a return to the original experience and an understanding of the problem of religious explication.

Harnack's *Dogmengeschichte* [*History of Dogma*][5] begins only with the third century. According to Harnack, Greek philosophy first dogmatized the Christian religion. But the actual problem of "dogma," in the sense of religious explication, lies in primordial Christianity. This here lies before us. The question of expression ("explication") seems to be secondary. Yet, with this seemingly external problem, we stand within the religious phenomenon itself. It is

5. Adolf V. Harnack, *Lehrbuch der Dogmengeschichte,* 3 volumes, Freiburg/Breisgau, 1886–90.

not a technical problem, separate from religious experience; rather the explication goes along with, and drives, the religious experience.

"Law" is here to be understood primarily as ritual and ceremonial law. Also intended is the merely secondary moral law. Therefore, there is a struggle of the Jewish-Christian community for the law, the law as that which makes the Jew a Jew. Ἔργον νόμου [the work of the law]: the attitude to the law. The opposition of faith and law is decisive: the *how* of faith and of the fulfillment of the law, how I comport myself to the faith and also to the law. Phil. 3:13 shows the fundamental posture of Paul.

The third chapter, in particular, contains a secure dialectical argumentation. Nevertheless, we are not dealing with a logical mode of argumentation. Rather it arises out of the consciousness of faith of this explication itself. The expression λογίζεσθαι [to consider, to speak] is characteristic for the articulation of the consciousness of faith, in the sense of making comprehensible the posture of faith for the individual himself, and being able to appropriate the specific-religious-comprehensible meaning. Paul shows his main theological card: the argument that Abraham himself would be justified only through faith. Accordingly, how does it stand at all with the law? 3:2: ἐξ ἔργον νόμου [the works of the law]—stands in sharp opposition to ἐξ ἀκοῆς πίστεως [by believing what you hear] (compare with Rom. 10:13, 14). The fulfillment of law is impossible; each fails in it, only faith justifies. Whoever thus stands under the law is condemned. 3:19 offers an accumulation of determinations that are supposed to suggest the inferiority of the law.

In studying the religious world of Paul, one must free oneself from drawing out certain concepts (such as πίστις, δικαιοσύνη, σάρξ, etc. [faith, righteousness, flesh]) and putting together their meaning from out of a heap of singular passages of the Pauline writings, so that one has a catalogue of fundamental concepts that say nothing. Equally mistaken is the thought of a theological system in Paul. Rather, the fundamental religious experience must be explicated, and, remaining in this fundamental experience, one must seek to understand the connection to it of all original religious phenomena. In order to win a guidance for this kind of study, we will initially emphasize the phenomenon that lies before us in the letter to the Galatians. Later we will reach out historically further, not so much forward into a later time as backward to the original Christian community and to Jesus himself. To be compared with the fundamental posture of Paul is Phil. 3:13: Self-certainty of the situation [*Stellung*] in his own life—break in his existence—original historical understanding of his self and of his existence. From out of this, he performs his feat as apostle, and as human being.

Chapter Two

Task and Object of the Philosophy of Religion

§ 17. *Phenomenological Understanding*

In which way are we to consider, for the philosophy of religion, that which we brought to attention, in an entirely primitive way, through a reading of the letter to the Galatians? That is to be decided only out of the leading aim of the task of the philosophy of religion. Therefore, we must sketch out what is most necessary in the method, and indeed in a brief, schematic treatment; thereby the connection with the general methodical introduction will be made as well. If one determines the task of the philosophy of religion entirely naïvely, one can say religion should be understood, grasped philosophically. Religion is to be projected into an understandable context. Thus the position of the problem of the philosophy of religion depends upon the concept of philosophy.

If one admits a limitation to primordial Christian religiosity, one must then observe that it is a historical fact. If one grasps the philosophical context as a determined, demarcated field—for example, as "consciousness"—the primordial Christian religiosity becomes a fact, that is, an example, a singular case in a range of possibilities, of types, of possible forms of religiosity. Because everything historical should come into consideration merely as example, it is clear that—as is entirely usual today, after all—a bare collection of material lies in the sense of this formulation of the problem. Through this formulation of the problem, the object to be recognized—for example primordial Christian religiosity—is already characterized; it is thereby sketched out in a particular sense of history. The historical types of religion are placed into a diversity of possibilities. They are a material to be drawn upon; in this way, they form an extra-temporal diversity.

Which presupposition lays at the bottom of this formulation of the problem? We do not ask this because we reject each and every positing of presuppositions, but because each philosophical positing of the problem must be clear about its presuppositions. Today's usual philosophy of religion makes the following presuppositions in its positing of the problem, about which it is not clear:

1. Religion is a case or an example of an extra-temporal lawfulness.

2. From religion only that which has the character of consciousness will be taken up.

And indeed the phenomena of consciousness, which correspond to the entirely particular concept of consciousness of the philosophy used as a foundation, standardize the entire formulation of the problem. Now if one describes as our task the phenomenological understanding of primordial Christian religiosity, so it sounds the same according to its wording. However, the former formulation of the problem understands away from its own object; it makes the object disappear. By contrast, it is the tendency of phenomenological understanding to experience the object itself in its originality.

§ 18. Phenomenology of Religion and the History of Religion

One will say that the usual philosophy of religion also holds on to the historical, to the religious-historical. But does the formulation of the problem of the usual history of religion attain to the genuine object of religiosity itself? So long as it is not certain that the religious-historical and the genuine religious-philosophical understanding, that is, phenomenological understanding, coincide, it is still not at all said that the history of religion can deliver material for the philosophy (phenomenology) of religion. To what extent does the religious-historical material, even if only as a starting point for the philosophy of religion, come into question? That is a problem that we cannot decide here; but it is a fundamental problem, which arises for all history of ideas [*Geistesgeschichte*]. Today's philosophy of history achieves nothing for positive historical research—and vice versa. It is the "merit" of Spengler to have compressed the comic effect of this situation into a philosophy. The problems of the philosophy of history are to be retrieved only out of the concrete historical sciences themselves.

Is then the material of the history of religion useable for phenomenology? In what way is the history of religion itself at all appropriate to its objects? One could say: If the history of religion clarifies religiosity from out of its religious environment, as [it does] out of its historical time, how can one then accuse it of not reaching its object? After all, it interprets, as objective science, free of prejudices and preconceptions, only on the basis of its material of sense that the contemporary sources offer, independently of all tendencies of the present. This argumentation has certainly an appearance of justification. On the one hand, one has to agree with it to a certain extent. But on the other hand, it must be objected that all objectivity of the science of history and the object-historical understanding offer no guarantee so long as the guiding fore-conception is not clarified.

It is to be shown, moreover, that all motives for historical understanding are always awakened through factical life experience. The science of history has only the task of employing them in formal formed-out-ness and in rigorous methodology. The tendencies of understanding arise from out of the living present, which are then merely formed out in science in "exact" methodology; the "exactness of method" offers in itself no guarantee for correct understanding. The methodical-scientific apparatus—critique of sources according to exact philological methods, etc.—can be fully intact, and still the guiding foreconception can miss the genuine object. Despite this, the modern history of religion accomplishes much for phenomenology, if it is subjected to a phenomenological destruction [*Destruktion*]. Only then can the history of religion be considered for phenomenology.

In this way, the history of religion accomplishes important preliminary work; at the same time, however, all of its concepts and results necessarily require phenomenological destruction. Yet this is still not a clarification of the context in which the material at hand forms the starting point for understanding. The guiding foreconception of which the historian is himself unaware— that is to say, the tendencies that already motivate the formulation of the problem—is decisive. It is often overlooked, especially in the specialized sciences, that already the formulation of the problem itself in no way offers itself out of the bare material; rather it is already foreconceptually determined. But phenomenology must always keep its eye exactly on this problematic of the foreconception, in connection with history.

§ 19. Basic Determinations of Primordial Christian Religiosity

Now in what sense should the material we have retrieved from the letter to the Galatians be used? What is the aim of our phenomenological understanding? It is not an interpretation on the basis of a historical kind of context, into which the letter to the Galatians would be placed; rather we want to explicate its own meaning. Already the basic determination of primordial Christian religiosity is decisive for this.

First, it is necessary to insert a remark that is important for all religious-historical study. It is therein customary today to work with the categorical opposition of rational and irrational. Today's philosophy of religion[1] is proud of its category of the irrational and, with it, considers the access to religiosity secured. But with these two concepts nothing is said, as long as one does not know the meaning of rational. The concept of the irrational, after all, is supposed to be determined from out of the opposition to the concept of the rational, which, however, finds itself in notorious indetermination. This pair of concepts is thus to be eliminated entirely. Phenomenological understanding,

---

1. [Cf. Rudolph Otto, *Das Heilige. Über das Irrationale in der Idee des Göttlichen und sein Verhältnis zum Rationalen,* Breslau, 1917.]

according to its basic meaning, lies entirely outside of this opposition, which has only a very limited authority, if at all. Everything that is said of the—for reason—indissoluble residue that supposedly remains in all religions, is merely an aesthetic play with things that are not understood.

Which basic determination do we give to the object of the philosophy of religion? The letter to the Galatians had delivered to us a confusing variety of things: Paul's apostolic calling, warning the community, etc. From that we have carried out an indifferent taking-cognizance, without understanding its guiding foreconception: in order to see that it cannot work this way—that is to say, in order to subject this taking-cognizance to destruction. We encountered a connection that seems to be self-evident: that Paul gives his doctrine and directs his warning wholly in the manner of the Stoic-Cynic wandering preachers of the time. Nothing special lies in the manner of his presentation. One may compare with this the words of the Athenians about him (Acts 17: 17 ff.). We, too, approach the letter to the Galatians similarly. The question arises whether this self-evidence is really such, and whether the connection of calling, proclamation, doctrine, warning does not have a motivated sense, one which belongs to the sense of religiosity itself. Thus for example the proclamation is itself a religious phenomenon, which is to be analyzed in all phenomenological directions of sense.

Now in the presentation our basic determinations run like propositions; but they are not to be understood as propositions that are to be proven afterwards. Whoever takes them as such misunderstands them. They are phenomenological explications. As basic determinations we state two for now:

1. Primordial Christian religiosity is in primordial Christian life experience and is itself such.

2. Factical life experience is historical. Christian religiosity lives[2] temporality as such.[3]

These fundamental determinations are for now hypothetical. We ask: If, with these, the basic meaning of Christian religiosity is hit upon, what follows from that methodologically?

§ 20. The Phenomenon of Proclamation

Now, from out of the indicated context, we single out the phenomenon of proclamation, because in it the immediate life-relation of the world of self of Paul to the surrounding world and to the communal world of the community

---

2. [Presumably, Becker, from whose notes this sentence is taken, misheard here, and instead of "live" [*lebt*] wrote "teach" [*lehrt*]].

3. [Marginal comment in F. J. Brecht's notations: transitive]

is able to be comprehended. It is thus a central phenomenon. Now in a purely formal manner, various questions can be posed: Who proclaims? How is proclamation done? What is proclaimed? etc. Here, too, there exists a certain complex out of which a unity is to be retrieved. And indeed we emphasize the How of proclamation. The enactment of life is decisive. The complex of enactment is co-experienced in life. Out of this it is to be made understandable that the How of the enactment has basic meaning. We are thus asking after the How of the proclamation of Paul. We are relatively conveniently situated for answering this question, for after all we have the How of proclamation before us in Paul's letters. Within the formulation of the question of the How of proclamation, the epistolary character appears, all of a sudden, as a phenomenon.

Theology—especially Protestant theology—influenced by the development of the historical humanities in the nineteenth century, has brought forth work on the history of style in regard to the literary forms of the New Testament. Further investigations may be eagerly expected, although the point of departure is misguided as much according to the science of history as phenomenologically. One approaches the matter entirely externally, insofar as one integrates the New Testament writing into world literature, in order to analyze its forms accordingly. Even if it were so that the forms of the New Testament are differentiated in no way from contemporary literature, still one may not proceed in this way. In analyzing the character of the letter, one must take as the only point of departure the Pauline situation and the How of the necessary motivation of the communication in letters. The content proclaimed, and its material and conceptual character, is then to be analyzed from out of the basic phenomenon of proclamation.

§ 21. Foreconceptions of the Study

The foreconceptions in the historical study extend in their effects into the critique of sources, the singularities of the assessment of the text, conjectures, questions of authenticity. One can illustrate this in the first letter to the Thessalonians, which was declared inauthentic by the Tübingen school which stands under Hegelian influence,[4] on the basis of its slight dogmatic content in comparison to other Pauline letters. Thus, the foreconception reaches all the way into the most minuscule aspects of historical research, indeed into the edition of sources. In this, the relations in art history are again different from those in the history of religion.

Thus, each pre-given historical material must be submitted to a forecon-

---

4. [Cf. F. C. Baur, *Paulus, der Apostel Jesu Christi,* 2nd edition, 1866–67, p. 107f.]

ceptual observation. But with that nothing is yet achieved for phenomenological understanding, because it has a different character than the object-historical. Object-historical understanding is determination according to the aspect of the relation, from out of the relation, so that the observer does not come into question. By contrast, phenomenological understanding is determined by the *enactment* of the observer. Despite the different origins of understanding, the connection of phenomenological understanding to the history of objects is closer than in other sciences.

Thus phenomenological understanding consists, *first,* not in the projecting of what is to be understood, which, after all, is no kind of object, in a material complex. It has, *secondly, never* the tendency of determining such a realm with finality, but rather is subordinated to the historical situation—insofar as the foreconception is even more decisive for phenomenological understanding than object-historical understanding. Thus, one has to begin at the starting point (the foreconception) of the phenomenological understanding. Such a starting point is not possible for every observer, for every phenomenon; it must be borne by a familiarity with the phenomenon. One proceeds methodologically securely if one approaches the basic determination purely *formally;* one intentionally affords the concepts a certain lability in order to secure their determination first in the process of phenomenological study itself. In this sense we have posited the following starting points for the sake of the determination of primordial Christian religiosity:

1. Primordial Christian religiosity is in factical life experience. Postscript: It is such experience itself.

2. Factical life experience is historical. Postscript: Christian experience lives time itself ("to live" understood as *verbum transitivum*).

One cannot prove these "theses." Rather they must prove themselves in phenomenological experience itself. The letter is something other than empirical experience. The basic determinations are thus hypothetical: "If they are valid, then such and such results for the phenomenon."

We initially consider the apostolic proclamation of Paul. If it represents a basic phenomenon, from out of it must be won a relation to the total religious basic phenomenon. In the enactment and through the enactment, the phenomenon is explicated. "Apostolic proclamation" is still too broad a characterization of the phenomenon. The apostolic proclamation is decisively clarified as soon as it is determined in its How, in its sense of enactment. This formulation of the question of the How is thus decisive. The character of the material—that we are dealing with letters—is convenient for these questions. The Pauline letters are, as sources, more immediate than the later-composed gospels. However, one may not isolate the epistolary character, nor bring into the problem the literary question of style. They are not primary. The epistolary style itself is the expression of the writer and his situation. Although the

Pauline letters lie so near to each other temporally, so that a Pauline development from one to another does not come into question, they are nevertheless really different. For example, the letters to the Romans and to the Galatians are much richer in dogmatic content than the letter to the Thessalonians. One must free oneself as well from the schematic classification of the letters.

§ 22. The Schema of Phenomenological Explication

How is a phenomenological explication of its material enacted? "Material" has a particular methodological sense. The explication of the phenomenon from out of the material is carried out in particular stages. Schematically speaking, the steps of the phenomenological explication are as follows:

1. Because the basic phenomenon is factical life experience, and because it is historical, so the first task is to determine the complex of phenomena object-historically, pre-phenomenologically, as a historical situation, but already from out of phenomenological motives.

2. The enactment of the historical situation of the phenomenon is to be gained. To this end: (a) the diversity of what may be encountered in the situation is to be characterized—and indeed in such a manner that nothing is to be decided about its actual connections (briefly: articulation of the situational diversity); (b) the "accentuating situation" of the diversity is to be gained; (c) the primary or "arch-ontic (reigning) sense" of the accentuating situation is to be ascertained; (d) from there to arrive at the phenomenal complex; and (e) from out of this to posit the study of origin.

But in doing this, we must remain conscious of certain limitations:

1. The basic comportment of the personal life experience of the observer (phenomenologist) is eliminated.

2. The study aims at the historical phenomena, but does not yet involve that which is decisive. One should note that the explication comes to a head ever more from step to step, becomes more and more individual, grows ever nearer to the peculiar historical facticity. This succession of steps becomes understandable only if one frees oneself from the theory of regions—unshakably.

Remarks on the schema of phenomenological explication:

Re: 1. Gaining the object-historical complex is already determined by the aim of the explication. It is not coincidental. The object-historical emphases should be studied; they yield an authentic emphasis and should be kept in mind. Re: 2. The application of the object-historical complex of occurrence to the original-historical situation encounters three difficulties.

A) Presentation through Language:

The language of the study of the material is not original. There is a more original conceptuality already in factical life experience, from out of which the material conceptuality that is common to us first derives. This reversal in conceptuality must be enacted, or else it is hopeless to ever grasp the situation. One may not simply take up self-evident concepts. (The question of the philosophical concepts has not been posed since Socrates.) At times, one believes to come closer to the problem through a "dialectic." But one may not posit life as "irrational" without being clear about the sense of irrationality. No material of explication has been understood as long as its indicated sense complex is not enacted. The complex of enactment itself belongs to the concept of the phenomenon. The philosophical concept has a structure incomparable to the material concept.

B) "Empathizing" with a Situation:

The problem of empathy does not budge as long as one grasps it epistemologically. But the motive of the problem of empathy is not epistemological at all. Empathy arises in factical life experience, that is to say, it involves an original-historical phenomenon that cannot be resolved without the phenomenon of *tradition* in its original sense. Today the environment of Paul is entirely foreign to us. But what is crucial for us is not the material character, the ideational of his surrounding world. This moment falls away entirely; the environment first gains its sense out of the understanding of the situation.

C) The Question of the Explication Itself:

Through the completion of the explication, that which is explicated becomes apparently independent, released from its enactment. But this is a distorted view. It is peculiar to the theoretical, attitudinal abstraction that what is abstracted is grasped as a moment of a material region, so that thereby the basic determinations of the region are won. What is abstracted is studied further without reference to that from which it is abstracted; the *fundamentum* of the abstraction does not matter. The abstraction as such, the transition from the *fundamentum abstractionis* to the abstracting is not co-experienced. Otherwise in the explication: if particular moments are explicated in the explication, those moments of sense to which the explication is not directed are not simply shoved aside; rather the How of their reaching into the just explicated, directional sense—or the direction of sense in the process of explication—is co-determined precisely by the explication itself. Here one could ask: Can one, with the relational sense (for example), study as well the "What" (the content) of that to which one is comported, and even the How of the enactment? But this objection is attitudinal. The directions of sense are all three grasped. The enactment of the explication is not a separated succession of acts, grasping determinations. It is to be gained only in a concrete life-context. One can thereby also, at the same time, have the directions of sense that are "not seen."

Chapter Three

Phenomenological Explication of the First Letter to the
Thessalonians

§ 23. Methodological Difficulties

The first letter to the Thessalonians was written in the year 53 A.D. (thus
twenty years after the crucifixion); it is the earliest document of the New
Testament. Its authenticity is now no longer doubted. We ask, according to
the stated method: What is the object-historical situation of Paul as he wrote
the letter? The letter was written on the first missionary trip in Corinth. The
trip led first to Philippi, from there for three weeks to Thessalonica. The
opposition of the Jews led Paul to leave the city secretly, and from there [he
went] to Athens, from which he sent Timothy back to Salonika and met him
again only in Corinth. Paul writes the letter just after his arrival in Corinth.
The situation is entirely determined by this. Compare for this I Thess. 3:6; 3:
2; Acts 18:5. On the first sojourn of Paul in Thessalonica see Acts 17:1–16.
If we present this object-historically, Paul appears as a missionary who talks
as a usual wandering preacher, without attracting too much attention.

Now we no longer observe the object-historical complex, but rather see the
situation such that we write the letter along with Paul. We perform the letter-
writing, or its dictation, with him. The first question: How does Paul, in the
situation of a letter-writer, stand to the Thessalonians? How are they experienced by him? How is his *communal world* given to him in the situation of
writing the letter? That is connected to the question, how *Paul* stands to this
communal world. The *content* of the communal world is to be seen in its
determination in connection with the How of the *relation* to this communal
world. Thus we must draw out the basic determination of this relation.

We have still another methodological difficulty to consider. One could say
it is impossible—or possible only in a limited way—to transport oneself into
Paul's exact situation. Indeed, we do not know his environment at all. This
objection arises from the view that what is given in the manner of objects is
primary for a situation with which one must "empathize." But one must judge
Paul's position with regard to his surroundings from out of his personality
and ask whether the surroundings are important for him at all. The "empathy"
problem is posed, for the most part, epistemologically, and is therefore misguided in its starting point. Scheler's view comes closest to the right one—
which, however, is still strongly epistemologically burdened. Furthermore, the

assertions of Paul are not different from an objective-historical report. That is a problem of presentation: through language, each expression falls into an attitudinal one. One must realize that it is misguided to cut concepts of objects to fit subjectivity.

Finally the problem of emphasis. How are the givenness of the surrounding world, the communal world, and the self-world, which flow into each other in factical life, emphasized? One can always observe only one at a time. This emphasis is not abstraction, because the other factors are nevertheless constantly co-given. The tendency is not toward the dissipation of historical facticity, toward gaining general religious-phenomenological assertions from one example. It is not the ideal of a theoretical construction that is aimed for, but the originality of the absolute-historical in its absolute unrepeatability. All questions of philosophy are, at bottom, questions about the How—strictly understood, questions of method.

The turn at which the object-historical situation becomes an enactment-historical one succumbs to a difficulty in presentation in the explication of the enactment-historical situation; and *there exists an immanent explication with a more original conceptuality* than that with which we are familiar, from which the usual conceptuality is first always derived, from which it originates. The actual preliminary question about the meaning of philosophical conceptuality has not been posed since Socrates. The conceptuality familiar to us tends toward the attitudinal, the study of matter. If one, from here, views only the problem of presentation, one sees that each thing to be explicated which is made known in talk, is not understood as long as one does not also grasp the complex of enactment in the concept. The material concept is absolutely incomparable to the phenomenological concept. An original consideration of the motives of the problem of empathy shows that it has nothing to do with epistemological questions. The problem of "empathy" is not to be solved without the phenomenon of tradition (of historical-factical life experience).

One difficulty is that we cannot at all, with our ideas, put ourselves in Paul's place. [Such an attempt] is misguided because what is crucial is not the material character of Paul's environment, but rather only his own situation. The problem of the *presentation, empathy*, and *explication* of "autonomized individuals" is badly posed. The explication differs from each material abstraction of the theoretical attitude. There abstraction is grasped as affiliated with and co-determining a material region: it is essential that the abstracted is fixed in further progress without regard to that *from which* it is abstracted, so that the "from which" remains a matter of indifference for the sense of the abstracted. Accordingly, the transition from the base to the abstracted is not important. Explication means: if it is explicated toward a particular direction of sense, the remaining directions of meaning are co-projected into it. In this, it is important to determine the How of the co-projection. If one claims it is not possible to explicate one direction and in the same stroke the others as well—as, for example, the content-sense, relational-sense, and enactment: attitudinal comportment of this objection. The individual directions of sense are not things. The complete disappearance of this difficulty can be seen only in a concrete situational context.

The turn from the object-historical complex to the enactment-historical *situation* itself derives from connections which can be shown in factical life experience. Does one, with this turning-around, at all emerge from history? Where does the phenomenological begin? This objection is legitimate, but it maintains as its background the conviction that the philosophical has a special dimension. That is the misunderstanding. Philosophy is return to the original-historical. This difficulty, therefore, does not burden our study.

§ 24. The "Situation"

The turning-around from the object-historical to the enactment-historical lies in factical life experience itself. It is a turning-around to the situation. "Situation" counts here for us as a phenomenological term. It would not be used for objective contexts (also not historically such as "condition"—for example, fatal situation or condition). "Situation" is thus for us something that belongs to understanding in the manner of enactment, it does not designate anything in the manner of an order. A diversity of situations or also within a situation should not be grasped as a complex of order. A situational series is not, moreover, a series in the manner of an order (compare to Bergson's "*durée concrète*"[1]). The question of the demarcation of a situation is independent of the determination of an object-theoretical section, of a historical period or epoch. And the object-historical period is also something other than a mathematically-physically determined particular period. A special investigation is needed in order to determine when an object-historical—and a situational—demarcation coincide. For the question of the unity or the diversity of the situation, it is important that we can gain them only in the *formal indication*. The unity is not formally *logical*, but merely formally *indicated*. The formal indication is in the "neither-nor"; it is neither something in the manner of an order, nor explication of a phenomenological determination.

We cannot project a situation into a particular field of being, nor into "consciousness." We cannot speak of a "situation of a point A between B and C." Language protests against this. And indeed we cannot do this because a point is nothing "like an I" [*Ichliches*]. "Being like an I" is understood entirely

1. Cf. H. Bergson, *Essai sur les données immédiates de la conscience.* 11th edition, Paris, 1912, pp. 75–79.

indeterminately. "Being like an I" belongs to each situation. With that it is not said that the "like an I" of a situation is that which unifies the diversity. Nothing is expressed about the relation of the I and the not-I. One should not here read into this a subject-object relationship, nor claim in the wake of Fichte that "The I posits the not-I."[2] About that, we express nothing. Apparently the Fichtean relation is entirely general, but it nevertheless prejudices already entirely particular connections; it says: "The I posits the form of non-I-ness"—not the factical world is posited. Fichte only grasped the Kantian situation more sharply. That which is "like an I" can stand in connection with the same and with the not-I, and the latter amongst itself.

The only differentiation we make between that which is "like an I" and the not-I is the following: "That which is 'like an I' *is* and *has* the not-I, the not-I merely *is* and does not *have*." This again as entirely formal indication; the *is* should not even be taken in the seemingly most general way, as predication, much less as existence, real occurrence, etc. The problem is the origin of the concepts of Being; the predicative *is* of theoretical explication arises out of the original "I am," not the other way around. Insofar as that which is "like an I" has something, the departure for the situation can be taken from here. For what is had seems to give itself objectively. It offers a starting point for the carrying-out of the explication.

"Situation" carries in itself, in the usual sense of the word, a sense of the static. This connotation must be disregarded. And yet a "dynamical" view misjudges the situation as well, in which one views the phenomenal context as a "flowing" and speaks of the flow of the phenomena. From that viewpoint, "situation" means a "shutting-down." But the situational complex stands beyond the alternatives of "static-dynamic." For the notion of flowing and streaming has the manner of an order as well; therefore homogeneity is at least implied, if not explicitly co-posited. The time of factical life is to be gained from the complex of enactment of factical life itself, and from there the static or dynamic character of the situation is to be determined.

We grasp situation purely formally as unity of a diversity. What makes up its unity remains indeterminate—but the situation is not a homogeneous field of relations; the situational structure does not run in one or more dimensions, but rather entirely otherwise. Already the starting point of a phenomenological study as having the manner of an order and the attempt of a material description fails because of the phenomenon itself. One must return ever again to the point of departure. The departure is to be taken from the having-relation of that which is "like an I." For what is had seems always still to appear as

2. Johann Gottlieb Fichte, *Grundlage der gesammten Wissenschaftslehre* (1794). New edition introduced by Fritz Medicus. Leipzig, 1911, p. 46.

something objectively characterizable: the relation of the people before Paul to him is how *he* has them.

§ 25. The "Having-Become" of the Thessalonians

Thus we will pursue *as what* Paul has the congregation in Thessalonica and *how* he has it. In doing so, we will go back to a particular moment of the object-historical report: Acts 17:4—to Paul's relation to the "few" who "fell to him" (καί τινες ἐξ αὦτῶν ἐπείσθησαν καὶ προσεκληρώθησαν τῷ Παύλῳ [some of them were persuaded and joined Paul). In turning to the "situation," is this object-historical relation retained, and in which way does it come to expression in the letter-writing? Paul is co-included in the state of the congregation (of the τινές [some]). The Thessalonians are those who fell to him. In them, he necessarily co-experiences himself.

We put forth formally the state of the relation of Paul to those who have "given themselves over to him." Paul experiences the Thessalonians in two determinations: 1. He experiences their having-become (γενηθῆναι). 2. He experiences, that they have a knowledge of their having-become (οἴδατε [you know]). That means their having-become is also Paul's having-become. And Paul is co-affected by their having-become. Showing this concretely from the letter is very easy. In the course of I Thess., the frequent use of (1) γενέσθαι [to come, to become] and similar words, and (2) οἴδατε [you know], μνημονεύσατε [you remember], among others, is striking. The thorough pursuit of the repetition of the same word seems external; but one must view this, in an enactment-historical understanding, as an ever-repeatedly surfacing tendency, as a motif. That is something other than the repetition of a natural event.

Re: 1. I Thess. 1:5, 6, 7, etc. The complex of the event is emphasized here in a particular way. The ἐγενήθη [became] enters it again and again. In writing, Paul sees them as those whose life he has entered. Their having-become is linked to his entrance into their life (εἴσοδος, 2:1 [coming]). 2:5 ἐγενήθημεν [came]: the "how" of this entrance is characterized (compare with 2:7, 8, 10, 14). These passages emphasize that for Paul the Thessalonians are there because he and they are linked to each other in their having-become.

Re: 2. "οἴδατε" [as you know]: 2:2, 5 in connection with γενέσθαι [came]. 2:9 μνημονεύετε [you remember]. 2:11 οἴδατε [as you know]. 3:6 ἔχετε μνείαν [you remember], 4:2 οἴδατε [you know], 4:9 οὐ χρείαν ἔχετε γράφειν ὑμῖν [you do not need to have anyone write to you]. 5:1 οὐ χρείαν ἔχετε γράφειν ὑμῖν γράφεσθαι [you do not need to have anything written to you]. This knowledge is entirely different from any other knowledge and memory. It arises only out of the situational context of Christian life experience.

Knowledge about one's own having-become poses a very special task for the explication. From out of this the meaning of a facticity is determined, one which is accompanied by a particular knowledge. We tear the facticity apart from the knowledge, but the facticity is entirely originally co-experienced. Especially in this problem, the failure of the "scientific psychology of experience" can be shown. Having-become is not, in life, [just] any incident you like. Rather, it is incessantly co-experienced, and indeed such that their Being [*Sein*] now is their having-become [*Gewordensein*]. Their having-become is their Being now. We can grasp that more closely first through a narrower determination of having-become. Can one explicate this meaning from out of the letter itself?

I Thess. 6: The γενέσθαι is a δέχεσθαι τὸν λόγον, an "acceptance of the proclamation"—ἐν θλίφει πολλῇ μετὰ χαρᾶς—"in great despair." The δέχεσθαι brought the despair with it, which also continues, yet at the same time a "joy" (μετὰ χαρᾶς) which comes from the Holy Spirit (μνεύματος ἁγίου) is alive— a joy which is a gift, thus not motivated from out of one's own experience. This all belongs to the character of the γενέσθαι. 2:13: λόγον θεοῦ [the word of God] is at the same time a subjective and objective genitive. The having-become is understood such that with the acceptance, the one who accepts treads upon an effective connection with God. 4:1: παρελάβειτε [learned], you have accepted the *how* of the Christian standard of living, etc. That which is accepted concerns the how of self-conduct in factical life.

Thus we have determined γενέσθαι through δέχεσθαι [to accept], further through παραλαμβάνειν [receiving]. That which is accepted is the how of self-conduct. The main passage which clarifies the connection is 1:9–10. It is about an *absolute turning-around*, more precisely about a turning-*toward* God and a turning-*away* from idol-images. The absolute turning-toward within the sense of enactment of factical life is explicated in two directions: δουλεύειν [serving] and ἀναμένειν [waiting], a transformation before God and an obstinate waiting.

Knowledge of one's own having-become is the starting point and the origin of theology. In the explication of this knowledge and its conceptual form of expression the sense of a theological conceptual formation arises. The δέχεσθαι is characterized in its how ἐν θλίψει (in despair). The acceptance consists in entering oneself into the anguish of life. A joy is bound up therewith, one which comes from the Holy Spirit and is incomprehensible to life. παραλαμβάνειν does not mean a belonging; rather it means an acceptance with the winning of a living effective connection with God. The being-present of God has a basic relationship to the transformation of life (περιπατεῖν [living]). The acceptance is in itself a transformation before God.

Now we give a *formal schematic* of the phenomenon. Without pre-understanding the entire context one cannot extract a singular reference. The formal schematic of the explication has meaning only in the formal articulation, [for] it does not emerge in the enactment of phenomenological understanding. In its formal elevation what is authentic is lacking.

On 1:9–10: The turning-toward God is primary. The turning-away from the εἴδωλα [idol] first arises from out of it and with it. This turning-away is secondary. ἐπιστρέφειν πρὸς τὸν θεὸν ἀπὸ τῶν εἰδώλων [you turned to God from idols] (εἴδωλον in classical Greek means "illusion," in the *Septuaginta* "idol images," where Paul has it from). For the explication, the task arises to determine the sense of the objecthood of God. It is a decrease of authentic understanding if God is grasped primarily as an object of speculation. That can be realized only if one carries out the explication of the conceptual connections. This, however, has never been attempted, because Greek philosophy penetrated into Christianity. Only Luther made an advance in this direction, and from this his hatred of Aristotle can be explained.

2:20: ὑμεῖς γάρ ἐστε ἡ χαρά. "You are my joy and my δόξα." οὔτε ζητοῦντες ἐξ ἀνθρώπων δόξαν οὔτε ἀφ ὑμῶν [nor did we seek praise from mortals whether from you or from others] (2:6) seems to stand in absolute contradiction to 2:20. Paul wants to win his own security through his success with the Thessalonians. Here is meant the opposition to the Greek wandering preachers, whom Lucian accuses of δοξοκοπία (addiction to fame). 3:8: Paul's life is dependent upon the Thessalonians' standing firm in their belief. He hands himself over entirely to the fate of the Thessalonians. The concepts ἐλπίς, δόξα, χαρά [hope, glory, joy] have a special meaning, or else one arrives at contradictions. In order to gain the sense of these concepts, we are forced to go to the basic context of the life of Paul himself. The entire conceptual structure is otherwise than one at first thinks. We are compelled, by the force of the phenomena themselves, to go back to what is original.

δουλεύειν and ἀναμένειν determine every other reference as fundamental directions. The awaiting of the παρουσία of the Lord is decisive. The Thessalonians are hope for him not in a human sense, but rather in the sense of the experience of the παρουσία. The experience is an absolute distress (θλίπις) which belongs to the life of the Christian himself. The acceptance (δέχεσθαι) is an entering-oneself-into anguish. This distress is a fundamental characteristic, it is an absolute concern in the horizon of the παρουσία, of the second coming at the end of time. With that we are introduced into the self-world of Paul.

§ 26. The Expectation of the Parousia

Paul lives in a peculiar distress, one that is, as apostle, his own, in expectation of the second coming of the Lord. This distress articulates the authentic sit-

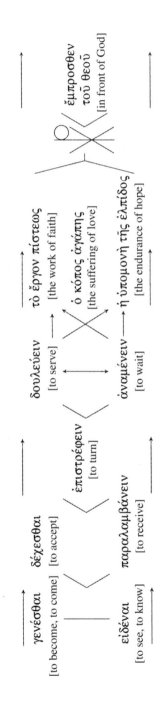

uation of Paul. It determines each moment of his life. He is constantly beset by a suffering, despite his joy as apostle. Twice in the text we find: μηκέτι στέγοντες "we cannot take it anymore" (3:1; 3:5). 3:10: the having-become of the Thessalonians is at the same time a new becoming. τὰ ὑστερήματα [is lacking] means: a supplement is needed.

2:17: For Paul, the Thessalonians have an absolute significance. One must proceed from his distress, in order to understand his letter-writing comportment. We take a further look into the self-world of Paul, in that we approach the passage II Cor. 12:2–10. Having been blessed with inspiration is not what is decisive; he excludes that and does not communicate it. The how of the enrapturement is unknown and unimportant. II Cor. 12:5: separation of existence as one who is enraptured and as apostle. Paul wants to be seen only in his weakness and distress. There is certainly a still more original reason why the difficulty belongs to the Christian. σκόλοψ τῇ σαρκί [a thorn in the flesh]— what that is is much discussed. It is to be understood more generally than Augustine does, who grasps it as *concupiscentia.* σάρξ, "flesh" is the original sphere of all affects not motivated from God.

2:18: ἐνέκοψεν ἡμᾶς ὁ σατανᾶς, "Satan hindered us." One may not stay with the idea that Paul is speaking of "Satan." The concept of Satan and his place in the life of the Christian cannot be explicated on the basis of this passage alone. In the Old Testament, "Satan" means simply *"adversary,"* "enemy in war," to get to the point, "the one who fights against what God wants." What is primary is not speculating whether and what the devil is. Rather one must understand how the devil stands in and affects Paul's life. Satan constantly hinders the work of Paul in exacerbating his distress, this absolute apostolic concern about his calling in this end of time. Cf. 3:5 ὁ πειράζων, the "tempter." 3:11: Paul then asks God in prayer (prayer in the decisive sense) to direct him to the path to the Thessalonians. Already in 2:17 he calls himself bereft, because, after all, he is far from them. The conclusion of the letter at 5:27 corresponds to the prayer: "I *implore* you to read the letter aloud to all." These moments—the impossibility of bearing it any longer, the devil, the call to prayer, the imploring at the end—all this makes possible, for the good will, an understanding of Paul's distress. In other letters cf. II Cor. 5:7.

The passages I Thess. 4:13–18 and 5:1–12 are to be compared in order to clarify the idea of the παρουσία. If the situation is now indicated, we come now to the letter-writing as a form of proclamation. The following interpretation should take care of several difficulties heretofore. The questions are these: 1. How does it stand with the dead, who no longer experience the παρουσία (4:14–18)? 2. When will the παρουσία take place (5:1–12)?

First we take up the second question. We can first gather how Paul understands the question from out of the how of the answer. Paul does not answer the question in worldly reasoning. He maintains a total distance from a cognitive treatment, but does not also, in that, claim that it is unknowable. Paul enacts the answer in juxtaposing two ways of life: ὅταν λέγωσιν [when they say] . . . verse 3, and ὑμεῖς δὲ [but you] . . . verse 4. What is decisive is how I comport myself to it in actual life. From that results the meaning of the "when?," time and the moment. The difficulties of phenomenological understanding are not only technical ones. The meaning of the individual as that of the infinitely complicated does not come into question here. The understanding is made difficult in its enactment itself; this difficulty grows constantly the nearer it approaches the concrete phenomenon. It is the difficulty of putting-oneself-into-another's-place, which cannot be supplanted by a fantasizing-oneself-into or a "vicarious understanding"; what is required is an authentic enactment.

II Cor. 12:2–10 gave us a preview of the self-world of Paul. The extraordinary in his life plays no role for him. Only when he is weak, when he withstands the anguish of his life, can he enter into a close connection with God. This fundamental requirement of having-God is the opposite of all bad mysticism. Not mystical absorption and special exertion; rather withstanding the weakness of life is decisive. Life for Paul is not a mere flow of events; it *is* only insofar as he *has* it. His life hangs between God and his vocation. The ways of "having" life itself, which belongs with the enactment of life, still increases the anguish (θλίψις). Each authentic complex of enactment increases it. What has been won heretofore is to be understood methodologically, in that from out of this it first becomes understandable what Paul has to say to the Thessalonians. What he says to them, and how he says it to them, is determined by his own situation. Schematically:

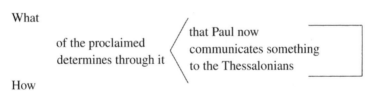

What

of the proclaimed
determines through it

that Paul now
communicates something
to the Thessalonians

How

It is this, the pressing situation, in which he writes the letter: cf. I Thess. 3:10: ὑπερεκπερισσοῦ [most earnestly] is a very strong expression for "urgent"; τὰ ὑστερήματα τῆς πίστεως [what is lacking in your faith]: important for the place of sins in Christian life. The proclamation is for Paul characterized formally by an intervention in the knowledge of the Thessalonians at a particular moment. Through the phenomenological characteristic of the proclamation the following must become apparent as authentic perspectives:

(1) A decisive understanding of the communal-worldly relation of Paul to the Thessalonians; (2) what Paul's situation authentically accentuates; (3) from this the solution of the problem of knowledge, which belongs with facticity;

(4) a preview of the richer structure of Christian life experience, which is, in its "What" and "How," always dependent upon the complex of enactment. Cf. with this from the summer semester 1919 lecture ("Über das Wesen der Universität" ["On the Essence of the University"]) the argument about the origin of perception and of knowledge from the explication of factical life experience[3]—and from the lecture in winter 1919–1920 ("Phänomenologische Grundprobleme" ["Basic Problems of Phenomenology"]) the developments regarding the concrete logic of a material region.[4]

The difference of our present study from that of the letter to the Galatians is important. It was only a mere taking-cognizance of the content, but it is a particular necessary step within the connection of access to understanding itself; this step will always be taken, if we attempt to carry out the authentic enactmental-historical understanding. The letter to the Galatians has a "dogmatic" content. This content is seen primarily in the exegesis. One must, however, be clear about how this content is to be understood as "believing knowledge." What Paul says is characterized by the fact that he says it *now* to the Thessalonians or the Galatians. One may not pounce upon the isolated content. The so-called dogmatic content of the letters is to be understood according to the entirety of how a communication of Christian knowledge is maintained. One errs if one grasps it in isolation.

What is the dogmatic form of the first letter to the Thessalonians? Paul answers two questions posed to him (see above page [German p. 99]):

Initially, the expression παρουσία has in its conceptual history a sense we do not intend here; the expression changes its entire conceptual structure, not only its sense, in the progress of its history. Christian life experience different in kind is evident in this conceptual transformation. In classical Greek παρουσία means arrival (presence); in the Old Testament (for instance in the *Septuaginta*) "the arrival of the Lord on the Day of Judgement"; in late Judaism "the arrival of the Messiah as representative of God." For the Christian, however, παρουσία means "the appearing again of the already appeared Messiah," which, to begin with, does *not* lie in the literal expression. With that, however, the entire structure of the concept is at once changed.

One could think, first of all: the basic comportment to the παρουσία is a waiting, and Christian hope (ἐλπίς) is a special case thereof. But that is entirely false! We never get to the relational sense of the παρουσία by merely analyzing the consciousness of a future event. The structure of Christian hope, which in truth is the relational sense of Parousia, is radically different from all ex-

---

3. Cf. Martin Heidegger, "Über das Wesen der Universität und des akademischen Studiums," in *Zur Bestimmung der Philosophie, Gesamtausgabe* vol. 56/7, ed. Bernd Heimbüchel. Frankfurt, 1987, p. 211 ff.
4. Cf. Martin Heidegger, *Grundprobleme der Phänomenologie. Gesamtausgabe* vol. 58, ed. Hans-Helmuth Gander. Frankfurt, 1993, pp. 72–75.

pectation. "Time and moment" (5:1: "περὶ τῶν χρόνων καὶ τῶν καιρῶν," always used in one) offers a special problem for the explication. The "When" is already not originally grasped, insofar as it is grasped in the sense of an attitudinal "objective" time. The time of "factical life" in its falling, unemphasized, non-Christian sense is also not meant. Paul does not say "When," because this expression is inadequate to what is to be expressed, because it does not suffice.

The entire question for Paul is not a cognitive question (cf. 5:2: αὐτοὶ γὰρ ἀκριβῶς οἴδατε [For you yourselves know very well]). He does not say, "at this or that time the Lord will come again"; he also does not say, "I do not know when he will come again"—rather he says: "You know exactly. . . ." This knowledge must be of one's own, for Paul refers the Thessalonians back to themselves and to the knowledge that they have as those who have become. This sort of answer determines that the question is decided in dependence upon their own life. Thus he juxtaposes two different ways of life (5:3: ὅταν λέγωσιν [when they say] . . . and 5:4: ὑμεῖς δὲ . . . [But you]). But this is not a juxtaposition of two different types; rather the motive lies in the How of the communication.

We will find this sort of juxtaposition again in the second letter to the Thessalonians. One observes: ὅταν λέγωσιν (5:3), "if you say," that is, they are such who realize at all to say something about that. εἰρήνη καὶ ἀσφάλεια (5:3), "peace and security" in factical life: this expression represents the How of self-comportment to that which encounters me in factical life. That which encounters me in my worldly comportment carries no reason for disturbance. Those who find rest and security in this world are those who cling to this world because it provides peace and security. "Peace and security" characterizes the mode of this relation to those who speak this way.

Sudden ruin overcomes them (5:3 τότε αἰφνίδιος αὐτοῖς ἐφίσταται ὄλεθρος [then sudden destruction will come upon them]). They are surprised by it, do not expect it. Or still better: they are precisely in the attitudinal expectation; their expectation is absorbed by what life brings to them. Because they live in this expectation, the ruin hits them in such a way that they cannot flee from it. They cannot save themselves, because they do not have themselves, because they have forgotten their own self, because they do not have themselves in the clarity of authentic knowledge. Thus they cannot grab hold of and save themselves (cf. 5:4 ἐν σκότει: "in the dark"). The comparison with the pregnant woman (5:3) characterizes the suddenness. It offers particular problems, namely what the comparison achieves in the sense complex, how far it can be "pressed," etc. In general, the use of the comparisons presents the explication with particular tasks.

5:4: ὑμεῖς δέ, ἀδελφοί, οὐκ ἐστὲ ἐν σκότει: "but you, brothers, are not in the darkness."—ἵνα ἡ ἡμέρα ὑμᾶς ὡς κλέπτης καταλάβῃ, "so that the day surprises you like a thief."—ἡμέρα has a double meaning: (1) opposite the darkness is the "brightness" of knowledge of oneself (ὑμεῖς υἱοὶ φωτός ἐστε 5:5 [for you are all children of light]). (2) ἡμέρα means "day of the Lord," that is, "day of the παρουσία." This then is the kind and mode of Paul's answer. Through this ("let us keep awake") we see: the question of the "When" leads back to my comportment. How the παρουσία stands in my life, that refers back to the enactment of life itself. The meaning of the "When," of the time in which the Christian lives, has an entirely special character. Earlier we formally characterized: "Christian religiosity lives temporality." It is a time without its own order and demarcations. One cannot encounter this temporality in some sort of objective concept of time. The when is in no way objectively graspable.

The meaning of this temporality is also fundamental for factical life experience, as well as for problems such as that of the eternity of God. In the medieval period these problems were no longer grasped originally, following the penetration of Platonic-Aristotelian philosophy into Christianity, and today's speculation which speaks of God increases the chaos. The pinnacle of the error is reached today in projecting onto God the concept of validity.

The present study takes up the center of Christianity: the eschatological problem. Already at the end of the first century the eschatological was covered up in Christianity. In later times one misjudged all original Christian concepts. In today's philosophy, too, the Christian concept-formations are hidden behind a Greek view. One would also have to draw on the gospels—the great eschatological sermon of Jesus in the gospel Matthew and Mark—out of which the basic position of the problem arises. The basic direction of eschatology is already late Judaic, the Christian consciousness [being] a peculiar transformation thereof. The origin of the meaning of the respective concepts is characteristic (cf. the apocalypse of Ezra[5]). The division of the directions of sense (form, relation, enactment) must be observed. The How of grasping reality, the How of understanding events is not to be carried out objective-attitudinally from out of the "reasonable human understanding." Rather, understanding the entire situation is necessary for understanding the phenomena. Here, how Paul answers the question of the "When" of the παρουσία is decisive; from this can one first judge what he said.

There is no security for Christian life; the constant insecurity is also characteristic for what is fundamentally significant in factical life. The uncertainty is not coincidental; rather it is necessary. This necessity is not a logical one, nor is it of natural necessity. In order to see this clearly, one must reflect on one's own life and its enactment. Those "who speak of peace and security" (5:3) spend themselves on what life brings them, occupy themselves with

---

5. [The so-called fourth Book of Ezra, from the end of the first century A.D., contains a Jewish apocalypse.]

whatever tasks of life. They are caught up in what life offers; they are in the dark, with respect to knowledge of themselves. The believers, on the contrary, are sons of the light and of the day.

Paul's answer to the question of the When of the παρουσία is thus an urging to awaken and to be sober. Here lies a point against enthusiasm, against the incessant brooding of those who dwell upon and speculate about the "when" of the παρουσία. They worry only about the "When," the "What," the objective determination, in which they have no authentic personal interest. They remain stuck in the worldly.

Chapter Four

The Second Letter to the Thessalonians

§ 27. *Anticipation of the Parousia in the Second Letter to the Thessalonians*

In his exegesis of both letters to the Thessalonians, the theologian Schmidt seeks to construct an opposition between the first and the second.[1] According to the second letter, the παρουσία is preceded by the arrival of the Antichrist with war and turmoil; but according to the first, peace and security reigns before the παρουσία, which arrives unexpectedly. According to the second letter, the Antichrist is to come as a warning and an intermediate sign. But this playing-off of different ideational [*vorstellungsmäßiger*] views against one another is not in the spirit of Paul. Paul is not concerned at all about answering the question of the When of the Parousia. The When is determined through the How of the self-comportment, which is determined through the enactment of factical life experience in each of its moments. Consideration of the second letter should confirm our results thus far. We will not go into the question of authenticity, nor the exegesis (cf. Hollmann in the *Zeitschrift für neutestamentliche Wissenschaft* [*Journal for Scholarship on the New Testament*], 1901 and 1904[2]). Only lack of understanding can disown Paul of the second letter to the Thessalonians.

Initially, we will get clear about the situation of the second letter. In what way did the first letter affect the Thessalonians? That is not so easy to see; but we can highlight some main features. The second letter presents a response to the present standpoint of the congregation. There are those in the congregation who have understood Paul, who know what is crucial. If the παρουσία depends upon how I live, then I am unable to maintain the faith and love that is demanded of me; then I approach despair. Those who think this way worry themselves in a real sense, under the sign of real concern as to whether or not they can execute the work of faith and of love, and whether or not they will hold out until the decisive day. But Paul does not help them; rather he makes their anguish still greater (II Thess. 1:5: εὔδειγμα τῆς δικαίας κρίσεως

---

1. Cf. P. Schmidt, *Der erste Thessalonicherbrief neu erklärt, nebsteinem Excurs über den zweiten gleichnamigen Brief,* Berlin, 1885, p. 111f.
2. [There is probably a confusion in the transcription. The correct details are: H. J. Holtzmann, "Zum zweiten Thessalonicherbrief," *Zeitschrift für neutestamentliche Wissenschaft* 2, 1901, pp. 97–108; G. Hollmann, "Die Uneichtheit des zweiten Thessalonicherbriefes," *Zeitschrift für neutestamentliche Wissenschaft* 5, 1904, pp. 28–38.

[evidence of the righteous judgment]). Only Paul himself could have written this. The overburdened nature (plerophory) of expression in the second letter has an entirely particular motivation, and is a sign of its authenticity.

1:11: κλήσεως [of his call]. Now at issue is to ask God that one will be dignified by the calling (κλῆσις). Christians must be κλητοί, those who are called, as opposed to those who are cast away (2:13–14: περιποίησις δόξης [obtain the glory]: the looking around for the δόξα of the Lord-concern). Paul sets those who have understood him up against those who, in more imminent expectation of the παρουσία, no longer work and loiter idly (3:11: μηδὲν ἐργαζομένους ἀλλὰ περιεργαζομένους [mere busybodies not doing any work]). They occupy themselves with the question (2:2), whether the Lord will come immediately. These people make an idling out of unconcern for the contingencies of life. They are concerned in a worldly manner, in all the bustling activity of talk and idling, and become a burden to the others (cf. I Thess. 4: 11). Thus they have understood the first letter otherwise.

One may not read the lines from II Thess. 2:13–14 as an isolated "apocalypse." Compare with 2:5! We are not dealing with a theoretical instruction. There, Paul reports the appearance of the people of unlawfulness, the son of ruin, of the adversary, and the like. He will come before the παρουσία (2:3: πρῶτον [first]). That is correct in terms of content. But that is not what is crucial primarily. The passage has been interpreted this way: Paul went back, became milder, no longer teaches the immediate imminence of the *Parousia;* he has become more careful and wants to comfort the people. Yet the entire tenor, the entire mode of expression of the second letter, speaks against this. This is not deprecation, but rather an increased tension, also in the individual expressions. The entire letter is still more urgent than the first: no taking-back, rather an enlarged tension. The Thessalonians are to be referred back to themselves. The overburdened character of the expression in Paul is to be understood first from out of this, [for] everywhere here precisely the complexes of enactment of factical life are emphasized. The following passages are characteristic of this:

II Thess 1:3 (and 2:13): εὐχαριστεῖν ὀφείλομεν [we must always give thanks].

1:3: ὑπεραυξάνει ἡ πίστις [your faith is growing]. The πίστις is not a taking-to-be true, or else the ὑπεραυξάνει would have no meaning; the πιστεύειν is a complex of enactment that is capable of increase. This increase is the proof of genuine consciousness.

1:4: ἐν ὑμῖν ἐνκαυχᾶσθαι [therefore we ourselves boast] is an increase of καυχᾶσθαι, praise.

1:11: πᾶσαν εὐδοκίαν (decision) ἀγαθωσύνης καὶ ἔργον πίστεως [every good resolve and work of faith] (cf. εὐδοκήσοντες τῇ ἀδικίᾳ).

2:8: τῇ ἐπιφανείᾳ τῆς παρουσίας [by the manifestation of his coming] (emphasis of what is current).

2:9: τέρασιν ψεύδους [lying wonders].

2:10: ἀπάτῃ ἀδικίας [wicked deception] (that is certainly a Hebraism). Everywhere the sense of enactment, here the love of truth, is emphasized through the overburdened expression.

2:10: τὴν ἀγάπην τῆς ἀληθείας [to love the truth].

2:11: ἐνέργειαν πλάνης [powerful delusion]. The particular vivacity. What is urgent in the situation is everywhere stressed in the πληροφορία [full conviction] of the expression.

2:13: ἐν ἁγιασμῷ πνεύματος καὶ πίστει ἀληθέιας [through the sanctification by the spirit and through belief in the truth] (ἔργον πίστεως πίστις ἀληθείας: truth stands in relational connection to faith). That shows that the πίστις itself represents a context of enactment, which can experience an increase.

2:14: εἰς περιποίησιν δόξης [you may obtain the glory], look about in the δόξα.

3:1: ἵνα ὁ λόγος τοῦ κυρίου τρέχῃ [so that the word of the Lord may spread rapidly]: so that the proclamation runs [?]

In order to understand this "overburdened nature of the expression" (plerophory), one must imagine Paul in the urgent anguish of his vocation. The ἀπολλυμένοις [those who are perishing] is missing a real enactment, which will not at all let itself be expressed positively; for the complex of enactment can be explicated neither positively as a mere course of happenings, nor negatively through some negation or other. The complex of enactment determines itself first in and with the enactment. Paul's kind of answer occurs in the same sense as in the first letter. Again, he opposes two modes of factical life. One does not see this if one focuses one's view only on the content. In the so-called "apocalypse" (II Thess 2:2–13) is found precisely (2:10) what is decisive: καὶ ἐν πάσῃ ἀπάτῃ ἀδικίας τοῖς ἀπολλυμένοις, ἀνθ᾽ ὧν τὴν ἀγάπην τῆς ἀληθείας οὐκ ἐδέξαντο εἰς τὸ σωθῆναι αὐτούς [and every kind of wicked deception for those who are perishing, because they refused to love the truth].

The decisive position is characterized through οὐκ ἐδέξαντο. The οὐκ ("not") is neither a non privativum nor a non negativum, but rather has the sense of the "enactmental not." The "enactmental not" is not a refusal of enactment, not a setting-oneself-outside of the enactment. The "not" concerns the position of the complex of enactment to the relation which is motivated from out of it. The meaning of the "not" can be clarified only out of the historical context. The δέχεσθαι without οὐκ has no relation. It would have to have a positive emphasis, but then a "yet enacting" would also be in error. Because then that which has the character of enactment would be characterized as a happening. But that which has the character of enactment is only co-possessed in the enactment itself, cannot for itself be objectified. The thoughts of negative theology grew from similar motifs of the "beyond yes and no." In order to escape the Antichrist as Antichrist, one must have first entered into the complex of enactment of the religious situation; for the Antichrist appears as God. The problem of negative theology appears, in a pale form, in medieval mysticism.

§ 28. The Proclamation of the Antichrist

The meaning of the proclamation of the Antichrist is the following: one must take the Antichrist for Antichrist. After all, he pretends to be a god. (Cf. II Cor. 4:4: ὁ θεὸς τοῦ αἰῶνος [the god of this world], after Irenäus Satan.) The facticity of knowledge is necessary for this. Whether one is a true Christian is decided by that fact that one recognizes the Antichrist. The event which should come before the παρουσία is thus, in its relational sense, one that is directed to the people (ἀπολλύμενοι—κλητοὶ εἰς δόξαν [those who are called into the glory]). With the arrival of the Antichrist, each must decide—even those who are unconcerned decide through this lack of concern. Already whoever remains undecided has removed himself from the complex of enactment of the anguish of expectation, and has joined the ἀπολλύμενοι (cf. II Cor. 4:3).

In the exegesis, the eschatological phenomenon is considered object-historically. It is said that people then had believed that the end of the world had come (millenarianism). Around 120 A.D. this stops; later millenarianism returns to life repeatedly in medieval millenarianism and in modern adventism. It is said that these millenarian ideas are temporally-historically determined, and therefore have no eternal validity. One attempts to examine the eschatological ideas according to their lineage. Thereby one is led to late Judaism, further to ancient Judaism, finally to ancient Babylonian and ancient Iranian notions of the end of the world. With that one believes to have "explained" Paul, freed from all churchly ties—that is to say, to have determined how Paul himself was to have looked.

We will see that precisely this "objectivity" is, in the highest sense, constructed. For this view never puts into question whether those who have eschatological ideas of this kind indeed have them as ideas. In talk without qualification of "ideas," one misrecognizes the fact that the eschatological is never primarily idea. The content of the idea may certainly not be eliminated, but it must be had in its own (relational) sense. The enactmental understanding from out of the situation eliminates these difficulties. It is a difficult problem for the history of culture—a problem that is very close to the concept of philosophy—to shed light upon how it so happens that the history of dogma (history of religion) has taken precisely this criticized ideational attitude. The main problem with this is not how the history of dogma entered in this ideational way, but rather why it never turned in another direction.

Origenes saw this problem in his *Commentaries* on *The Gospel of John* and on the individual writings of the Old Testament. Equally well did *Augustine* see this problem of the historical that lies in Christian life experience.[3] It is a false conception to form a general concept of the historical and then impose it onto the individual formulations of problems, rather than proceeding from the respective complex of enactment (for example, from that of artistic creation or of religious experience). Likewise, the philosophical methods corrupt the sense of the history of religion. That which Paul says has a peculiar expressive function, from which one cannot tear out the "ideational content," in order, for instance, to compare it with the content of ancient Babylonian ideas. The original complex of enactment, in which the eschatological is found for Paul, is important, independently of connections that exist between Persian and Jewish eschatological ideas. The "obstinate waiting" is not some ideational "expectation," rather a δουλεύειν θεῷ [serving God].

The obstinate waiting stands in the complex of enactment of the entire Christian life (see Schema in § 26 "The Expectation of the Parousia" p. 67). Thus the second letter to the Thessalonians is easy to understand, despite some difficulties. The situation is, in relation to the first letter, changed insofar as the words "the day of the Lord comes like a thief in the night" are understood correctly by some (calm [?] obstinate waiting) and incorrectly by others. These latter set the work aside, stand around and chat, because they expect him every day. But those who have understood him must be despairing, because the anguish increases, and each stands alone before God. It is these to whom Paul now answers that the anguish is an ἔνδειγμα [proof] of the calling; the others he sharply rejects. The event of the Parousia is thus directed, in its sense of happening, toward the people who bifurcate into the called and the rejected. Of the rejected ἀπολλύμενοι, the Lord of this world—that is, Satan— has blinded their sense. They *cannot* δοκιμάζειν [testing] (I Thess. 5:21), that is to say, test.

§ 29. Dogma and the Complex of Enactment

It is noticeable *how little* Paul alleges [*vorgibt*] *theoretically or dogmatically;* even in the letter to the Romans. The situation is not of the sort of theoretical proof. The dogma as detached content of doctrine in an objective, epistemological emphasis could never have been guiding for Christian religiosity. On the contrary, the genesis of dogma can only be understood from out of the enactment of Christian life experience. The allegedly dogmatic doctrinal content of the letter to the Romans is, also, only understandable out of the en-

---

3. [Cf. the lecture "Augustine and Neo-Platonism" in this volume.]

actment in which Paul stands, in which he writes to the Romans. His procedure of proof is nowhere a purely theoretical complex of reasons, but is rather always an original complex of becoming of the kind that, in the end, is also merely shown in a proof. What reigns here is the opposition of basic comportments of practical life: σωζόμενοι and ἀπολλύμενοι, which does not mean "the rejected ones," but rather "to be in the state of becoming rejected," etc. The *participium praesentis* instead of *participium perfecti* emphasizes the enactment that is still in process. At issue is an acceptance, which is a final deciding.

The οὐκ δέχεσθαι has a positive sense, in disabling knowledge. This δέχεσθαι thus grounds the εἰδέναι [to know] and δοκιμάζειν [testing]. Paul sees these two types of people under the pressure of his calling as the proclaimer. The δέχεσθαι ἀγάπην (love as enactment) ἀληθείασ [truth] means a complex of enactment, which enables for the δοκιμάζειν of the divine. On the basis of this δοκιμάζειν, the knower first sees the great danger in store for the religious person: whoever does not accept the enactment cannot at all see the Antichrist who appears in the semblance of the divine (ἀντικείμενος ἐπὶ πάντα λεγόμενον θεόν [he opposes above every so-called god]), and becomes enslaved to him without even noticing it. The danger becomes apparent only to the believers; the appearance of the Antichrist is directed precisely toward the believers, the appearance is a "test" for those who know. The ἀπολλύμενοι believe (2:11) the ψεῦδος [delusion], they are deceived precisely in their highest bustling activity with the "sensation" of the Parousia, and fall from their original concern for the divine. For this reason, they will be *absolutely annihilated*—Paul knows no mere afterlife [*Postexistenz*] for the damned away from God—and they lose ζωή [life]. The appearance of the Antichrist in godly robes facilitates the falling-tendency of life; in order not to fall prey to it, one must stand ever ready for it.

The appearance of the Antichrist is no mere passing occurrence, but rather something upon which each one's fate is decided—even that of the already-believing. As ἀντικείμενος who opposes himself to the divine, he is the enemy of the believer, although he makes his appearance in the form of the divine itself. The revelation (ἀποκαλυφθῆναι) is only a revelation for one who possesses the possibility of distinguishing. Thus the warning (II Thess. 2:3) that they should not let themselves be deceived. 2:11: The rejected believe the lie; they are not indifferent; they are highly busy, but they are deceived and fall prey to the Antichrist. Thus, they do not neglect what is Christian as irrelevant, but rather show a peculiar increase, which fulfills their blindness and completes the fall [*Abfall*] to the anti-godly, so that a return is impossible. In Paul, to be damned means an absolute annihilation, absolute nothingness; there are no levels of hell, as in later dogma. The recoiling and increasing reformulation of Christian life experience into objective form was effected through the apologetic reaction of defense against paganism and its science.

The πρῶτον ἔλθῃ [comes first] (2:3) does not mean extension of the deadline, rather precisely, in the sense of Christian facticity, an increase of the highest anguish. Thus Paul concludes in 2:15, with a summary of his eschatological account: ᾽ Ἄρα οὖν, ἀδελφοί, στήκετε καὶ κρατεῖτε τὰς παραδόσεις (tradition?) ἃς ἐδιδάχθητε εἴτε διὰ λόγου εἴτε δι᾽ ἐπιστολῆς ἡμῶν [so then, brothers and sisters, stand firm and hold fast to the traditions that you were taught by us either by word of mouth or by our letter]. To the Christian, only his τὸ νῦν of the complex of enactment in which he really stands is to be decisive, but not the anticipation of a special event that is futurally situated in temporality. In late-Judaism, the anticipation of the Messiah refers primarily to such a futural event, to the appearance of the Messiah at which other people will be present. Ezra IV shows already acquaintance with the Christian prevalence of enactment, as opposed to the event-complex that is expected. From this complex of enactment with God arises something like temporality to begin with. II Thess. 2:6–7: καὶ νῦν τὸ κατέχον [and you know what is now restraining him] (that, which holds back the Antichrist) οἴδατε.—τὸ γὰρ μυστήριον ἤδη ἐνεργεῖται τῆς ἀνομίας [for the mystery of lawlessness is already at work].

Theodoret,[4] Augustine, and others see in κατέχον the precipitous order of the Roman Empire, which suppresses persecution of Christians by Jews. This passage could be regarded as an objection to our argumentation. Paul would be here concerned with the objective. *But:* the secret of sin (μυστήριον τῆς ἀνομίας) is already at work; that is what is decisive. Sin is just as much a mystery as faith. μόνον ὁ κατέχων ἄρτι ἕως ἐκ μέσου γένηται [but only until the one who now restrains it is removed]. The verses 6–7 encompass the problem of the Christian attitude toward a non-Christian surrounding world and communal world, and thus the problem of salvation history. From this context I Thess. 4:13 can be understood: οἱ λοιποὶ οἱ μὴ ἔχοντες ἐλπίδα [as others do who have no hope] (ὑπομονὴν ἐλπίδος). That is to say, all who stand outside the Christian context of becoming are without guidance as to the question of the dead. The way in which God resurrected Christ, so too will he bring the dead to him along with Christ. "That we believe." (πιστεύομεν). But we do not have to concern ourselves with such curious questions, for faith gives us certainty. Mark 9:1: Individuals among you will not die, before the βασιλεία τοῦ θεοῦ [the kingdom of God] comes ἐν δυνάμει [has come to power].

Paul, too, still expected the Parousia before his death. The great presentation [*Aufmachung*] in which the Antichrist appears facilitates faith for the believers,

---

4. [Bishop of Kyrrhos in Northern Syria, 393–ca. 466 A.D.]

if they already *are* decided. The decision itself is *very* difficult. The expectation must already be such that through faith, the deception of the Antichrist will be recognized as deception. The "before" is thus here increase of the highest anguish. That is why (2:15) Paul says only: stand firm and master the traditions that you have experienced. The questions of content may not be understood detachedly. The opposition of dogmatism and morality is actually misguided, too. The title "eschatology" is just as oblique, because it is taken out of Christian dogma and designates the doctrine of final things. Here we do not understand it in this theoretical-disciplinary sense.

Chapter Five

Characteristics of Early Christian Life Experience

§ 30. Factical Life Experience and Proclamation

On the object of proclamation: we must differentiate between the proclamation of the synoptics and that of Paul. In the synoptic gospels, Jesus announces the *kingdom of God,* ἡ βασιλεία τοῦ θεοῦ (Luke 16:16). In Pauline gospel, the proper *object of the proclamation is already Jesus himself as Messiah.* Cf. I Cor. 15:1–11. Here the essential teachings of Paul are found, but they are and remain entwined with the *How,* with life; they are not concerned with a specifically theoretical teaching. Cf. Rom. 1:3, Rom. 10:9: the resurrection and the faith in the son of God as Lord is the basic condition of salvation. The concept of the gospel as we know it today arises first from Justin and Ireäus and is entirely different from the Pauline concept (character of enactment). The first sentence of the gospel of Mark still has the original sense. (Beginning of the gospel of Jesus Christ, ἀρχὴ τοῦ εὐαγγελίου Ἰησοῦ Χριστοῦ, whereby Jesus Christ is to be understood as gen. obj.)

The factical life experience of the Christians is historically determined insofar as it always begins with the proclamation. The connection of the Christian with the surrounding world is discussed in I Cor. 1:26–27; 7:20. The significances of life remain, but a new comportment arises. We want to follow further the problem of proclamation in such a way that we leave matters of content entirely aside; now it must be shown that Christian religiosity lives temporality. What meaning communal-worldly and surrounding-worldly relations have for the Christian must be understood; and if they do, in what way. Christian factical life experience is historically determined by its emergence with the proclamation that hits the people in a moment, and then is unceasingly also alive in the enactment of life. Further, this life experience determines, for its part, the relations which are found in it.

For all its originality, primordial Christian facticity gains no exceptionality, absolutely no special quality at all. In all its absoluteness of reorganizing the enactment, everything remains the same in respect to the worldly facticity. The accentuation of the Christian life has the manner of enactment: I Thess. 3:3; 5:9. All primary complexes of enactment lead together toward God, are enacted before God. At the same time, the ἀναμένειν [waiting] is an obstinate waiting before God. The obstinate waiting does not wait for the significances of a future content, but for God. The meaning of temporality determines itself out of the fundamental relationship to God—however, in such a way that only those who live temporality in the manner of enactment understand eternity. The sense of the Being of God can be determined first only out of these complexes of enactment. To pass through them is the precondition. Further, it must be asked how dogmatic conceptuality arises out of such complexes of enactment. It is essential that the proclamation always remains co-present as alive, not only as a thankful memory.

In this having-become, how should the Christian comport himself to the surrounding world and communal world (I Cor. 7:20; 1:26 ff. σοφοί, δυνατοί, εὐγενεῖς [wise, powerful, of noble birth])?—Τὰ ὄντα: the reality of worldly life is targeted. The reality of life consists in the appropriative tendency of such significances. But these do not at all become dominating tendencies in the realm of the facticity of Christian life. Rather ἐν τῇ κλήσει μενέτω [remain in the condition in which you were called]! At issue is only to find a new fundamental comportment to it. That must be shown now in the manner of its enactment-structure. The indeed existing [daseienden] significances of real life are lived ὡς μή, as if not.

§ 31. The Relational Sense of Primordial Christian Religiosity

The relational sense of primordial Christian religiosity to the surrounding world, communal world, and self-world is to be determined; the authentic self is still to be differentiated from the self-world. Precisely the relations of the self-world are hit the hardest: self-worldly concern carries the semblance within itself. Paul is clear about the fact that these relational directions demand a peculiar characterization, which he renders in apparently common terms: πνεῦμα, ψυχή, σάρξ [spirit, soul, flesh]. Precisely these concepts typically illustrate that a wrong direction of understanding is entirely unable to hit upon the genuine meaning. One grasps them as qualities and thingly [dingliche] determinates. Only the correct explication of the sense-complexes allows a religious-historical comparison. Before this, all such compilation of material is not useful even for a modicum of understanding.

The explication must be maintained on its first level. There are subjective limitations of understanding: καινὴ κτίσις [a new creation], Gal. 6:15 (κλῆσις, call). I Cor. 7:20 stands out. One should remain in the calling in which one is. The γενέσθαι is a μένειν [remaining]. In all the radical reorganization, something remains. In what sense is the remaining to be understood? Will it itself be taken into becoming, indeed in such a way that the sense of remaining is, in its What and How, first determined out of having-become? With this, a peculiar complex of sense is indicated: these relations to the surrounding world receive their sense not out of the formal significance they indicate;

rather the reverse, the relation and the sense of lived significance are determined out of the original enactment. Put schematically: something remains
unchanged, and yet it is radically changed. Here we have a playground of
clever paradoxes, but that does not help us! Pointed formulations explain nothing.

The relational sense is not changed, and still less the content. Thus: the
Christian does not step out of this world. If one is called as slave, he should
not at all fall into the tendency [to suppose] that something could be won for
his Being in the increase of his freedom. The slave should remain a slave. It
is a matter of indifference in which surrounding-worldly significance he
stands. The slave as Christian is free from all bonds, but the free one as
Christian becomes a slave before God. (The γενέσθαι is a δουλεύειν before
God.) These directions of sense which refer to the surrounding world, to one's
vocation, and to that which one is (self-world) determine in no way the facticity of the Christian. Nonetheless they are there, they will be maintained and
first authentically assigned [zugeeignet] there. The significances of the surrounding world become, through having-been, temporal possessions. The
sense of facticity determines itself in this direction as temporality. Until now,
the relational sense of the surrounding world and communal world was purely
negatively determined. Insofar as these relations have no possibility at all to
motivate the arch-ontic meaning of primordial Christian religiosity, the positive question arises regarding the relation of the Christian to the surrounding
world and the communal world.

Now for the relational sense in which the Christian stands to the surrounding world. These are difficult connections, because the relations to the self-
world are precisely hit the hardest through the Christian having-become. In
Paul himself these connections are only briefly, yet sharply, touched upon
(Cor. and Phil.). Paul is clear about the fact that this relational direction requires a unique characterization (πνεῦμα—spirit, ψυχή—soul, σάρξ—flesh).
Usually, these concepts are grasped as conditions [als zuständliche]. The
surrounding-worldly and communal-worldly connections co-constitute facticity; but they are temporal possessions, insofar as they are lived in temporality.

I Cor. 7:29–32: We know the γενέσθαι as δουλεύειν and ἀναμένειν. Here:
καιρὸς συνεσταλμένος [the appointed time has grown short]. There remains
only yet a little time, the Christian living incessantly in the only-yet, which
intensifies his distress. The compressed temporality is constitutive for Christian religiosity: an "only-yet," there is no time for postponement. The Christians should be such that those who have a wife, should have her in such a
way, that they do not have her, etc. Τὸ σχῆμα τοῦ κόσμου [the present form
of this world]: the form of the world passes away; σχῆμα is not meant so very
objectively, rather as ordered toward a self-comportment. Rom. 12:2 shows
how σχῆμα [form] should be understood: καὶ μὴ συσχηματίζεσθε τῷ αἰῶνι τούτῳ

[and do not be conformed to this world]. Here one can gather the enactment-character of σχῆμα. The connections Paul [makes] should *not* be *ethically* understood. That is why it is a misperception when Nietzsche accuses Paul of *ressentiment. Ressentiment* in no way belongs to this realm; in this context one cannot speak at all of *ressentiment.* If one enters into that kind of talk, one shows only that one has understood nothing.

One is tempted to translate the ὡς μή by "as if," but that will not work. "As if" expresses an objective connection, and suggests the view that the Christian should eliminate these relations to the surrounding world. This ὡς means, positively, a new sense that is added. The μή concerns the complex of enactment of the Christian life. All of these relations experience a retardation in the respective enactment, so that they arise out of the origin of primordial Christian life experience. Christian life is not straightforward, but is rather broken up: all surrounding-world relations must pass through the complex of enactment of having-become, so that this complex is then co-present, but the relations themselves, and that to which they refer, are in no way touched. Who can grasp it, should grasp it. The isolation of Christian life sounds negative. Properly understood, the complex of experience can be grasped only out of the origin of Christian life-context. In Christian life there is, however, also an unbroken life-context, on the level of spirituality [*Geistigkeit*]—which has *nothing* to do with the harmony of life. With brokenness, the anguish and the gloominess of the Christians is still intensified; it has entered into the inner-most realm. The aforementioned passage can apparently be easily interpreted, and yet a genuine understanding renders it ever more difficult. The Christian life should, on the side of the surrounding world, receive a character of self-evidence (I Cor. 4:11–13).

§ 32. Christian Facticity as Enactment

Christian life experience is not modified by having-become itself. The relational sense of Christian life experience is different from that of the surrounding-worldly. If the surrounding-worldly relational sense were independent of Christian life experience, then certain passages in Paul would be incomprehensible. The conversion to Christian life experience concerns the *enactment.* In order to raise the relational sense of factical life experience, one must be careful that it becomes more "difficult," that it is enacted ἐν θλίψεσιν. The phenomena of enactment must be entwined with the sense of facticity. Paul makes of enactment a theme. It reads: ὡς μή, not οὐ. This μή indicates the tendency toward that which has the character of enactment. μή refers back to the enactment itself.

Articulating the phenomena gives rise to the necessity of setting aside any psychological schema. One must allow the phenomena to present themselves in their originality. Nothing is accomplished yet in merely "bringing to giv-enness"; this succeeds only through phenomenological destruction. Cf. I Cor. 4:11: Paul says: "Become my descendants!" He gives up all worldly means and significances and yet fights his way through. Through the renunciation of the worldly manner of defending oneself the anguish of his life is intensified. Entering into such complex of enactment is almost hopeless. The Christian is conscious that this facticity cannot be won out of his own strength, but rather originates from God—the phenomenon of the effects of grace. An explication of these complexes is very important. The phenomenon is decisive for Au-gustine and Luther, cf. II Cor. 4:7 f.: τοῦ θεοῦ καὶ μὴ ἐξ ἡμῶν [to God and does not come from us], then the oppositions; θλιβόμενοι, ἀλλ᾽ οὐκ etc. "We have the treasure (of Christian facticity) in earthen vessels." What is available only to us Christians is not sufficient for the task of arriving at Christian facticity.

Without Christian facticity, the significances of life would be decisive and would modify the relational complex. But here the course of the sense of factical life runs opposite. The enactment exceeds human strength. It is un-thinkable out of one's own strength. Factical life, from out of its own re-sources, cannot provide the motives to attain even the γενέσθαι. Through the over-intensification of a significance, life attempts to "gain a foothold." This concept of a "foothold" is meaningful in an entirely particular structure of factical life experience. One cannot apply it to Christian factical life experi-ence. The Christian does not find in God a "foothold" (cf. Jaspers[1]). That is blasphemy! God is never a "foothold." Rather, "to have a foothold" is always accomplished in view of a particular significance, attitude, view of the world, insofar as God is, in giving a foothold and in winning a foothold, correlative to a significance. Christian worldview: actually a contradiction! It does not arise from a complex of a historical kind, like the Christian. Thus whoever has not "accepted" (δέχεσθαι) is unable to sustain facticity or to appropriate the "knowledge." Cf. I Cor. 3:21 f.; Phil. 2:12 f. In Christian life experience, it arises from the sense of the surrounding world, that the world does not just happen to be there. It is no ἀδιάφορον [indifferent]. The significance of the world—also that of one's own world—is given and experienced in a peculiar way through the retrieval of the relational complexes in the authentic enact-ment.

§ 33. The Complex of Enactment as "Knowledge"

The χρᾶσθαι κόσμους [to deal with the world], the μὴ συγχρηματίζειν [do not have dealings] requires a particular mode of deciding: δοκιμάζειν [testing],

1. Cf. K. Jaspers, *Psychologie der Weltanschauungen,* Berlin, 1919, Chapter III c: Der Halt im Unendlichen.

εἰδέναι [to know]. As long as one begins from contemporary psychology and epistemology, stipulating phenomena of consciousness, one arrives at a false understanding of "knowledge." Characterizing it as "practical knowledge" brings one no closer to its sense-structure. One cannot simply presuppose, as understood, "knowledge *per se*" and then adapt it. The question as to which basic complex "knowledge" refers back, is thus answered: in that of the δου-λεύειν [serving] and ἀναμένειν [waiting]. Knowledge does not run alongside and freely in abeyance, but is rather always present. The complexes of en-actment themselves, according to their own sense, are a "knowledge." Cf. I Cor. 2:10: ἡμῖν γὰρ ἀπεκάλυψεν ὁ θεὸς διὰ τοῦ πνεύματος. τὸ γὰρ πνεῦμα πάντα ἐραυνᾷ, καὶ τὰ βάθη τοῦ θεοῦ [these things God has revealed to us through the spirit; for the spirit searches everything, even the depth of God] etc.

According to its own essence, "knowledge" requires πνεῦμα ἔχειν. In mod-ern exegesis, the meanings of the word πνεῦμα have been researched in the contemporaneous and in the ancient literature further back, all the way back to Plato. One sees analogies to this especially in certain passages of the "Her-mes Trismegistos" (in the so-called "Corpus Hermeticum"). These lines co-incide linguistically-stylistically and chronologically with Paul. It is said that, in the above-cited passage (I Cor. 2:10 ff.), Paul characterizes himself as a "pneumatic." The human being becomes God himself. Ἀνὴρ πςευματικός [human spirit] is said to be the godly, ἀνὴρ ψυχικός [human soul] the human, in him. This passage serves as argument for a connection of the Pauline writ-ings to the Hellenistic mystery-religions.[2] But this is misguided. Object-historically, no objection can be made, but from the enactment-historical interpretation, πνεῦμα, ἀνακρίνειν, ἐραυνᾷ, τὰ βάθη τοῦ θεοῦ [the spirit, search-ing, things, the depth of God] (I Cor. 2:10) mean something entirely different.

The πνεῦμα in Paul is the basis of enactment from which knowledge itself arises. πνεῦμα is in Paul connected with ἀνακρίνειν and ἐραυνᾶν (I Cor. 2:15; cf. also II Cor. 4:16, the "external" and "inner" human being; Rom. 8:4 ff. πνεῦμα-σάρξ). Σάρξ is a φρόνημα (8:6), a conviction; that is to say, a tendency of life. Gal. 2:20; Phil. 1:22: σάρξ is the complex of enactment of authentic facticity in surrounding-worldly life. Its opposite πνεῦμα is thus the δουλεύειν and ἀναμένειν. There is in Paul no πνεῦμα εἶναι [being spirit] (as in Corpus Hermeticum), but rather a πνεῦμα ἔχειν, ἐν πνεύματι περιπατεῖν [having spirit, living in spirit], or ἐπιτελεῖσθαι [being subject to]. Thus it is false to view πνεῦμα as a part of the human being; rather ἄνθρωπος πνευματικός is one who has appropriated a certain peculiar property of life. That means the πάντα ἀνακρίνειν. In sharp opposition to this is the theoretical cognition, the πάντα γνωρίζειν in the hermetic writings, cf. II Cor. 3:3. There remains a deep op-

2. Cf. Reitzenstein, *Die hellenistischen Mysterienreligionen nach ihren Grundgedanken und Wirkungen,* op. cit.

position between the Mystics and the Christians. The Mystic is, through manipulation, removed from the life-complex; in an enraptured state God and the universe are possessed. The Christian knows no such "enthusiasm," rather he says: "let us be awake and sober." Here precisely is shown to him the terrible difficulty of the Christian life.

Real philosophy of religion arises not from preconceived concepts of philosophy and religion. Rather, the possibility of its philosophical understanding arises out of a certain religiosity—for us, the Christian religiosity. Why exactly the Christian religiosity lies in the focus of our study, that is a difficult question; it is answerable only through the solution of the problem of the historical connections. The task is to gain a real and original relationship to history, which is to be explicated from out of our own historical situation and facticity. At issue is what the sense of history can signify for us, so that the "objectivity" of the historical "in itself" disappears. History exists only from out of a present. Only thus can the possibility of a philosophy of religion be begun.

Appendix

Notes and Sketches on the Lecture

Letter to the Galatians
[on § 16]

Paul in struggle—not only for his mission, but for the Galatians themselves; against the "law" not only as *law,* but rather as belonging to the world era [*Weltzeit*]. A push away into the unredeemed, not a radical seizing of the spirit.

The conflict about circumcision: question of the conditions for the entry into Christian life; external sign of inner belonging to the "alliance" [*Bundeswelt*] after exile. Not law, with its works and morals, distinguishes, but rather, *faith in Jesus Christ.* Superfluousness, harmfulness [...]* In law a "way to salvation" is embodied (view of existence!) (Way to salvation in upholding the commandment!) Meaning of the entire *law:* to refer man to his doings; the works of his doings [?], the reward will be of the law. For Paul: God alone acts in the sending of Christ! Thus: not the works of human beings, but rather grace!

Law—grace (at issue is existing, "living"), whether ἐκ νόμου [of the law] or (ΞΨΖ) ἐκ πίστεως [of faith], either/or of the *paths,* to life not itself the aim. Thus πίστις → δικαιοσύνη → ξωή (δόξα, τίμη, ἀφθαρσία [glory, honor, immortality]).

Thus for now as regards the letter to the Galatians: drawing out an understanding of the direction of sense, the arch-ontic, the *phenomenological fundamental dynamic*! At issue is whether what is Christian explicates itself, originally of itself becomes its own existential [*existenziell*] possession, *or* atrophies in worship [?]. *Passion of the apostle* disseminating [?] in this letter; behind this the eschatological! Faith not empty as a state and as yielding a final bliss, rather enactmental relation of the concerned entry to the future; being-extinct since the beginning of the end of time! Christianity something with an entirely new principle of existence: Christian salvation!! *Explicated in struggle* and through struggle. Faith: is *dying with Christ;* and indeed faith as recognition of the redeemed Christ, *that he is the Messiah.* That, however, has its essentially eschatological turn, thus includes within it running toward *the aim*! So he is, at the same time, *hope* for the *completion of the beginning.*

---

*[Two words, illegible.]

Religious Experience and Explication
[on § 17]

Religious experience—its sense, and insofar as it has concrete effects; its way of explication. Genuine or imposed schematic ordering! Unemphasized explication—emphasized, pre-dogmatic—dogmatic.

Religiosity and religion grow into a factical life-world, grow up in the language that belongs to it. New creation of the language only limited. Against this its function of meaning—the conceptual structure receives a reorganization from within, whereby the fallen-away frame of language, despite the reorganization, maintains itself even more strongly (*dialectic*—Paul! The development of Paul; the paradox reorganized, sublated [*aufgehoben*] by a *systematics*).

In order to understand that originally, one needs to emphasize the basic experiences and the experiencing foreconception—the authentic *dynamic of sense*. One has always confused this with the system, and through the rejection of a schematic systematization, one has delivered oneself over to individuation [*Vereinzelung*], and for the individuated phenomena searched for religious dependencies.

"Methodical" problems, not in the technical, but in the philosophical sense. The phenomena [form] their own proper "complex." "Religious attitude"—*register!*

The "structural complex" of the religious is the "first thing"; it must be found. But no "descriptive" task, rather one of *ex-plication*. (That is to say, the taking-out of the pre-enactment and the basic enactment, the taking-out [being] interpretive [*verstehende*]. "Out" is attitudinally and regionally thought; it is a simpler, originally more authentic foreconceptual enactment; through this the order is not created, but all explicative enactment- and situational-movements and steps are won in the *fundamental guidance* of the explication (Terminus)).

Now one can be absolutely interested *in* the explication and *to* it directly, and *must* be so actually, but it does not need to be communicated, above all not if the calling is missing; but it can also have the consequence that the *explicational structures* are understood *destructively* and historically: then arises an *a.f.m.* [?] that is not a preparation and relief, but is a first forcing toward the difficulty—and then motivated as such out of factical life.

Methodological Considerations regarding Paul (I)
[on §§ 18 and 19]

A short methodological instruction. To understand Paul and his apostolic pronouncement phenomenologically and from it decisive sense-complexes of

Christian life. Already itself an isolated, crude way of speaking. But adopting it does not mean dividing it up into philosophical concepts, making it accessible, thereby neutralizing what is foreign to "us today." We would then precisely move away from that which is to be the object, and turn the "object" into a case, an individuation of religious consciousness in general, whereby it is itself entirely questionable from where the latter arises as a standard in the first place. *Historical life as such* does not let itself be shattered into a non-authentic thingly manifold which one now exhaustively studies; and in particular the meaning of our special object protests against this.

One must even claim that a religious-historical study that fuses the object into a general religious-historical framework, researches according to contexts of emergence and motives of development, and strives for a general interpretation of the former time, comes still closer to the object—insofar as this approach is at least *historical,* if also attitudinally historical and object-historical (and in this case engenders principal difficulties in the history of religion).

The observational relation that is characterized as "historical" is closer. Only an indication for the authentic, for at its basis, the latter also, like every primarily attitudinally motivated observation, runs against any phenomenological understanding.

The introduction must explicate the sense of the phenomenological relation of access, the starting point, the possible starting points, the concretely required beginning that is not at all left to philosophical flirtations,—the inner connection of all of this with phenomenological (enactmental) understanding.

For the following effort the instructions can only be laid out so far: what is crucial is not to have our understanding led away from the object—that is to say, interpreting the object on the basis of a ready-made framework and inserting it therein, just as little as in the abundance of the contemporaneous material that is brought up for comparison. What is the object at all according to its fundamental determination? Do not ask *in this way,* theoretically constructively, but rather only the starting point of determination for analysis. Factical life does not belong to a region, it is itself also not a region; it is, moreover, not in opposition to all that is regional; *rather it is crucial to make an effort to show the object in itself in a particular way and to lift it into an explicitly phenomenological understanding.*

This understanding remains outside of the differentiation of rational-conceptual grasp and irrational letting-be of an indissoluble law;—presumably one believes to have left the object undisturbed; the opposite is the case, for the aforementioned irrational law has the sense of its irrationality from a concept of the rationality of life that is itself unclarified and, moreover, factically fundamentally misguided.

It is peculiar to phenomenological understanding that it can understand the *incomprehensible,* precisely in that it radically *lets* the latter *be* in its incomprehensibility. That is itself comprehensible only if one has understood that philosophy has nothing to do with the scientific study of object and subject. (Again a question of the introduction.)

The access is essentially determined by the fact that the *phenomenon* to be reached (Christian religiosity—Christian life—Christian religion) is *grasped, in its basic sense-direction, already in the starting point of the explication.* At first, as they come to understanding in the starting point, these sense-complexes can still be far removed from authentic philosophical understanding. It is enough if they are recklessly grasped hold of and, for the enactment of explication, not let go of, but ever more radically secured. (In this, the evidence of securing is not determined by the sense of scientific general validity and rational necessity, but rather through originality of the concern and measured against this, as is absolutely required.) (Cf. Methodological Considerations regarding Paul (II).)

With this it is said: it is crucial to emphasize sense-relations of the appropriation (first of all the emphasis proper to experience, entrance in predominating relations, which also already offer themselves in their content), to make them apparent and to explicate them radically originally, in absolute distance to that which is to be appropriated and to the enactment of appropriation [?] and still also taking it *a.f.m.* [?]

One such basic determination is as a starting point: *Christian religiosity is in factical life experience, it actually is this itself.* We attempt to understand this *from out of the apostolic proclamation of Paul.* (1. Manner: How of the proclamation—to *place* the apostolic mission into the *life* of the *communal world.* 2. Accentuation of the sense-complexes: the *eschatological*—"absolutely teleological.")

Methodological Considerations regarding Paul (II)
[on §§ 20 and 21]

Factical life: in which basic phenomenological direction? Accentuation of the directions of sense; "that which exists" [*das Bestehende*]—factical meaning?

The proclamation, εὐαγγέλιον [gospel], in terms of *content, relational, enactmental.*

When is *proclaimed*—to the individual, in which *communal-worldly* (factical life) tendency?

How is *proclaimed*—apostolic, for appropriation.

What is *proclaimed*—not doctrine, worldly wisdom.

Who proclaims, and as *which*?

The *What* meets *what in which way*? The historical. (Jesus Christ, cross, resurrection.)

The *proclamation* in its authentic accentuation of sense and *tendency of enactment* and *mission* [?] (demanding).

How of the *demanded* appropriation; revolution of factical life through proclamation, insofar as it is appropriated.

What *is* triggered in factical life experience, awakened, disturbed, *forced* in the basic *self-worldly* experience, also in the resistance?

Which new basic articulation of life is raked up, and whereto and how? This articulation is such that, through itself, it demands con-frontation [*Auseinander-setzung*] from all those who *run* into it!

Out of this the meaning of the undertakings must be understood: the writings of the New Testament—*form of literature!*—sense of one's own explications—*New Testament theology*!

Our study is subject to a *limitation:* from the New Testament, only the *Pauline letters*. The problems that arise in regard to the entire ending, whether the Jesus-Paul question (indeed chronologically the oldest and at the same time most immediate record) is at all properly posed, and other questions have not even been touched upon.

In this the historical situation of the letters is also to be observed much more carefully, how in it the direction of proclamation is motivated enactmentally. Thus one may not simply take them as doctrinal writings on equal footing, much less can one strongly emphasize *the historical* (as objective situation) while forgetting the real motivational connection with the proclamation or while treating it only as an aside. *It is what is decisive.* That is why such an exposed position in the letter to the Galatians must be treated first; although it must precisely be said, that *this* situation is not such that it carries within it, fully apparently, what is authentic; rather the reverse. The proclamation has made a turn in regard to, or is stuck on, the problem of ὁδός [path].

The height of the literary form has here not the tendency of independent integration into world literature and comparison, but rather the opposite: the retreat to the enactment of proclamation. That surrounding-worldly motives and forms are taken up speaks precisely *to the originality* of the basic driving motive of proclamation as a Christian motive. (To be won only from out of the explication of origin. Compare Norden, Weiß, Bultmann: *Theologische Rundschau;*[1] Wendland. "Form"—"style" are not aesthetically typologizing;

1. Rudolf Bultmann, "Neues Testament. Einleitung II" in *Theologische Rundschau. 17. Jahrgang*, Tübingen, 1914, pp. 79–90. [Literary Review of:] E. Norden, *Agnostos Theos. Untersuchungen zur Formengeschichte religiöser Rede*. Leipzig, 1913.—J. Weiß, "Literaturgeschichte des Neuen Testaments," in *Die Religion in Geschichte und Gegenwart III*. Tübingen, 1912. column 2175–2215.—P. Wendland, "Die urchristlichen Literaturformen," in *Handbuch zum Neuen Testament*, 2nd and 3rd ed., Tübingen, 1912. I, 3; pp. 257–448.
[Cf. further: J. Weiß, *Paulus und seine Gemeinden. Ein Bild von der Entwicklung des Ur-*

rather the How of explication, concern, appropriation of the enactmental understanding—decision!)

In the same way all *problems of interpretation* remain peripheral, in part
because they burden the study; above all, however, because they are not decisive, perhaps not even radically posed. Due to the neglect of the hermeneutical problem. (*Dilthey* crudely understood, but for him specifically, no problem. *Spranger, Volkeltfestschrift;*[2] cf. supplement "Das Historische"[3].)

One must observe above all the following: that drawing out "concepts" and
"ideas of content"—and still more the comparison of these to what is contemporaneous or previous (Greek-Hellenistic, Jewish-Israeli)—is misleading.
Apparently real scientific knowledge and yet burdened with a wide-ranging
presupposition that in Christian experience there is to be found "ideas of
content" and "concepts" at all. *The "expressions" are always to be taken as
a "cluster" of relations, of sense-complexes.* We may not approach it with the
attitude that we will encounter things and the bare juxtaposition of things, and
order them according to a schema of our healthy and small understanding.
The *"mood"* is precisely that which is decisive; everything depends upon—
and phenomenological investigation must show precisely this—understanding
the peculiar phenomenal complex "factical life experience," and especially the
Christian one. The genuine foreconception will then also have been developed
first of all for the object-historical, attitudinally understanding study.

In reference to the phenomenological radicalization, one need not fear the
objection that it is thus "modernized"; every understanding modernizes insofar
as it, in the explication, *uncovers* something new that lies "in the sense." If
one only hangs on to the "ideas of content"—the picture of the world and its
erstwhile theoretical interpretation and order—then modernization may appear
very crass; but holding on to ideas of content is, precisely, no real grasping
at all, and is entirely illegitimate as a measure for modernizing reinterpreta-
tion.

Methodological Considerations regarding Paul (III)
[on § 22]

Significance of the study for theology. (Not as praise of its importance, but
rather positive demand for a new posing of the problem which actually drives

christentums. Berlin, 1914.—P. Wendland, "Die hellenistisch-römische Kultur in ihren Beziehungen zu Judentum und Christentum" in *Handbuch zum Neuen Testament*, 2nd and 3rd ed.,
Tübingen, 1912, I, 2; pp. 1–256.]

2. Eduard Spranger, "Zur Theorie des Verstehens und zur geisteswissenschaftlichen Psychologie" in *Festschrift Johannes Volkelt zum 70. Geburtstag. Dargebracht von Paul Barth, Bruno
Bauch, Ernst Bergmann, Jonas Cohn, u.a.* Munich, 1918, pp. 357–403.

3. [The manuscript of the supplement has not been preserved.]

me!) The concept of theology remains entirely suspended in this. The outdated concept might indicate: it cannot be avoided that the discovery of the phenomenal complexes changes from the ground up the problematic and the formation of concepts and offers authentic measures for the *destruction* [Destruktion] of Christian theology and Western philosophy.

The pre-Christian—the Christian revolution [*Umbruch*]: how are they both in themselves determined, how comparable are they, and how are they to be brought, *phenomenologically*, in which basic determination? To determine from this determination also the meaning of the "opposition" and of "development" (revolution). "*Christian*" not simply a determination, according to which different things meld together and dominate something. (That holds precisely in reference to the eschatological! Compare criticism regarding the lecture.[4])

***

Phenomenological explication and "psychologization,"—"spiritualization" [*Vergeistigen*], "rationalization."

In principle to be distinguished: the coarse in content, attitudinal substitution of "psychologically-meant contents" with the physical—the phenomenological return to the sense-complexes.

1. Must be observed, that perhaps the opposition physical-psychical has been misread into it from out of the attitude for which there are no problems of access.

2. The phenomenological explication poses a problem, but not an unsolvable one and above all no such internal hermeneutics of bare science, but *the* problem of basic existence—in the context of the *destruction*. Compare the *outline* in the "Introduction to the Phenomenology of Religion": "History of Ideas," "Foreconceptual History."[5]

3. The phenomenological explication does not aim at isolated contents, and only and primarily at them; rather, it aims at the relations and *enactments,* which are readable off the content (in each temporally conditioned form). However, these relations and enactments are, in turn, not to be elevated in an a priori perpetual armamentarium; rather, they are to grasp the sense from the appropriation of one's own factical *existence*!

4. Above all one may not spread out the "phenomena" like pieces on a stage of consciousness and let them dwell there indifferently;—falling attitude! The radical idea of constitution also does not change this; *on the contrary!*

---

4. [The manuscript of the supplement has not been preserved.]
5. Cf. text of the lecture course, above p. 61.

***

Pronouncement of the existential communication to the community, I Cor. 1.

Paul shows: the gospel is strength for those who are called and it has the fundamental enactment of faith. Thus from out of this as fundamental experience, the entire factical life experience is determined, and all *significances* in it must be determined radically therefrom. It is a falling if one turns to other extra-wordly means and the "wise" of the world bring confusion.

In principle (only concretely); the called should περισσεύειν μᾶλλον [do every move], permanent concern, authentic appropriation in factical life experience, that is to say, live temporality authentically, as what and how it is, out of Christian fundamental enactment. That means: the "proof" [*Beweis*] and the *showing* [Erweis] of what is proclaimed lie not in having-had insight; rather, the proclamation is "showing" (ἀπόδειξις) of the "spirit," "force," I Cor. 2:4. Faith should, after all, be no human wisdom, cf. there [2:5]. Communication of existence; and the apostle is only a tool of this *showing*.

The Hermeneutical Foreconceptions
[on § 22]

Origin of the hermeneutical relation. Which direction of sense is at all the arch-ontic in the hermeneutical? To what motive-(original-)complex does it refer back?

Phenomenology of Pauline Proclamation (I)
First Letter to the Thessalonians
[on §§ 23–26]

In the study of the letter to the Galatians (cf. methodological considerations regarding Paul (II)) in the first, initial taking-cognizance-of the "content" of apostolic [. . .]* Paul in the situation (objective historical situation), and indeed far into the middle of his apostolic activity: struggle, theological confrontation. Going back into factical life and grasping the situation (factical) step by step more sharply.

First letter to the Thessalonians a "piece" of apostolic *proclamation* itself. It shows itself in its incipience [?], to lift the fundamental situation from out of itself. To radicalize the phenomenal complex itself, out of which one may no longer step. "Form" of the *proclamation*—content of proclamation—*How*

---

* [Two words, illegible.]

of the proclamation; this last being the decisive, and indeed enacted in which factical situation, how it arises therefrom; enacted *in* it and breaking *into what, How* of the breaking-in.

Not to be separated from the "literary form"! As a special problem! Expression *as* communication! In this, the explication of the *proclamation* does not have the aim of a peripheral contribution toward *an image of the personality as type;*—a fundamentally mistaken measure which is inappropriate to the being, the life, of Paul.

How of the proclamation: enactmental complex in his life, how the proclamation is positioned in his life, and how it perpetually occupies him (the "hurry") 2:2; proclamation in broad, great struggle of effort. "The warning [*Vermahnung*]" may not be separated, no practical, usual appendage, rather corresponds to the fundamental sense of Christian existence of perpetual and radical concern (μᾶλλον). I Thess. στηρίξαι [to strengthen] 3:2; so they do not trouble themselves for nothing, everything toward παρουσία.

How does *Paul* see the Thessalonians? Those who have passed away [*Entschlafenen*]! Not coincidentally! 3:10 καταρτίσαι [restore], 3:12; 3:13. Yet they who, in the night, urge themselves toward the *facticity of the end of time.* 2:19 Fear of not being able to praise, of not having fulfilled the vocation. Belongs essentially to the warning! The *uncertainty* (3:2: wavering in sadness) can become great, for instance those "who have passed away": what will become of us? νεκροὶ ἐν Χριστῷ [the dead in Christ], not θάνατος [death]! "Serious," their "constant determination" ("Intensity" [?] for instance Christlessness [?]) *constitutive* for *the decisive* in *what is Christian!* Phenomena, where and how of their connection and situation!

It so proceeds in the memory of the "beginning," which is to be kept in mind; it concerns only the unfolding of this! Factical life: surrounding-worldly, communal-worldly, self-worldly relations determined from the enactment of the end-of-time facticity; in this there is for him only *proclamation,* everything depends on *their* failure or success; what is *decisive* never καύχησις [a boasting], thus also about him *as apostle!* εἴσοδος ὁποία [our coming] 1:9; 2:1 was not κενός [not in vain]; we know, you are *chosen, you stand* in the expectation, it depends on you, each of you.

The proclamation must have constant determination, because the *proclaimed* is not to be "assimilated" into the [secular] world, it does not *penetrate, from itself,* it is only [?] beginning [?]; ever more στηρίξαι, devoured; building back to the foundation, not building up and building further and falling. For this reason, the apostle: ἀδιαλείπτως μνημονεύοντες, μηκέτι στέγων, 3:1; 3:5: *he is always to them in the How of the apostle!* εἰδότες τὴν ἐκλογήν! Knowledge of distress ("the certainty of eternity"—not poor on movement), that does not stop and let rest, but the opposite (2:18 ff.; 3:5 decisive), precisely now, despite all this, the last concern and we thank God for that! He considers his apostolic responsibility before God and only this. 1:5 ἐγενήθη. Responsibility: in this the proclamation is concerned and in this his factical life-relation to the Christians. *Communal-world* has arrived in this becoming at the situation. That the gospel stands in their life, that they can no longer avoid it! 3:3. Their relationship to Paul—*faith!* μίμηται ἡμῶν! μνεῖαν, *thinking on* [Gedenken] the *How* of having-become-Christian through him is decisive, 2:9; 3:6! (Problem, whether the connections [?] do not have a new fundamental sense *despite* the schema.)

Phenomenology of Pauline Proclamation (II)
First Letter to the Thessalonians
[on §§ 23–26]

The letter a *concerned existential* "contemplation" of the *situation!* Arising out of this, therefore "nothing special."

Construction and presentation still uncertain. Each letter singly in its *situational structure?* And then not some sort of generalization! Rather an original complex of enactment, so that what is *authentically* historical comes to be expressed!

Where do I stand and go and with me you, you who are called! (Essential discrimination in factical life experience, particularly phenomenological?) This situational structure not coincidental, but to the fundamental sense of factical life experience of the Christian. How and in how far? Cf. 2:18; 3:5; here what is decisive in his existence: ἐλπίς [hope]!

You are also my hopes in the Parousia. *You,* in what you have now become and are becoming, are so through my apostolic proclamation, my concernful enactment in regard to you, that is to say, *you are* my real *being* (3:7)! For if you were not so, I would have been missing, my concern and accomplishment would have been missing. (That I am apostle, and that God works through me, is certain.) If it fails, it is *my* fault (failure in Phillipi; new confidence created, 2:1); and therefore I can*not bear* it, I am restless concerning you, for I do not know where you and I 'lie'—in the θλίψεσιν[oppression]— and that the *tempter* is at work! And indeed the more so, the closer to the decision—thus my struggle (2:2). All the more must I *see* you, that is to say, have you in person in front of me (3:10: ἰδεῖν καὶ καταρτίσαι[see and restore]).

Always again the absolute *end* [*das* Letzte]: Parousia! Stands *ominously* in its *place.* How is this *standing* phenomenological? Or articulation of enactment! And that phenomenologically back to existential fundamental concern! *Life ↔ death.* Not to become ἀθέτων τὸν θεόν, not to eliminate God, that is to say, the ἁγιασμός—a calling!

Phenomenology of Pauline Proclamation (III)
First Letter to the Thessalonians
[on §§ 23–26]

Opposition of the Jews: Indication, that something "new," different faces them, against which they rebel. It touches upon something in the factical life experience of the Jews and of the inhabitants of Thessalonika in general. For πρὸς ἐκληρώθησιν, from—to, that is to say, in they themselves something must have been turned around; ἐπείσθησαν, again convinced. So the communal world in Thessalonika stands for Paul also. That certainly only for one *moment;* not yet (*eschatologically*) determined, neither the communal world, nor the communal-worldly fundamental relation of *Paul.*

What is the apostolic enactment of the mission in its fundamental direction, motive, and tendency? (Explicational structure, later.) How, in this congregation in Thessalonika, stand: (a) the communal-worldly relation of Paul to the congregation. Communal world: 1. How the Thessalonians themselves, as *what determined,* how experienced, their "existence" for Paul. 2. How for Paul the relation is enacted. This also means: brought to that through him, that is to say, the turning-around triggered through him. (b) *Self-world.* (c) Surrounding world.

In the sphere of this communal-worldly situation and under [?] it, belonging to it, for it itself a particular decisive *before* [?], *becoming* (T.) in all phenomena of such religious fundamental sense?

Re (a) communal world (Thessalonians): such as he writes to. Is that the fundamentally determining, independent character? No, rather only on the basis of . . . Are they distinguished in a special way through this? Yes and no; no, in that they are ἀδιαλείπτως [unceasingly] in their "being"; yes, but this stands in question for him primarily as apostle and for *them,* insofar as the urgency of their awakening continually and urgently imposes itself, that is to say insofar as it urges *eschatologically.*

Articulation of the communal world, which *through* call, faith; eschatological, phenomenal basic sense of what is communal-worldly experienced. *Previously* the pagans, no link in a complex of significance or even in a practical "earthly" purpose! Those who received the gospel through him, and who show themselves as called in their acceptance of it, thus those who met him in his ownmost factical life experience, "those to whom he came." (As which is it motivating the writing of the letter to them, possible basic motive, cause, starting point (cf. the return of Timothy).)

ἐγενήθη τὸ εὐαγγέλιον εἰς ὑμᾶς [the gospel came to you]. How this came to be—its setting-in—so decisive, that also here in the reverse, Paul himself does come from "memory," they are thus "standing in a history" (the entire meaning of which is enactmentally co-given within them; (eschatologically) *chosen*).

To contrast: in that, unique *encounter* with others, entering into factical life; can be an occasion for the eruption of new enactments; but never so much as here, where existence grounds itself in this *encounter.*

Phenomenology of Pauline Proclamation (IV)
[on §§ 23–26]

Εἰς ὑμᾶς τὸ εὐαγγέλιον ἐλενήθη [to you the gospel came], thus κληθέντες [summoned], and thus as such, they who are troubled in torment know constantly, 3:2: given in the historical basic posture, παρουσία! This becomes clear in that he is writing to them. Alone in that: ever more περισσεύειν μᾶλλον [increasingly abounding]; what is decisive is the increasing concern. It as "each individual," 2:11; 5:11, 14, 15; everywhere as παρακαλεῖν ἀλλήλους [encourage each other].

Factical life emerged out of a genesis and became in an entirely special way historical (enacted). Such a *fundamental character* that makes possible absolutely no single ideational relation, or at all a primarily concern-free one. But that means the coming and encountering are not something peripheral. How not?

The phenomenon of proclamation—*center of motivation* of the *enactment.* Their "genesis" is at once and stands in that of his own; he belongs with that to them, stands now with them in their fate in an entirely determinate sense. From this, now, the longing to "see" them, καὶ: 3:10 καταρτίσαι; because he is bound as apostle, because they have been entrusted to him, and that in this time.

εἴσοδος [path] (Aristotle) of Paul I 5:9; 2:1–12. 3:17 ff. expelled from them, but from physical distance, not the heart.

His ἐλπίς—the end [*das Letzte*] with καὶ ὑμεῖς (2:19) his existence. χαρᾷ ἔμπροσθεν τοῦ θεοῦ [the joy that we feel before our God], 3:9.

Regarding the motivation of the *letter-writing.* Himself *in* struggle against life, that is to say, has in his life a decisive meaning, not coincidental mood, enjoyment [?], pleasure, lovableness, or personal concern [*Anteilnahme*]. Necessity of his apostolic existence 2:18. 3:5: πειράζων [blocked]: κενόν, μηκέτι στέγων [when I could bear it no longer]. The urgency of time! 4:8: ζῶμεν, when you stand in this anguish and distress? (not earthly!). 3:11: *God* may clear the way. 5:27: entreat you to read the letter to all brothers.

How does Paul experience the surrounding-world? Is that what is discussed here? The "not" characteristic! *Eschatology;* here falsely "localized."

How is his self-world given to him?

Phenomenology of Pauline Proclamation (V)
[on §§ 23–26]

Directions of explication: communal world as receiving. Communal world as "receiving" world into which the gospel *strikes*. How is it to receive it, take it up, "re-act"? Communal world: each individual. For this, how is the structure to be gained from out of the enactment of proclamation? For this, how is the structure to be gained from out of the resistance and its How? (Cf. supplement proclamation[6]).

Sermon of the Cross—its *How.* 2:18 shows: there must be a fundamental situation there, one decisive for the communal world.

Paul in struggle against factionalization, that is to say the advancing of opinions of individuals, pomposity. ("I think," I Cor. 1:14, that I have no longer baptized, that is to say, that I cannot brag about it.) For baptism is also not what is decisive, but rather proclamation, and indeed *how:* not in wise talk—so that the cross will not be emptied out through so much chatter—rather simply through his appropriately plain speech. That is the only thing, and here there is no possibility of chattering, if one has only grasped the How; cross and the corresponding sermon of the cross, I Cor. 1:17 f.

It is exactly such, that upon its basis absoluteness, unaffectedness is decided; it introduces an either/or and leaves no room for half-wayness and opinions—big talk, which covers over the authentic.

The initiation may not be softened and weakened by a mode of reception that, through talk and wisdom overlooks it, which thus does not hold itself radically open. The situation of the existential concern is radically prepared. To take up the preparatory [*disponierende*] situation of the sermon of the cross. The self-worldly situation of the apostle. (Eschatology—and How of Paul in this.)

In the face of this falling tendency of life and attitude in communal-worldly tendencies (wisdom of the Greeks) is required a radical restraint, in order to preach in the simplicity demanded; always see the cross only as such. The cross is such that with it, one takes an inferior position in the communal world, that one would actually have to hide it, that one would have to be ashamed for it. But Paul Rom. 1:16: οὐ γὰρ ἐπαισχύνομαι τὸ εὐαγγέλιον [for I am not ashamed of the gospel]. That is to say an absolute faith is the basis, and the above is able to follow how faith (absolute concern) determines the *accentuating situation* as *arch-ontic sense;* no juxtaposition in a series, but a motivational complex of factical life.

***

---

6. [The manuscript of the supplement has not been preserved.]

How of the Thessalonians: having-become, concrete life-complex of the same. For Paul ἐλπίς—χαρά—δόξα [hope—joy—glory]; he experiences them *in this way,* as themselves waiting obstinately, living towards. In his nature, [he is] an essentially other. From this distress the absolute concern. (Entry—3:10, prayer!) From this [?] what is seen in this letter-writing in such a situation is—determination of the *What* of that which is written from out of the How of existence and from that, in particular, the *How of this What*! 4:13: οὐ θέλομεν ὑμᾶς ἀγνοεῖν [we do not want you to be uninformed], you should know. Starting with the οἴδατε and its fundamental fullness; developing the attitude toward [*einstellen in*] their factical world or its own explication. With this Paul meets them in their own *facticity,* to which, after all, the "knowledge" belongs. 5:11: the θέλομεν itself arises out of his ownmost self-worldly experience (urgency). The Thessalonians are those who know in becoming, indeed so, that *he* (as apostle) must want that they *also* know.

Factical life experience has its genuine own explication, co-determined by the fundamental experiences. Insofar as Paul conducts himself only in absolute concern to the Thessalonians and sees them in their authentic How, will he move in the "intercourse" with them openly in the self-explication, not only this; rather there is for him no other possibility at all in this urgency. What came to be spoken between them is as factical life experience's own explication, and indeed in its *facticity* itself, not doctrinal about it, in the slickness and detachment of theory; rather, the explication takes up the turns and breaks of factical life in all its sadness and no more. (*Or-igin of theology.*) And what the Thessalonians are: υἱοὶ φωτός—ἡμέρας; starting point for the explication of the authentic knowledge of facticity. ("Dogmatic"! connections; τὸ πνεῦμα μὴ σβέννυτε [do not quench the spirit], 5:19; cf. Deißner!⁷)

The other letters [are] to be understood in this way, too. Therefore letter to the Galatians is to be regarded in advance as a whole, in order to avoid always comparing; and indeed so, that in the study it will become apparent how it has absolutely not carried out the means of understanding such that in even so wide-reaching an explication what is decisive has been missing.

The "content of the letter in a narrower sense," that about which he writes—and the How of this writing, insofar as it is understood correctly from the beginning and is not alienated [?] from the outside, is able to also explicate authentically the communal-worldly life-complex in its articulation and with that the factical life of the Thessalonians, and above all that of Paul.

To explicate the *How of the proclamation* such that from out of itself under the force of the phenomena, that is to say from their enactmental mobility. . . .

At the same time the eschatological is thereby also brought more originally

---

7. Kurt Deißner, *Auferstehungshoffnung und Pneumagedanke bei Paulus*, Naumburg/Saale, 1912. (Theol. Diss., University of Greifswald, 1912.)
[Cf. further: Kurt Deißner, *Paulus und die Mystik seiner Zeit*, Leipzig, 1918.]

to a preliminary understanding. Eschatology *and facticity* as experienced in factical life; the facts of salvation history.

The "screaming at" expresses the urgency, also that he sees the Thessalonians as *on the way;* the having-become—being [is] a *new* becoming; they have become—and absolute—*becoming* (which has ὑστεπήματα, must στηρί-ξαι). Because Paul experiences in himself the absolute anguish and *moves from out of [?] it* (II Cor.) and only so does he *understand authentically.* That is to say at once: he cannot bear it, that is to say, he must say to them—and therein he finds himself again authentically. 3:7 ff.: the *anguish,* in which he rejoices, and which makes him ever more inexhaustible. The higher they stand, the greater the danger.[. . .]*

Enactmental-Historical Understanding
[on § 24]

The object-historical complex of happening should be understood enactmental-historically. The approach to this turn *such* that the complex of happening will be experienced, at any point, situationally. Thus "situation" means no object-historical concept, but a phenomenological term (literally!), although it is often used object-historically.

Limits of the event-complex—limits of the situation do not coincide (= problem). The later question, how that pertaining to event will be experienced by the situational complex.

Question of the How of proclamation—questioning that opens up! Questions somehow always there—the question that always *explicitly* takes cognizance-of!

Diversity of the *situation.* (Principal things about the situational "structures.") (f.) and (f.) "I," that lives the situation and to whom it belongs (f.). Self-world (I) lives "away from" and "towards";—no longer formal, but important. "I" posited in the manner of formal indication, as unity-forming; with that it is not said that it already actually captures the situation. Formal indication of the schema of the situational diversity and unity. I in relation to that of the I [*Ichlichem*] and that of the not-I [*Nichtichlichen*] (self-world, communal world, surrounding world). Formal indication of the situational diversity, a relational complex; likewise nothing concluded about the unity and diversity.

"I" "is" and as such it "has"; already a closer determination of the relational complex, not formal, rather formal indication. The "is" of the theoretical predication and "is" of the enactmentally radical [?] self-ness [?] (existence) [?]

---

* [Illegible insertion.]

[are] incomparably separate, hence the employment here is formal-in-dicational. [It is] a fundamental error to think that one can *gain* what is existential and enactmental through concretization [?] and specification and material completion of the predicative "is." *The other way around:* the theoretical and predicative only a falling, and indeed that of the *pure* attitude!

To lay out what is *had.* Since this relational diversity and unity of the situation is not one *of order,* so that no *determination* can be given in such a way that elements of diversity can be studied in isolation, and these [...]* lay as diversity in *one* region, with the starting point of the explication is already. . . . From here precisely the situational structure is to be understood, for which there is no *regional* a priori, but a *historical originality and decision against it and for it,*—not theoretical, but enactmental, because each enacts on its own.

How, for instance, is the eschatological? Not encompassing, not common, but *reigning throughout* enactmentally. What through—where to? What and how [is] reigning and on what grounds?

Because the enactmental understanding is also in danger of falling, compressed into an attitude or interspersed with attitudinal moments, it is difficult at times to grasp what is authentic in the situation. Mostly that of *what* is given; it still has something of attitudinal being-had and can be directly so.

The *What* for the *Thessalonians* apparently *again* characterized attitudinally, to be sure, *in* the situation, in *having, but still not authentically.* What they "are" (surrounding world) and "have" (surrounding world) as that belonging to the "I" [*Ichliches*]. What they are: that is to say, for Paul in the situation, to which we [...]** place, and what they *have as such beings,* do not *separate*—one thing determines the other, is *the same,* that is to say, existential fundamental determination is indicated!

Eschatology I (I Thess.)
[on § 26]

I Thess. 4:13–5:11 concerns 1. fate (factical life, being) of those who have passed away, in relation to ([...]***) the παρουσία; 2. the When of the παρουσία. Thus: to something that stands in essential relation *to them,* to their factical life, to that of their now Christian life, initially in their communal world; from out of which some are torn—what does this mean? But why for the others, not for oneself? *Because they themselves* can die—and what will

* [An illegible word.]
** [An illegible word.]
*** [An illegible word.]

happen then? Everything depends upon the meaning of the παρουσία. What does it mean, so that the Thessalonians begin to mourn and have no hope, that is to say, actually *fall*?

This meaning is *something* which decides their factical life; their hope, the having-of-hope, and the How of this having. That is, the authentic How of their being (cf. Schema[8]).

Paul intervenes in their "knowing," in which the παρουσία is at stake, at stake is that for which they *obstinately wait,* at stake is their *obstinate wait-ing*—an essential determination of the How of their factical life.

Indeed, he intervenes so originally and genuinely [?] in their knowing, that he gives them knowledge precisely by way of the *How* (by way of the en-actmental sense of the same). Insofar as the How is decisive,—which emerges more and more clearly in the progress of the explication. We realize here what was formally indicated earlier, and do not follow the order of the letter's content, which itself, as it presents itself object-historically, *is something ex-ternal* after all, even if not in isolation and merely external.

παρουσία-"event," "how," "who"? The relation to them—what is *coming.* How is it *there,* which objectivity is involved in its *cognition*? This itself is a *faith*!!

The How of the *relation* is motivated essentially in the *enactment* (factical life)!

4:13, ff. A certain grief is to be resisted. Is this warranted in Christian [terms]? How does Paul *resist* this "practical purpose?" For this reason, no decoration, which is otherwise common in apocalyptics—that is *forbidden* for Paul, cf. 5 ff. "no curiosity," "no drive for communication"!

Paul says nothing about the fate of those who have passed away (now), what has become of them since, where they are, but only what is decisive again: they will not be "passed up." Here everything is condensed only into the simple line: in his urgency and in his authentically Christian existence, he, as it were, does not hear at all the broodings of hopeful, falling speculation.

Difficulty: if death, following II Cor. 5:8 and Phil. 1:21, is an immediate transition to community with Christ, why is the motif of consolation first sought in the future Parousia? Is not death already equivalent? Stählin 183.[9]

5:1–11. On *time* and *moment* [Augenblick] (biblical use of the terms not coincidental; the explicit characterization of the When, not an objectively in-different When; καιρός decisive). And how does he determine this When? Not through objective temporal specifications, but through the *How*, and indeed

---

8. Cf. text of the lecture course, above p. 68.
9. Cf. Wilhelm Stählin, "Experimentelle Untersuchungen über Sprachpsychologie und Reli-gionspsychologie," in *Archiv für Religionspsychologie*, ed. W. Stählin, vol. I, Tübingen, 1914, pp. 117–194.

How as referred, at the same time, to the relation to the *How*. For the relation or the enactment, is what is decisive in the *When*! You do not need [it], you know that the *When* in your factical life, and precisely in this aforementioned *How* of its enactment.

This relation or enactment is grounded in a being chosen! Because you *are* called, the basic sense of your *Being is*. Take to περιποίησις σωτηρίας [acquiring a safeguard] (that is to say ἀναμένειν [awaiting], put on the armor! *Strife* [Kampf]).

For *those* who have no hope and thus despair, but have seeming happiness and security, it comes as "sudden" and inescapable; *unexpected,* unprepared for it; no means for overcoming and taking a stance; they are *handed over* to it. The corresponding relation is a falling one, absorbed in (εἰπήνη, ἀσφάλεια [peace, security]), finding sufficiency [?]. Corresponding relation pushed away, not even seen. They cannot *escape;* they want to save themselves but can no longer do so. To be *taken absolutely*! They are mired in darkness such that they themselves (enactment) are hidden. They do not "look" *at* it, and run away from themselves.

Opposition: ὅταν λέγωσιν [when they say ...] 5:3—ὑμεῖς δέ [but you ...] 5:4; such that it characterizes two ways of relating to it. For the wise the day does not come (like the thief in the night)—not suddenly and inescapably, 5:5.

ἡμέρα, *the* day and *on* the day for the Christian! ἡμέρας ὄντες νήφωμεν, sober in contrast to exaggeration, *an errant falling*! (Those who drink, who are drunk) No erroneous enthusiasm (rather ἐλπίδα σωτηρίας), which runs in the same direction as *sleeping,* being reasonable!!

Eschatology II (I Thess.)
[on § 26]

The *hope* that the Christians have is not simply faith in immortality, but a faithful *resilience* grounded in Christian factical life. Hope: it is experienced not as boasting (and thus no concern for one's self) but rather precisely ἐλπίδα [hope] in coping, ὑπομονή [endurance] of the θλίψις [oppression]!

"*Having hope*" and mere *attitudinal expectation* [are] essentially different. To have "expectation" as hope, faithful, loving, serving expectation in sadness and joy. Cf. 4:5, esp. Eph. 2:12: ἐλπίδα μὴ ἔχοντες καὶ ἄθεοι ἐν τῷ κόσμῳ [having no hope and without God in the world].

To what extent do the Thessalonians (which?) suffer a "loss," such that they are despairing, such that they have no hope, that is to say, step out of the special sense of enactment? They should by no means *concern* themselves with brooding, that is to say, they should not speculate about problems, that is to say, mere attitudinal expectation, εἰ γὰρ πιστεύομεν. *Faith*! πιστεύειν not

mere attitudinal acceptance (as true) of a fact! Still emptier and less appropriate (or more one-sided) than the Protestant, exclusive emphasis on *fiducia*.
Both read off a relational moment, but see neither the authentic nor the enactmental.

Unmistakably, the expressions that Paul uses in his teaching refer to the fear
of a merely partial and temporal exclusion. He holds up to them not the
assurance that a resurrection stands before even those who have passed away,
but rather that which God, through Jesus (at the coming about of the messianic
realm) will bring with him: ἄξει σὺν αὐτῷ (4:7) (*ut ei aggregentur et eius
gloriae fiant participes* (Turrettini)[10]).

At the same time, or priority, of the living, or of the reception of salvation,
thus *again* a *When, not so much an objective one in general*. The care was
directed only to the advance of the living, or the *disadvantage of the dead*.

If we have faith (central fact!), then is given in this faith a self-relation to
the question (resurrection), that neither speculates nor, above all, comes into
doubt. Those who have passed away, as long as they are believers, will not
be lost; they will *be present also, and that is what is decisive*. If we believe,
then we have the right hope, that is to say, the genuine relation to that which
is meant in the question. (Faith in the dead and resurrected (Christ) means
with regard to its content: the *How* of the factual! Salvation-*historical*!) (The
"*modified*" eschatological expectation: II Cor. 5:9, 10; I Cor. 6:14; II Cor. 4:
14; Phil. 1:21 f.; 2:17; 3:10 f. *On the contrary:* I Cor. 15:51; 7:29–31; 1:7,
8; 16:22; Rom. 13:11; Col. 3:4; Phil. 4:5.)

One must take care not to reinterpret the expectation of Paul object-
historically, as one of his generation that also concerns him. The *complex of
enactment* is primary; that is the decisive "When," that he is prepared for it.
Is that not a paraphrasing modernization? *Paul believed* (cf. above) (means!!!),
he believed, however, not "falsely"; here there is no true and false. The question of the "development" of his view is to be treated correspondingly.

The *How* of the coming of the Lord itself determines the How of the entrance of the living and the dead, ἐν κελεύσματι—φωνῇ—σάλπιγγι [by command—call—trumpet]. "*The* day" is thus characterized, the sign of *this* day.
Reawakening and ascension coincide with the παρουσία. κέλευσμα [com-
mand—order], orders to the rowers, call of the field marshal; in the hunt the
dogs directed to the prey! God *calls* the dead to stand up. (κέλευσμα not call
for battle against enemies!)

Eschatological symbols: trumpet (double meaning: (1) a revelation of power

---

10. Francisci Turrettini, *De Satisfactione Christi Disputationes. Accesserunt Ejusdem Disputationes duae: I. De circulo Pontifico, II. De Concordia Pauli et Jacobi in Articulo Justifi-
cationis.* Geneva, 1691.

that makes everything tremble, (2) signal for the gathering of the god of the people!) Do future time and the days of the Messiah coincide?

αἰὼν μέλλων: (either) authentic eternity; or the time of the Messiah, only better as opposed to that of the present, but still worldly [*irdisch*], not actually *of the end of time*, and yet futural!

In late-Judaism: the time of the Messiah still worldly, but worldly completion of the Old Testament "theocracy."

Eschatology III (II Thess.)
[on §§ 27 and 28]

Resonance of the ways of the Determination of the How of the When or fate in II Thess.

1. Increased *uncertainty*, still more radically urged to enactment, that is to say, thus (possibility) of doubt as to the capacity to hold out—*this* sadness and in such way; always concerned in a Christian way, but not authentic; still attitudinally stealing a glance at sadness.

2. In emphasizing the enactment, at the same time emphasis on the unimportance of worldly life; thus only from this side *unconcerned about worldly matters*, but in a worldly sense; doing nothing [?] and concern about the Parousia in a worldly way. Much bustling activity of talk and speculation.

To see from the lack of understanding how the Thessalonians should have understood and *how* Paul now in the second letter helps them along. Chapter I: the *keeping-oneself ready*, chapter II: again the two ways of comportment.

"Plerophory" in II Thess. means what? What does it aim at? At the *emphasis of the existential enactment in the letter*, which is what is crucial!

εὐδοκία—resolution, fulfilling [*vollmachen*] the enactmental tendency to the good; II Thess. 1:11: ἔργον πίστεως [work of faith]; 2:12: εὐδοκήσατες τῇ ἀδικίᾳ [took pleasure in unrighteousness] (sin!), cf. 3:5.

μὴ ταχέως σαλευθῆναι [not to be quickly shaken] 2:2: ἀπό—to be shaken up, confused, uncertain, to lose clear (knowledge) (the basic orientation of our knowledge), and with that be terrified; through nothing, which may impose itself in talk; "the day has come" ' that would be an "objective" determination. θροεῖσθαι, in particular in false terror, not to be confounded with religious fear and trembling!

That cannot be given.

The new question as to the When of the Parousia, II Thess. 2:1–12. We understand already, from I 5:1 ff., how the When is to be understood, what in it is decisive. Now *Paul* does not want to measure out the When, fix the "soon" or the "not soon" (that is to say, halt, or even take back what he said earlier);

rather you should not, in false concern, cling to people who *deceive* you, but *understand* everything *salvation-historically*, just as I *explicated* from out of faith, in fundamental comportment to *God*, or to the opponent (sin).

No one, and above all not the speculators and chatterboxes, can say: "the day has come"; "now" is grasped as "the now" when it comes, because "before" this the Antichrist must appear. (No "story" that then still happens, an "accident," rather something essential, if also negative, encountering God and Christians. It does not at all come to a mere before and after. "Before" is nothing of an *order* or attitude, but rather concern—something existentially significant.) And who recognizes him? Only the *believers*, for he precisely deceives! Thus the When is always uncertain even for the believer; for them what is crucial over and against the Antichrist is only resilience.

Take note of the introduction of the question of the *Antichrist* through the decisive (existential) παρουσία-problem, and indeed under the aspect of the pure, faithful holding firm. As a *"sign of the time"* which [gives] the meaning of "time" and of experience of time-day, the experienced understanding (believing, insofar as it is decided) also takes its meaning.

ἀποστασία [apostasy], its coming, that itself means standing-firm and it can be recognized only from out of this firm standing. And how is it *recognized*? Not as worldly *sign*.

Antichrist: adversity to God signifies as *sign* the end of time!?

ἄνομος (initially: not Jew), son of ruin, he falls to ruin. "Final fate of the god-adverse undertaking." ἀντικεῖσθαι, to oppose; ὑπεραίεσθαι, to rise (again). To sit in the temple is the decisive sign of unbelief against God; thus only the meaning of *adversity to God* is the decisive in all concepts; decisive "sign" of the "time."

Eschatology IV (II Thess.)
[on §§ 28 and 29]

2:5, 6; You remember the knowledge of faith, so *you* also know now and must know τὸ κατέχον, that which forces-down and restrains. 2:9 Antichrist, παρουσία of the lost.

So the Antichrist must come first, the time of testing, of the highest anguish and decision, the most stringent either-or. It is not so simple and comfortable as the chatterboxes think. Do not let itself be deceived by them, that is to say, be brought into the wrong fundamental posture toward the Parousia, *confusing the obstinate waiting, letting oneself fall*. Rather, it is a highest anguish, and it is not the most important thing that you take note of the objective When, rather that you *stand firm* in it, do not falter, be concerned about the sign of the time *in this way*, and do not forget the most important matters by observing what happens and the like, by speculating cognitively about it.

ψυχή

μιᾷ ψυχῇ συναθλοῦντες τῇ πίστει τοῦ εὐαγγλίου [striving side by side with one mind for the faith of the gospel], Phil. 1:27. The existential fundamental posture of the Jews according to Paul. Cf. Rom. 1; the "existential" fundamental posture of the pagans according to Paul.

AUGUSTINE AND NEO-PLATONISM

Early Freiburg Lecture, Summer Semester 1921

Motto

Curiosum genus ad cognoscendam vitam alienam,
desidiosum ad corrigendam suam.

[The human race is inquisitive about other people's lives,
but negligent to correct their own.]

Augustine, Confessiones X 3,3

INTRODUCTORY PART

Interpretations of Augustine

The task set before us is a limited one; to what extent it is limited will become clear, at least negatively, in its demarcation from other interpretations and evaluations of Augustine. These latter ones concur in their high esteem of Augustine's cultural-historical impact.

Medieval theology is based on Augustine. The medieval reception of Aristotle was able to assert itself—if at all—only in a sharp confrontation with Augustinian directions of thought. Medieval mysticism is a vivification of theological thought and practical-ecclesiastical religious ritual which, in essence, goes back to Augustinian motifs. In his decisive years of development, Luther was under the strong influence of Augustine. Within Protestantism, Augustine remained the most widely esteemed Father of the Church.

Augustine was subject to a renewal in the Catholic Church, in particular in seventeenth-century France (Descartes, Malebranche, Pascal, Jansenism, Bossuet, Fénélon). He remained especially at home there until the modern Catholic school of apologetics in France, which at the same time appropriated Bergsonian ideas (which, in turn, were determined by Plotinus). What is at work in this is not really Augustine, but an Augustinianism which is more appropriate to the doctrine of the Church, and which slightly violates the dogmatic boundaries only in ontologism. (What Scheler is doing today is merely a secondary reception of these circles of thought dressed up in phenomenology.)

Augustinianism has a twofold meaning: *philosophically,* it means a Christian Platonism turned against Aristotle; *theologically,* a certain conception of the doctrine of sins and of grace (freedom of the will and predestination).

Augustine was subject to a reconsideration through the awakening of the critical science of history in the nineteenth century—that is, through the emergence of a real history of dogma and of the Church, as well as of a history of Christian writing and of Christian philosophy. Of the research of the last decades, we might characterize briefly the three most prominent interpretations and evaluations from which the following attempt distinguishes itself, and with regard to which it essentially limits itself.

§ 1. Ernst Troeltsch's Interpretation of Augustine

E. Troeltsch presented the most recent interpretation in his work *Augustin, die christliche Antike und das Mittelalter. Im Anschluß an die Schrift* De Civitate

Dei [*Augustine, Christian Antiquity, and the Middle Ages, following* De Civitate Dei; 1915]. Troeltsch interprets Augustine from the perspective of a general, universal-historically oriented philosophy of culture. "Since the Christian movement [. . .] [left] the realm of education, property, and society [. . .] the problem of culture became the great problem of Christian thinkers,"[1]— that is, the question of how the world and the real goods of culture are to be integrated into Christian salvation. (The problem of culture: How one is to establish oneself in the world, make oneself at home in it with decency and adjusted to progress, after one has already fallen for paganism.)

Troeltsch sees the real significance of Augustine in his having become the great moral thinker of Christian antiquity with his ethics of the *summum bonum*. Augustine "is the last and greatest conjoinment of the dying ancient culture with the ethos, myth, authority and organization of the early Catholic Church."[2] (An old shelf-warmer, translated into the phraseology of universal history and philosophy of culture!) Thus, Augustine, "in his essence, could not at all be taken up on the soil of another culture."[3] He is more conclusive for antiquity and less foundational for the Middle Ages.

In this way, one of the most important demarcations of the great periods and main formations of the Christian idea has been achieved.

The course of this study runs entirely within the method of the history of religion which Troeltsch had already determined (cf. "Introduction to the Phenomenology of Religion," Winter Semester 1920/21[4]). According to this method, the research into, and presentation of, the "religious formation of ideas" is to be separated from the background of a determinate, theological dogmatism; and these ideas have to be viewed in their fusion with "the respective general situation of culture."[5] The method of the history of religion must be one of the history of culture, which also includes the method of social history. Troeltsch does not mean to say "that the great religious movements themselves derive immediately from the general situation of culture."[6] (But belong to it? This misunderstanding would be even worse, because the "derivation" could really have a meaning in the end! But assertion?!) "The opposite is the case. But its possibility of assertion is founded upon it, and its institutional fixation as a religion of the masses is conditioned by its integration into a given system of culture."[7] (Thus, Troeltsch is concerned with this

---

1. Ernst Troeltsch, *Augustin, die christliche Antike und das Mittelalter. Im Anschluß an die Schrift* De Civitate Dei, Munich and Berlin, 1950, p. 50.
2. Ibid., p. 7.
3. Ibid.
4. Editor's note: In this volume, pp. 14–21.
5. Ernst Troeltsch, *Augustin, die christliche Antike und das Mittelalter,* preface [*Vorbemerkung*].
6. Ibid., p. 172.
7. Ibid.

problem—that is to say, since he establishes the problem of culture as the essence of a universal-historical study of history, the study becomes, to a considerable extent, "encompassing," but equally blurred and merely the material of an educational orientation. This is so, particularly, if one takes into account what such orientation is supposed to accomplish: a general philosophy of religion and of culture. Everything remains suspended in mid-air, as long as this background has not really been determined or has not seriously been problematized. Cf. "Introduction to the Phenomenology of Religion."[8])[9]

Instead of a theological dogmatism, a general philosophy of religion and of culture is supposed to form the background of this manner of consideration. One can easily see that the determination of the "essence" of Augustine depends entirely on the meaning and legitimacy of this background.

§ 2. Adolf von Harnack's Interpretation of Augustine

Harnack understands Augustine and his significance differently. Harnack's presentation is based on a much greater familiarity with Augustine's writing than is found in the case of Troeltsch and his—in this respect—*too* universal presentation. Harnack's presentation has to be understood on the basis of the task of a history of dogma, as he formulated it.

Within the problematic of the history of dogma thus conceived, what is peculiar to Augustine does not, according to Harnack, appear as the formation of a new dogmatic system, but as the re-vivification of the old one on the basis of personal experience and piety, and, in closest connection with this piety, the integration of the new fundamental thoughts of the doctrine of sin and grace. This results in a double task for the study of the history of dogma: on the one hand, the presentation of his piety, and on the other, his effect as a teacher of the Church.

In his general evaluation, Harnack emphasizes the first aspect and characterizes Augustine's peculiarity as the "reformer of Christian piety."[10] Augustine rediscovered religiosity in religion. "He led the religion from the congregational and ritual form into the hearts as a gift and a task."[11]

What Augustine formed as dogmatism and the doctrine of faith connected with the old Catholic symbol. "In this way, the peculiar outline of this doctrine emerged, one which continued to have an impact in the West in the Middle Ages, and which even forms the basis of the doctrine of reformation—a com-

---

8. Editor's note: In this volume, pp. 19–21.
9. Editor's note: The text in parentheses has been added from the Troeltsch excerpts.
10. Adolf von Harnack, *Lehrbuch der Dogmengeschichte, vol. II 3: Die Entwicklung des kirchlichen Dogmas II/III* (Tübingen, 1910, 4th ed.), p. 59.
11. Adolf von Harnack, *Dogmengeschichte,* Tübingen, 1914, 5th ed., p. 284.

bination of old Catholic theology and the old Catholic schema [Christology] with the new fundamental thought of the doctrine of grace, pressed into the framework of the symbol."[12] In this, with regard to the work on the formation of the doctrine, Augustine distinguished himself by having been the theologian within the old Church who most ardently strove for the unity of a system of the doctrine of faith.

§ 3. Wilhelm Dilthey's Interpretation of Augustine

A third interpretation was presented by Dilthey in his "Einleitung in die Geisteswissenschaften I" ["Introduction to the Human Sciences I"; 1883] in the context of a historical pursuit of the formation of historical consciousness and an epistemological basis for the human sciences.

[Oskar Becker's notes]: He traces knowledge back to descriptive psychology, to "experience" (in the sense of self-observation, internal perception).—Now, what is the significance of Christianity, and of Augustine in particular, for the foundation of the human sciences?—A change in the life of the soul goes along with Christianity. The life of the soul turns back to itself. A new vivacity comes to humanity through the experience of the great model of the personality of Jesus.—What is the significance of this alteration for the purposive complex of science? With Christianity, the limit of ancient science, which merely concerned itself with the representation of the outer world, has been overcome: the life of the soul becomes a scientific problem. By virtue of God's revelation in historical reality (salvation history), he is torn out of the theoretical transcendence in Plato and enters into the complex of experience. The origin of historical consciousness lies here.—Dilthey pursues this connection further; he shows how Christianity becomes a doctrine and a philosophy under the influence of ancient science.—What is Augustine's significance in this process? In the face of ancient skepticism, Augustine ascertained the absolute reality of internal experience (in the form of a precursor to the Cartesian "cogito, ergo sum"). But the turn to metaphysics follows immediately: The *veritates aeternae* [eternal truths] are the ideas in the absolute consciousness of God. Knowledge is an aspect of the essence of substance. The human soul is changeable; it requires an unchangeable basis. This is the internal experience of God's existence (Augustine, *De trinitate*).—Dilthey says that what Augustine wished to accomplish was accomplished first by Kant and by Schleiermacher. Thus, Dilthey entirely misunderstands the inner problem of Augustine.

---

12. Adolf von Harnack, *Lehrbuch der Dogmengeschichte,* p. 95.

§ 4. The Problem of Historical Objectivity

The question as to which of the three interpretations is the objectively correct one—the interpretation of the *history of culture,* of the *history of dogma,* or of the *history of science*—is badly formulated. The attempt to create agreement among the interpretations, or to refute one or the other by bringing contradictory material to bear, would represent a complete misperception of the meaning of historical objectivity. The distinction between "true" and "false" in the usual, mostly uncritically accepted sense must not simply be transferred to history. However, an argumentation on the basis of a skepticism resulting from this would be equally erroneous. For the meaning of skepticism in its usual conception is valid only in opposition to the aforementioned concept of truth; with this concept, skepticism belongs to the same level of enactment [*Vollzugsstufe*] of a theoretical determination and securing, and to the norms immanent to their meaning. (Skepticism only states that it[13] does *not* attain *its* goal which—according to its opinion, too—it "really" ought to attain.) Just as that concept of truth is inapplicable, so too is an argument on the basis of skepticism. In other words, the bringing-together of the historical and the relative is absurd. This remark is merely to indicate that questions and decisions about historical objectivity lie within an attitudinal direction [*Einstellungsrichtung*] very much their own.

If one wished to draw the quietist conclusion, seeing all interpretations as equally justified, this opinion would be of the same origin as the skeptical one. (The solution comforts and contents itself with the *bringing together,* the "replacement" of what ought to be! "*Idea*" is customary today! What is comical about philosophy [is] that, on top of everything else, it supplies the sanctioning theory to all of this.)

Thus, if historical experience and knowledge are not to remain deliverable over to traditional standards of knowledge, then we have to seek a decision positively, in the sense of historical experiencing and determining, a decision which itself can only be a historical one.

The yielding of such a decision, along with its genuine appropriation, dominates the following considerations, which, however, are meant to be merely preliminary work. In their concrete execution, they might be the most likely considerations to open up an understanding of the sense of enactment of the historical experience effective therein, and of the peculiarities of the problems that arise. A brief discussion of the three interpretations of Augustine characterized above, however, may immediately remove us, negatively speaking, from those perspectives not in question here. (We will consider: 1. The sense

---

13. Editor's note: The manuscripts of notes agree: "it" = "objective, historical knowledge."

of access [*Zugangssinn*]. 2. The motivational basis for the starting point and the enactment of access [*Zugangsvollzug*]. Important [is] first of all the distinction itself; an assistance to the understanding, no discussion on our own.)

§ 5. *A Discussion of the Three Interpretations of Augustine according to*
Their Sense of Access

The *sense* of access is the same in the three interpretations, however different the *directions* of access to their object may be, insofar as it is in each case a different content, a different, holistic determination of the "whatness" [*inhaltliches Wasbestimmtheitsganzes*] of the "result"—ethics, religiosity, epistemological foundation—which is dominant. The object (Augustine) is viewed [*gesehen*] from different per-spectives [*Hin-sicht*] (it is viewed [*hin-gesehen*] with regard to different "sides" of it); but it is viewed as an object, in an objective complex of a determinate order. The framework of this order differs according to its breadth, whether it is thought as a developmental complex or not.

Troeltsch provides the broadest, universal-historical framework. In the succession of periods of the Christian formation of ideas, and thus at the same time of the development of European culture, Augustine is subjected to a position and a fixation of meaning—what is here most essential about him— as the concluding moralist of the culture of Christian antiquity, and he is determined as *essential* on the basis of this cultural-philosophical framework. What is at issue is less the formation itself of Christian ideas or the person, but, in a philosophy of culture, the cultural-social (objective) process of effective influence and of prevalence [*Auswirkungs- und Durchsetzungsprozeß*]. Corresponding to the so-called "comprehensive" framework and the so-called "depth of thought" of all cultural-philosophical orientation, such a presentation always moves along the thinnest margins of thoughts and catchwords. Given the lack of a living familiarity with historical life, and the compulsion to universality, such a presentation is almost necessarily merely a thin reworking of secondary literature.

In Harnack, too, the perspective on the object is in a prefixed complex of order: the emergence of the dogma of the old Church and its development. Augustine as a "re"-former, viewed in regard to what lies ahead and fixed as the source of effects on that which follows.

The same holds for Dilthey. The framework here is the development of the human sciences in European cultures.

Insofar as, in these historical interpretations, the dominant perspectival sense [*Sinn der Hinsicht*] is that of viewing [*Hinsehen*] the object as placed in a historical complex of order objectively posited, we designate this perspective the *object-historical attitude*. What is presented has the sense of the object [*Gegenstandssinn*] of the objectively drawn image, and the conditions of access focus on the control of the possible material that will come into question. The determination of the object which has been made primarily in this way first of all underlies all further evaluations and claims.

§ 6. A Discussion of the Interpretations of Augustine according to Their Motivational Basis for the Starting Point and the Enactment of Access

a) The Motivational Centers of the Three Interpretations

So far, only the sense of access of the three studies has been characterized. The attitude tends toward the object-historical characteristics of order. This does not exhaust the discussion. (The objective framework of order is essentially co-founded in the positing of the chronological sequence of historical time. "Time" functions in objective history: (1) as a methodologically regional means of determining material. As such, it is enacted in the attitude in the manner of such regional means; according to its origin; however, it is already a *specific* kind of "orientation"; (2) as itself an objective material object, a determinate time: an *age*. The possessive relation to time is the relation of the objective distance of contemporary time from earlier time,[14] of the objective and qualitative structural difference of the contemporary age from an earlier one.[15])

The sense of access as the object-historical perspective is, to be sure, the same, but the motivational basis for the starting point and the enactment of the access is different still. With Troeltsch, this basis is the effort toward a specifically characterized philosophy of culture—more precisely, the "conviction" to assist the resurrection of contemporary mental life, and religious life in particular, through a system of cultural values which is universal-historically oriented. With Harnack, the effort is directed toward the theological understanding of faith, the "conviction" that a critical historiography of dogma shows how an ecclesiastical theology which originally does not agree with Protestant Christian theology came about.[16] And Dilthey's effort strives for the foundation or the structure of the historical human sciences—in the end, the "conviction" that in the mental-historical penetration of what is past

---

14. and these under one another.

15. is had in the re-moving of . . . , and only in passing through this removing is it re-possessed!

16. "Pure knowledge of the history of knowledge" must help us "to accelerate the process" of "disentangling" ourselves from alien forms which it has to assume. (Adolf von Harnack, *Lehrbuch der Dogmengeschichte,* vol. I, 4th ed., 1909, p. 24.)

(what is objective), a concrete mental task of life in the present is given.[17] How these "convictions" are to be understood and to be judged as motivational centers and in their relations of historical enactment [*vollzugsgeschichtliche Beziehungen*]—what they themselves really "are"—cannot be determined here. (Insofar as the claims of the three aforementioned conceptions reach beyond the material interest and problem-solving of a singular discipline— and this is the case here—they subject themselves to philosophical or theological criticism. This criticism must judge their motivational basis with regard to its originality, and then it has to pursue the question as to what extent and in what sense an "objective" study is philosophically meaningful.)

b) Demarcation from Object-Historical Studies

At this point, we only say the following with the intent of negative demarcation: 1. None of the constellations of motives mentioned above is relevant to our investigation. 2. Insofar as such a constellation is a living one, its meaning prohibits us from viewing the particularly emphasized, real philosophical-phenomenologically founded goal in an objective-historical study. With a different set of motives, a different sense of historical experience is given. How this set of motives is (only?!) connected to the object-historical set of motives—and what it means at all—is difficult to determine, and even more difficult to convey, given the contemporary state of philosophical means of explication and customs. It may suffice that it attempts the enactment in a concrete manner. Above all, one has to guard against hasty constructs, and should not think that the "opposite" of object-historical study is "subjective," "non-scientific," and the like, or rather is founded on a "subjective" perspective and a subjective purpose. This supposition achieves nothing but a stunted and inferior form of historical study—which, in itself, is entirely legitimate—for exactly in this, the meaning of the relationship between history and science remains undiscussed.

In its demarcation from the object-historical attitude, this means for our study that, although we speak of the object in apparently the same manner, regarding it in this direction of understanding fails to follow its sense.

The intention here is not directed toward a comprehensive image of the "life and work" of Augustine; nor are these works understood as the "expression of the personality" in the sense of an imagistic presentation. When we will speak of development and the like, this is done without the purpose of providing an image.

This negative demarcation can be grasped still more specifically. The title of this investigation reads "Augustine and Neo-Platonism." Speaking object-

---

17. against the construction, against naturalistic and one-sided natural-scientific orientation.

historically, this is the question of the extent and manner of influence of Neo-Platonic philosophy upon Augustine's philosophical-theological dogmatic work. In more recent research into Augustine, this question is discussed constantly. Harnack, too—under the theological influence of Ritschl[18]—precisely focuses on the process of the Hellenization of Christianity in tracing the emergence of Church dogmas and their development. Likewise, Dilthey—under the unmistakable influence of Schleiermacher and Ritschl—has spoken of the penetration of Greek metaphysics and cosmology into inner experience. But Dilthey has not given us really concrete evidence, nor are the existing proofs more than statements of a literary-historical kind, findings which report the adoption of concepts and terms. (A juxtaposition of philosophy and dogma-historical schemata in which Neo-Platonism appears as material and means of education.) But even if this problem of the object-historical context had been grasped more sharply, it would not befit the problem which guides the following study and which is to be worked out in it.

The study bears this title because we take as our orienting starting point the aforementioned question of the object-historical context, and because we will guide ourselves through this question in order to throw into relief certain crucial phenomena which determined themselves decisively in the historical situation of enactment of that time, and which still "carry" us in this determination. That does not mean, however, that the question of the relation between Neo-Platonism and Augustine represents a special case of the general problem of the relation between Greek antiquity [*Griechentum*] and Christianity, as if "the general problem" could be illustrated and decided on the basis of the concrete situation of the material—to say nothing of the fact that such formal-logical shattering of the historical [*Geschichtlichen*] in general into extra-temporal problems and determinate, accidental realizations goes against the meaning of the historical [*Historischen*], divisions which cannot be removed by Hegelian manipulation once one has made them, or if one retains as a starting point the idea of a Hegelian, or any other specially formed, system. The historical context in question here is the most inappropriate ground for the problem "Greek antiquity and Christianity," once this problem has been admitted. Firstly, because the Christianity into which Augustine grows is already entirely permeated by what is Greek, and secondly, because what is Greek in Neo-Platonism has already been subjected to a "Hellenization" and orientalization, if not also, as seems very likely to me, to a Christianization.

We want to gain access to sense-complexes which are precisely covered up by such formulations of the problem as Dilthey's. In the end, we are not dealing with Greek metaphysics and cosmology, nor with "experience" as the

18. and that of Luther!

psychological taking-cognizance-of, nor, above all, with a mere penetration of the latter by the former. (We are also not dealing with the foundation of the sciences in inner experience.) The fact that, for Dilthey, the question takes a very different direction results from his conviction that the problem Augustine did not solve has, at least in principle, been decided by Kant and Schleiermacher.

In the objective form of Greek metaphysics and cosmology lies the problem of the meaning of object-theoretical, material science; and the question of the inner experience and the essence of the factical connection harbors a much more radical phenomenon—merely the defining title here: "factical life"; and, above all, the relationship between the one and the other is different from a penetration of one into the other or, to put it positively, the epistemological foundation (constitution) of the former [science] in and from the latter [inner experience]. (Only from the outside can one see a "problem-lying-in-the-objective-historical-form"; it does not exist in historical enactment. But the task and difficulty of enactment consists precisely in twisting the problem out of this manner of posing the question—immanent perception, adequate description.)

c) Demarcation from Historical-Typological Studies

But precisely from this, one would like to conclude that we are dealing with a general problem, and that "Neo-Platonism and Augustine" constitutes only a *typical* form of it. This is not the case. And if we understood the historical in this sense, the real meaning of the study would be lost. (The concept of "type" and the complex of experience and conception which carry it, turn back into the object-historical manner of posing the question.)

Neo-Platonism and Augustine will not become an arbitrary case, but in the study their historicity [*Historizität*] is precisely to be raised into its own, as something in whose peculiar dimension of effect [*Wirkungsdimension*] we are standing today. History hits us, and we are history itself; and precisely in our not seeing this today, when we think we have it and control it in a heretofore unattained objective study of history, precisely in thinking this and in continuing to think and construct on this opinion culture and philosophies and systems, history gives us, every hour, the heaviest blow. Speaking of "standing in the dimension of effect" has nothing to do with the platitude that one is always dependent on tradition. On the contrary, precisely this view tempts us to seek to make "new culture" and a new age in a false manner, precisely in the manner of epigones.

This is only to indicate the direction, in itself a negative manner. It is meaningless to give general speeches about this if the factical situation [*fak-*

tische Stand] is not already somehow compelling, or if it is not seen in the genuine direction of appropriation.

This manner of posing the problem leads us, in the treatment of Augustine, to draw on the theological, just as much as on the philosophical, very concretely and determinately, and not, for instance, to extract a philosophy which we then use as a basis. The boundaries between the theological and the philosophical are not to be blurred (no philosophical blurring of theology, no "intensification" of philosophy pretending to be religious). Rather, precisely going back behind both exemplary formations of factical life ought to (1) indicate in principle how and what lies "behind" both, and (2) how a genuine problematic results from this; all this not extra-temporally and for the construction of an approaching or not approaching culture, but itself *in historical enactment.*

MAIN PART

Phenomenological Interpretation
of *Confessions;* Book X

§ 7. *Preparations for the Interpretation*

a) Augustine's Retractions of the *Confessions*

Toward the end of his life, around 426 or 427 (he died in 430), Augustine wrote *Retractionum libri duo.* "*Retractationes*"—that is, a taking-up again of his *Opuscula* (*libri, epistolae, tractatus*), a re-examination *judiciaria severitate* ["with judicious severity"][1] in which he notes, corrects, and improves what, to him, now seems problematic. In the preface (*prologus*), where he thus determines the task of the *Retractationes,* he also gives an account of the motives which provoked this reassessment.

> Illud etiam quod scriptum est, *Ex multiloquio non effugies peccatum* (Prov. X, 19) [. . .] sed istam sententiam Scripturae sanctae propterea timeo, quia de tam multis disputationibus meis sine dubio multa colligi possunt, quae si non falsa, at certe videantur, sive etiam convincantur non necessaria. [It is also written there: "Much talking does not avoid sin" (Prov. 10:19) . . . But I fear this sentence of the Holy Scripture, for with so many writings of mine, one can without a doubt gather many passages which, if not false, may certainly be seen as, or convince one of being not necessary.][2]

(The preface is to be explicated from an existential perspective.)

On the *Confessions,* Augustine writes:

> Confessionum mearum libri tredecim, et de malis et de bonis meis [in my good and my bad *being, life, having-been*][3] Deum laudant iustum et bonum, atque in eum excitant humanum intellectum et affectum; interim quod ad me attinet, hoc in me egerunt cum scriberentur, et agunt cum leguntur. Quid de illis alii sentiant, ipsi viderint; multis tamen fratribus eos multum placuisse et placere scio. A primo usque ad decimum de me scripti sunt: in tribus caeteris, de Scripturis sanctis, ab eo quod

---

1. *Retractationes,* Prol. 1, in *Patrologiae Cursus Completus,* Series Latina, accurante J.-P. Migne (Paris: 1861/1862), vol. 32, p. 583. Henceforth, the *Patrologiae Cursus Completus* will be cited as PL followed by volume and page number.

2. *Retractationes,* Prol. 2; PL 32, p. 583 f.

3. Editor's footnote: The square brackets within the citations from Augustine reproduce Heidegger's attempts at a translation or his explanations.

scriptum est, *In principio fecit Deus coelum et terram,* usque ad sabbati requiem (Gen. I, 1, II, 2).

[The thirteen books of my *Confessions* praise God as just and good for my bad and my good actions (in my good and my bad *being, life, having-been*), and they excite the human intellect and affect. As for me, they had this effect on me while I wrote them, and still have this effect when I read them. What others think about this, is their concern. I know, however, that they greatly pleased, and still please, a great many Brothers. The first ten books deal with me; the other three books deal with the Holy Scripture according to what is written there: "In the beginning, God made heaven and earth" until the rest on Sabbath (Gen. 1:1; 2:2).][4]

b) The Grouping of the Chapters

To begin with, a registering overview of the content of Book X should be made, so that we have at our disposal the knowledge of what is written in the book. (It is divided into forty-three small chapters; the serial order breaks down later and reunifies itself in a very different "How"—cf. the (objectively) long excursus on *memoria* has a fundamental function!) While the meaning of such a taking-cognizance-of and its function in factical life seems obvious, it is so far from obvious that we cannot say anything about it at the outset, but will have to do so in later contexts. Later "considerations" (formal!) will differ from these in ways not exhausted by the later ones' being "more thorough," "more detailed," "more complete," "more secure," and "better"; but rather the *direction, means,* and *enactment* of their grasping will finally change, and will change abruptly. (The exposition [*Referat*] is not meant to supplant or improve upon the original, but to surrender it to a genuine explication, to articulate it in a special way. This requires a detour through an ordering putting-away, so that a thing is more easily accessible to us at the outset. A pure exposition, as description, does not exist. That could be, at most, a bad *interpretation* which is unclear about itself, which takes itself to be absolute. "Exposition" is still the primarily, "objectively" oriented point of departure for the actually intended explication, one which also articulates itself in a falling manner [*abfallend*]. Only this gives it its meaning.)

As a starting point, we have an orientation about "what at all is actually stated there," "what it is all about." In this respect, Book X can be easily demarcated from the other books, as Augustine here no longer relates his past, but rather tells what he is now: "[I]n ipso tempore confessionum mearum," quod sim [what I am "in the very time of the making of my confessions"].[5]

---

4. *Retractationes* II 6, 1; PL 32, p. 632.

From a linear and objective viewpoint, the book thus gives a "supplement" and a "completion"—although we have to observe that, objectively speaking, there is a "gap" between the years of 388 and 400. (No "gap" if what is at stake is not at all, or certainly not primarily, biographical and objective representation.)

For the "overview" we may utilize the division into chapters, a division which is not unimportant for the following articulation. The distribution and combination into groups of the single chapters will, at first, appear arbitrary: (1–4), (5), (6), (7), (8–19), (20–23), (24–27), (28–29), (30–39), (40–42), (43).

§ 8. The Introduction to Book X
Chapters 1–7

a) The Motif of *confiteri* [to confess] before God and the People

(1–4) Beginning with a call to God, Augustine wants to become clear about what it might mean to confess before God, from whom, as the all-knowing, nothing can be concealed, and who thus cannot really be informed of anything which he does not already know. What does it mean *to confess in the face of God,* and what does it mean *to confess to one's fellow human beings?* And what is that good for? In regard to the confessions about his past, the profit is clear. First of all, by showing that grace assists even the weakest one, it shakes up the weak without leaving them in despair. And the good and the strong ones will rejoice, not that evil and sin occurred, but that what *was* is now *no* longer. But why give a report about the present condition? To justify the publication, Augustine writes:

> An congratulari mihi cupiunt cum audierint quantum ad te accedam munere tuo, et orare pro me cum audierint quantum retarder pondere meo? Indicabo me talibus. [Do they desire to congratulate with me when they hear how near, by your gift, I am now come to you, and to pray for me, when they hear how I am held back by my own weight? To such I will reveal myself.][6]

b) Knowledge of Oneself

(5) So Augustine wants to dare confess himself. And he will only confess what he "knows" about himself. Augustine admits not knowing everything

5. *Confessiones* X, 3, 4; PL 32, p. 781.
6. *Confessiones* X, 4, 5; PL 32, p. 781.

about himself. He wants to confess that too. (*Quaestio mihi factus sum.* [I have become a question to myself.] "To comprehend is the range of man's relation to the human, but to believe is man's relation to the divine."[7] *Terra difficultatis.* [Difficult territory.] Observe the different relational sense [*Bezugssinn*]! "Tamen est aliquid hominis quod nec ipse scit spiritus hominis [. . .] quibus tentationibus resistere valeam, quibusve non valeam." [Yet there is something in the human being which is unknown even to the spirit of man [. . .] I do not know which temptations I can resist and which I cannot.].)[8]

Yet one thing is certain for him: that he loves God. "Quid autem amo, cum te amo?" [But what do I love, when I love you?][9] Augustine attempts to find an answer to this question by investigating what there is which is worthy of love, and by asking whether there is something among them which God himself is, or what gives a "fulfilling intuition" if he lives in the love of God, what suffices for, or saturates, that which, in the love of God, he intends. ("Cum te amo" already indicates an existential stage here—the stage which has experienced mercy and, in this mercy, has been pulled out of deafness, the stage which can "hear" and see, that is, the stage in which loving, in such loving, is opened up for something definite[10]; and only from here on, in the "*cum,*" do *coelum et terra* [heaven and earth] announce God's praise—not, however, when my attitude is that of natural-scientific research.)

c) The Objecthood of God

(6) I do not love physical shape, gracefulness, brightness of light and the pleasantness of sound, nor the fragrance of blossoms and ointments, nor earthly limbs in embrace; and yet I love something like this when I love *Deum meum* [my God]: "lucem, vocem, odorem, cibum, amplexum interioris hominis mei" [light, voice, fragrance, food, and the embrace of my inner man].[11] But what now is this? He queries the earth, nature, the seas, and the abysses and whatever animals live in them, and the whole cosmos, the sun, the moon, the stars. And they respond: We are not what you are looking for. But we may reveal something of this to you, the "questioner": *Ipse fecit nos.* [He made us.] (Ps. 99:3). "Interrogatio mea, intentio mea; et responsio eorum, species eorum" [My questioning with them was my attention to them; and their answer was their beauty].[12]

---

7. Søren Kierkegaard, *Sickness unto Death,* trans. Howard Hong and Edna H. Hong, Princeton, N.J.: Princeton University Press, 1980, p. 95.

8. *Confessiones* X, 5, 7; PL 32, p. 782.

9. *Confessiones* X, 6, 8; PL 32, p. 782.

10. God—above all world [?] powerful [*Welt[?]mächtig*].

11. *Confessiones* X, 6, 8; PL 32, p. 783.

12. *Confessiones* X, 6, 9; PL 32, p. 783.

And he turns to himself and asks what a human being is. An outside and an inside. "Corpus et anima *in me* mihi praesto sunt" [*In me* I see a body and a soul].[13] (This is not simply an objective characterization, a "synthesis.")

What should he query? The corporeal world has been gone through already, so "melius quod interius" [what is inward is better].[14] For the messengers—that is to say, the senses—report to this interior, and the *homo interior* [inner man] decides about the message. The *homo interior* really poses the questions, and to him the response *ipse fecit nos* is given. Yet this is accessible to all those who are of a sound mind. Why does nature not speak to all beings in this manner—for example, to animals? They cannot ask, "animalia [. . .] interrogare nequeunt" [animals cannot question it].[15] Questioning is already a judging and a standing-over; the subjected, "*subditi,*" cannot do this. They only answer to the "judging" questioner—that is, only to him who can internally decide, by way of comparison. To him "truth" speaks and decides: Your God is not heaven, not earth, is no corporeal mass at all; here, the "part" is less than the whole.[16] However, alongside the exterior, the interior is experienced[17] in the human being as permeating, moving, and giving life to the body: *anima, melior es, vitam praebes* [the soul, the better part, gives life]. "Deus autem tuus etiam tibi vitae vita est" [But your God is to you the life of your life].[18,19] (This does not have to be understood, as Dilthey would have it, in an objectifying, Greek-metaphysical manner. Cf. *lumen, vox interioris hominis* [light, the voice of the inner human being]! And the concept *vita* [life]!—But in any case, an unclarified entanglement of motifs and explicating tendencies remains here.)

d) The Essence of the Soul

(7) Thus God is something which surpasses the soul, and indeed, the soul in particular ("sur-passing": new meaning! *Quis est ille super caput animae meae?* [Who is he who is above the top of my soul?] Not only the idea of objective having-been-created!) And thus it is necessary to go through the soul itself. Augustine finds the "power" by which the soul is attached to the body and with which it moves its mass. "Non ea vi reperio Deum meum: nam

13. Ibid. (Heidegger's emphasis).
14. Ibid.
15. *Confessiones* X, 6, 10; PL 32, p. 783.
16. So the considering and seeing—experiencing—peculiar! (Always asking "How"! Under the aspect of a "How.")
17. And the soul itself moves the *moles* [mass].
18. *Confessiones* X, 6, 10; PL 32, p. 783.
19. In the *transire* [passing] and the *ascendere ad Deum* [rising up to God], *Deus* is: *is qui fecit me* [He who has made me]. (Cf. X 8, 12.)

reperiret et equus, et mulus, quibus non est intellectus (Ps. XXXI, 9); quia est eadem vis qua vivunt etiam eorum corpora" [It is not by that power that I find my God: for then the horse and the mule, which have no intellect, could find him (Ps. 31:9); since it is the same power by which their bodies live also].[20] Apart from the life-giving power, Augustine finds the power which makes possible sensuous perceptions and which assigns to every "organ" its peculiar, unique achievement (*officium*), the "organizing" power in a restricted sense: "jubens oculo ut non audiat, et auri ut non videat; [. . .] quae diversa per eos ago unus ego animus. Transibo et istam vim meam: nam et hanc habet equus, et mulus; sentiunt enim etiam ipsi per corpus" [commanding the eye not to hear, the ear not to see; (. . .) I who act through these diverse (senses) am one soul. I will rise beyond this power of mine: for even the horse and the mule have this, they also perceive through their bodies].[21] (Here we already have the "displacement" of the question—cf. 10:20—under pressure from the phenomena: the question is no longer whether this or that *is* God, but whether I can find God "therein" = "thereby" = "living therein."[22,23] This happens by comparison with other living beings—objectively—which are in *possession* of the same power. Of them it is then claimed (cf. the word of Scripture at Ps. 31:9)[24] that they have no intellect by which, apparently, God is to be found somehow, foreconceptually [*nach Vorgriff*]. Cf., in the following, the back-and-forth of the considerations regarding experience as the means objectively present-at-hand, and as interpretation regarding enactment! The wavering itself is an expression of what? The starting point for the existential break-through of the order and object-relation—psychology, or interpretation and grasping of the problem from factical life concretely historical-existentially.

§ 9. *The* memoria
Chapters 8–19

a) Astonishment at *memoria*

In the progressing-transcending ascent, Augustine arrives in the wide field of *memoria*. At first, untranslated. Our presentation does now not strictly follow

---

20. *Confessiones* X, 7, 11; PL 32, p. 784.
21. Ibid.
22. "in" and "thereby" cf. in reference to *memoria* [memory]—*gaudium* [inner joy].—
23. The motivation of *progredi* [progressing, rising above] also in *memoria*. The meaning of "going through"? The path and the way stations of the "going through" are predelineated through obsolete traditional psychological classifications. How to break through and render a different sense?
24. "Do not be like horses and mules which have no understanding, into whose mouths one has to put the bit and the bridle if they do not want to come to you."

the order of chapters but—for the purpose of overview—is deliberately kept still more schematic. With Augustine himself, the "disorder" has a certain sense of expression: the always new unlocking of "contents" and enigmas of enactment. (What phenomena Augustine brings forth, regarding the content only, and, above all, *how* he explicates the phenomena and in what basic contexts and determinations—e.g. *beata vita* [the happy life]—shatters the framework and the structure of the usual concept.)

In the *memoria* are numerous images of things, and all that we simultaneously think about them—expanding and contracting them by thinking them through, working on them: "penetrale amplum et infinitum" [a vast and infinite interior].[25] All this belongs to me and I myself do not grasp it. The mind is too narrow to contain itself. Where should that be which the mind cannot grasp of itself? "Stupor apprehendit me. Et eunt homines admirari alta montium, et ingentes fluctus maris, et latissimos lapsus fluminum, et Oceani ambitum, et gyros siderum, et relinquunt se ipsos" [I am seized by amazement. People are moved to admire mountain peaks, and vast waves of the sea, and broad waterfalls of rivers, and the vast extent of the ocean, and the circular motions of the stars, but they pass themselves by].[26] And they do not marvel at the fact that right now, when I am speaking about it, I do not see it myself, and that nonetheless, I could not speak about it if I did not see it in myself in the same enormous dimensions. (Viewed objectively: Augustine lets himself go, loses himself in intense meditation on the *memoria.*)

And when I am dwelling in *memoria,* I demand at will that, in the situation of recounting something—"cum aliquid narro memoriter" [when I recount anything from memory][27]—this or that becomes present [*gegenwärtig*] to me. Some things come quickly, some take more time, some tumble over me without order, in piles. And in the case that something definite is being presently sought, it offers itself: "Perhaps I am what is sought?" I refuse it *ab manu cordis* [from the hand of my mind] until the one I want has been awakened ("donec enubiletur quod volo" [until what I want be freed of mist][28]). Other things, by contrast, surface in order, one by one, upon demand. Thus it happens when I recount.

b) Sensuous Objects

Not only what and *how* something marvelous here occurs, however, but also the diversity of the contents which enter the *memoria,* and *how* they do so,

25. *Confessiones* X, 8, 15; PL 32, p. 785.
26. *Confessiones* X, 8, 15; PL 32, p. 785.
27. *Confessiones* X, 8, 12; PL 32, p. 784.
28. Ibid.

generates astonishment.[29] What enters is ordered according to its respective way of access, genuinely and in kinds: colors, sounds, smells, tastes, hardness and softness, warmth and cold; what comes from material bodies outside, what comes from one's own bodily interior. (If it is only there—having freed itself, as it were, from its manner of access—it does not matter. I represent [*vergegenwärtige*] only its *meaning* anyway.)

Even in darkness I can distinguish between black and white, can determine something about colors, and no sounds force themselves in the way. And I "sing" when tongue and larynx are at rest. Without presently smelling, I distinguish between the fragrance of lilies and that of violets. Not the objects themselves are present, but "images," as it were. (*Within* representation I am able to distinguish.)

c) Nonsensuous Objects

However, not only sensuous objects are at one's disposal in this way, but, for example, *propositions* and *rules, theses* and the *questions* of the sciences— for instance, when I hear: There are three kinds of questions: whether something is, what it is, and how it is constituted. To be sure, I do retain the images of the sounds of the words in which the proposition is presented, even if I know that the sounds have already passed, but what I have in this way is not "the proposition." I have not received the thing itself, the meaning I understand through the "senses," by way of hearing; and I have not seen it somewhere outside of consciousness; and I do not have an image of the meaning of the proposition in my consciousness, but the meaning itself. How did it get into my consciousness? I go through and query all entrances and passageways. Seeing responds: If it has color, it is from me. And I have not taken them from an alien consciousness while learning, but have cognized them within myself. But hitherto they have not been in *memoria*. Where then have they been?

So the *memoria* also encompasses relations of numbers and laws of spatial relations (*mathematical objects*). These are neither of color nor do they sound, nor do they possess any other sensuous determination. To be sure, I hear the words in which they are presented and in which we speak of them, but these change (Greek—Latin); mathematical objects do not at all belong to the class of linguistic expressions. When I see the most thinly drawn line, as thin as a spinning fiber, it is not the mathematical line itself. Only he who has it knowingly present to himself—without thinking sensuously-corporeally at the mo-

---

29. Not only representation [*Vergegenwärtigung*] but also presentation to myself [*Gegenwärtigung*].

ment—grasps it. I count colors and sounds, I measure heavy and light bodies. What counts and measures, and what is counted as such in its being-counted (determinateness of numbers) are not of color, etc. "Et ideo valde sunt" [And that is why they truly are][30]—and precisely because of this they possess being in high degree.

d) The *discere* [to learn] and Theoretical Acts

If we now grasp the "scientific objects" in this way, not in images, but possessing them themselves, what then actually is the *discere,* the *gaining of knowledge* (how does something become *notitia* [being-known, knowledge]?), learning? Nothing other than the taking-together, the ordering, of what "lies" in the *memoria*—in this respect of thinking—without order, dispersed and neglected. (*Discere* here really means to *search,* to lift up the true.) It is such ordering which renders what is learned, and what is determined thus in the order, in each case "jam familiari intentioni facile occurrant" [now easily occurring to the attention familiar with them][31] (meeting halfway the corresponding sense of foreconception of a field [*Gebietsvorgriffssinn*]—usefully corresponding to a predelineated order!).

What is thus "*ad manum positum*" [posited at hand], what is at one's disposal as ordered, is that which is known, that which has been learned. If it remains unattended for a longer period of time, it submerges, and yet does not fall entirely outside of consciousness, and has to be taken out again as something new, and as if for the first time: "quod in animo [ex quadam dispersione] colligitur, id est cogitur" [what is gathered together in the soul (from its dispersions), that is thought upon].[32]

I "know" even what is false, I *have it at my disposal;*[33] if there are falsities, it is still not false, *that* I know this. And I know this by having distinguished the truths from it, by way of comparison. It is one thing whether I know that I am now differentiating, and a different thing whether I remember to have differentiated. Thus, my own doing, too, is at my disposal in my representation, even the representing and the having-been-represented themselves. (The manner of knowing current enactments—self-world?—and the manner of knowing that one *has* enacted [*Vollzogenhaben*]—theoretical acts.)

Thus, in the *memoria* I can have not only the vast field of things, materials, and objects, but myself too ("mihi praesto sum" [I am present to myself]; no. 20, 21, 22, 14), and, to be sure, not only the *discernere* [to differentiate],

---

30. *Confessiones* X, 12, 19; PL 32, p. 787.
31. *Confessiones* X, 11, 18; PL 32, p. 787.
32. Ibid.
33. This would not in itself reveal the *memoria* in its "value."

colligere [to gather], *cogitare* [to think] in the more narrow sense of *meminisse* [to remember],[34] but "affectiones quoque animi mei eadem memoria continet" [the affects of my mind are also contained in the same memory][35] (and noematically!).

e) The Affects and Their Manner of Givenness [*Gegebenheitsweisen*]

The manner in which the affections are had in the *memoria* is very different from the manner in which they are had in current experience, "cum patitur eas" [when it experiences them].[36,37] The manner corresponds to the essence of the *memoria*. When I represent to myself a joy or a sadness, I am not, or do not need to be, joyful or sad myself. I am not full of fear when I remember a fear. Yes, I can joyfully represent to myself now a sadness, and vice versa. (The representation of affects is not conditioned by the character of affects of the represented situation.) This peculiarity is not astonishing when what is remembered or represented is an affect of the body. Since the body is not the same as the soul, an affect of the body—a corporeal pain, for example—can very well be different from the psychic condition, for example the joy of having overcome the pain. But the enigma concerns the psychic conditions themselves. The *memoria* is certainly nothing outside of consciousness but is consciousness itself. How can I have sadness in a joyful mood? (I "have" sadness. And at the same time: I "have" the joy. In both cases: "I.")

The *memoria* is, as it were, the stomach: the food taken in, sweet and bitter, is still there, but does not have any taste any longer. It is ridiculous (*ridiculum*) to claim a really existing similarity, but they do have something in common.

And when I find out something about emotions and classify and define them—*cupiditas, laetitia, metus, tristitia* [avarice, joy, fear, sadness]—I take them out of consciousness itself; there they are at my disposal. (Thus, Augustine does see the having as something on its own after all!) And when I have them like this, I am not perturbed ("*perturbatur*") by their presence. (What is represented does not itself determine the situation of representation.) Who would want to be able to cognitively or theoretically determine something about it if he constantly had to live in these emotions—as if the phenomenologist of hate or fear constantly had to be fearful. And again, when I state something about the affects and describe them, not only the words are there, but the affects themselves are intended. And I can characterize them

---

34. *augere* [increasing]—*minuere* [decreasing]: enriching analytically—synthetic, simplifying, reducing the manifold.

35. *Confessiones* X, 14, 21; PL 32, p. 788.

36. Ibid.

37. Distinction important! From *gaudium* [joy] and *beata vita* [the happy life] which are not currently in possession. Existence!

only if I myself have them. (How do I "have" them?) "Et tamen non ea loqueremur, nisi in memoria nostra non tantum sonos nominum secundum imagines impressas sensibus corporis; sed etiam rerum ipsarum notiones inveniremus, quas nulla janua carnis accepimus, sed eas ipse animus per experientiam passionum suarum sentiens memoriae commendavit, aut ipsa sibi haec etiam non commendata retinuit" [And yet we would not speak about them unless, in our memory, we could find not only the sounds of the names according to their images imprinted in it by the senses of the body, but also the notions of the things themselves which we never received by any of the gateways of the body. The mind itself, perceiving them by the experience of its own passions, has committed them to memory, or the memory itself has retained them without being committed to it].[38]

f) *Ipse mihi occurro* [I meet myself]

"Ibi et ipse mihi occurro, meque recolo, quid, quando, et ubi egerim, quoque modo cum agerem affectus fuerim. [. . .] ex his [what is at my disposal] etiam futuras actiones et eventa et spes, et haec omnia rursus quasi praesentia meditor" [There also I meet myself and recall myself, what I have done, when and where I did it and how I was affected when I did it. [. . .] and on the basis of this (what is at my disposal), I meditate upon future actions and events and hopes as if they were present now].[39] (What is to come, what is expected—*quasi praesentia* [as if present].) And thereby that in which I live is not itself—in the flesh—present; and yet, it is not nothing, otherwise I could not say anything at all about it.

But what, now, really is this "not nothing"? I say "stone," "sun," "cum res ipsae non adsunt sensibus meis" [when the things themselves are not present to my senses][40] (res—imago) [thing—image]. I have their image in the representation to myself. Thus, a sick person could not distinguish between sickness and health if health were not somehow present for him; and yet, he is sick.

And if, while saying "sun," the *image* is *present,* then it is not an image of the image, but the image itself. And when I mean *memoria* itself, is it *itself* present or by way of an image? (The same with numbers.)

g) The Aporia regarding *oblivio* [forgetfulness]

And when I now speak of "forgetting," I do understand what I mean. Thus, forgetting itself must be present. When I represent *oblivio* to myself (*oblivio:*

---

38. *Confessiones* X, 14, 22; PL 32, p. 788 f.
39. *Confessiones* X, 8, 14; PL 32, p. 785.
40. *Confessiones* X, 15, 23; PL 32, p. 789.

the having-forgotten-something *and* what has been forgotten), is *praesto* [present]: "memoria qua meminerim, oblivio quam meminerim" [the memory which I have remembered, the forgetfulness which I have remembered].[41] (This is not playfulness or sophistry; but rather, the problem has been posed as clearly as possible at the level of the problematic and the material and explicative tendencies of Augustine's time.—The "praesto est" concerns, in an undifferentiated manner, the *content* which has been represented, and the *enactment* of the representation of *memoria* and *oblivio;* their existence— being actual "in"—as consciousness has not been distinguished.—Now, *oblivio* is *relational,* a fact we have not yet considered: *not* having present to oneself—something which had been present to oneself and which should be present now—as presently not having something at one's disposal, as the *absence* of *memoria.* Located in the relational sense, this being-absent *is grasped*—and, indeed, enactmentally—as non-presence in the aforementioned sense of the not-being-*praesto* [present]—but for this, the being-absent has to be itself seen. The antinomy stems from this: if *memoria* is present—representation to myself—then *oblivio* cannot be present, and vice versa. If the latter is present, then I cannot represent something to myself; in terms of content, it itself is not present.)

"Sed quid est oblivio, nisi privatio memoriae?" [But what is forgetfulness but a privation of memory?][42] Thus, when *memoria* is present—that is, when I remember *oblivio*—*oblivio* cannot be present, or when it is there, I cannot represent it to myself.

"Adest ergo ne obliviscamur, quae cum adest obliviscimur." [Present therefore it is lest we forget what, when it is present, we do forget.][43] Can one conclude from this that *oblivio* itself is not present but rather its image is,[44] since, if it were present itself, it would "cause" forgetting? Who is able to see clearly here? ("Quomodo ergo adest ut eam meminerim, quando cum adest meminisse non possum?" [How then is it present for me to remember when, if it is present, I cannot remember?][45] Thus, we have to represent to ourselves the *oblivio—meminisse.* "Memoria retinetur oblivio." [Forgetfulness is retained in the memory.][46] Forgetting is represented as such.)

But even if we admit that only the image of the representation were present, it must still itself be present for me to get the image. But how can that be, since precisely the forgetting, according to its sense, extinguishes that which

---

41. *Confessiones* X, 16, 24; PL 32, p. 789.
42. Ibid.
43. Ibid.
44. When I am living in forgetfulness, I do not represent.
45. *Confessiones* X, 16, 24; PL 32, p. 789.
46. Ibid.

was to become available as *notatum* [known]? "Et tamen [. . .] ipsam obli-vionem [the having-forgotten] meminisse me certus sum, qua id quod mem-inerimus [what we want to represent to ourselves] obruitur." [And yet . . . I am certain that I remember forgetfulness itself (the having-forgotten), by which what we remember (what we want to represent to ourselves) is con-cealed.][47]

h) What Does It Mean to Search?

This *memoria* is "tanta vitae vis" [a great force of life],[48] and I am myself *memoria.* (Do I find You "in" the *memoria?*) What should I do, what do I want? God—*vera vita* [true life]; "volens te attingere unde attingi potes, et inhaerere tibi unde inhaerere tibi potest" [desiring to reach you in the way you can be reached, and to hold on to you in the way one can hold on to you].[49,50] I must transcend the *memoria,* for animals (like the fish and the bird) have it, too; "habent enim memoriam et pecora et aves" [for even beasts and birds have memory],[51] since they find their dens and nests and whatever else they are used to. For habit is only possible through *memoria.*

"Transibo ergo et memoriam, ut attingam eum" [So I will pass beyond my memory to reach him].[52] Where should I find You? Outside of *memoria* which I am about to transcend? But then I am *immemor tui* [unmindful of You].[53] And how can I search for You if I do not somehow have You, if I do not know about You? (Thus, I cannot say at all that I do *not* have something, and so I also "have" God in some way?) What does "searching" mean?

The woman who searched for and found the lost drachma—how could she search for and find it if she did not somehow still have it present to herself? If, while searching for something, different things offer themselves, and I reject each and everything until I "have" found the "right" thing I am search-ing for, then I must "have" what I am searching for and that according to which I evaluate what I find. And even if what I search for were there, and I did not recognize it as such, it would not be *found.* (Being found ≠ objec-tively—thought—being-there [*da-sein*]. To have—having it prior to having found it!) So if something which escapes the eye is being sought, it is present to the *memoria* in searching and in being sought. (Cf. the lecture course

---

47. *Confessiones* X, 16, 25; PL 32, p. 790.
48. *Confessiones* X, 17, 26; PL 32, p. 790.
49. Ibid.
50. *Unde attingi potest*—cf. above: *unde quaerere debui* (*Deum meum*) [in what way should I have questioned (about my God)]! (s. *Confessiones* X, 6, 9; PL 32, p. 783!)
51. *Confessiones* X, 17, 26; PL 32, p. 790.
52. Ibid.
53. If "outside" of *memoria,* then I am "immemor tui."

"Phänomenologie der Anschauung des Ausdrucks" ["Phenomenology of Intuition and Expression"], summer semester 1920,[54,55] "being" = having.—Really having = not having lost it; having in relation to *possibly* losing it—in anxiety—possibility—intentionality!—being-there [*Da-sein*]—objectively—is a theoretically formed-out character which can really lack the factical appropriation, but this means that it cannot itself be used to determine the meaning of factical reality.)

But what if we search for that which has dropped out of the *memoria,* which is not in it, which has been forgotten? Where do we search in this case? Certainly in the *memoria* itself.[56] But it is not there! Or is partly there and partly forgotten—so that we still have, as it were, a remainder in our consciousness which we are trying to complement in order to remove the mutilation? (If it had dropped out altogether, a reference to it could not be of any use, either.) So, for instance, when we are concentrating on the name of a person which we encounter as somebody we know, we reject all the names which force themselves upon us, until we come across that *one* which we are accustomed to associate with that person. But even what had been forgotten surfaces *from* and *in* consciousness. So it cannot have dropped entirely from consciousness. Indeed, we look very closely at the meaning when we speak of something forgotten: "Neque enim omnimodo adhuc obliti sumus, quod vel jam oblitos nos esse meminimus. Hoc ergo nec amissum quaerere poterimus, quod omnino obliti fuerimus." [For we have not yet utterly forgotten that which we remember ourselves to have forgotten. That which we have forgotten entirely, therefore, we will never be able so much as to search for.][57] (It is still there in the consciousness of having forgotten, that is, forgetting is no radical privation of *memoria,* that is, it has its *intentional relational sense.* Understood relationally: As long as we have still lost something, we still "have" it.—What does "omnino oblivisci" [having forgotten entirely] mean? Not at all living in the enactment of the representation, not at all having at one's disposal the direction of access, to have shut oneself off against it, or having covered oneself up to the point of not seeing that it is still there in certain relational directions. But this one does not grasp!)

[Two questions:] 1. What does "searching" really mean? 2. What am I really searching for? More precisely: what, while searching, is still at my disposal? (That I have it, how I have it.) At what am I directing my effort, and what escapes me? (In anticipation [*im Vorgriff*]: God as *vita vitae* [the life of life].

---

54. Martin Heidegger, *Phänomenologie der Anschauung und des Ausdrucks. Theorie der philosophischen Begriffsbildung* Early Freiburg Lecture Summer Semester 1920. *Gesamtausgabe* vol. 59, ed. Claudius Strube. Frankfurt: Klostermann, 1993.
55. Factical life—meaning: "Being"
56. If we find something, we must have presence in the *agnoscere* [knowing].—Even–Even what has been forgotten must be in the *memoria.*
57. *Confessiones* X, 19, 28; PL 32, p. 791.

But this does not have to have the formed-out, concrete, traditional sense, but really has an existential sense of movement.) Or as whom do I experience myself, who has forgotten what and how [. . .]* ? That is, in my search of God, something in me does not only reach "expression," but makes up my facticity and my concern for it. (According to what do I recognize and grasp something as God? What gives the fulfillment of meaning: "*sat est*" [it suffices]? *Vita* [Life].) That means, in searching for this something as God, I myself assume a completely different role. I am not only the *one from* whose place the search proceeds and who moves toward some place, or the one *in* whom the search takes place; but the enactment of the search itself is something of the self. What does it mean that I "am"? (The self gains an "idea" of itself, what kind of idea I have of myself. Kierkegaard)

§ 10. Of the beata vita
Chapters 20–23

a) The How of Having *beata vita* [the happy life]

Questions up to this point: What do I love when I love You? *In qua vi animae* [in what power of the soul] do I find [You]? I have to transcend the *memoria* as well. On the other hand, what I search, what I love, must be "in" the *memoria.* I must somehow have it in order to search. What then do I seek when I seek God? "Cum enim te Deum meum quaero, vitam beatam quaero. Quaeram te ut vivat anima mea. Vivit enim corpus meum de anima mea, et vivit anima mea de te [vita vitae meae]." [For when I seek you, my God, I seek the happy life. I will seek you that my soul may live. For my body lives by my soul, and my soul lives by you, (the life of my life).][58] Tradition—not, or not entirely, destructed [*destruiert*]! Then, the question *quomodo quaero Deum* [how do I search for God] becomes the question *quomodo quaero vitam beatam* [how do I search for the happy life].[59,60] (Augustine immediately gives an answer to the question: "Quid autem amo, cum te amo?" [But what do I love when I love you?]:[61] *beata vita.* This answer does not follow from what preceded it. But the latter does motivate the question as to the How of the search. The search and, above all, the search for God, have become problematic! Thus, the question turns into a general *theory* of access, and not into a

---

*[One word is illegible here.]

58. *Confessiones* X, 20, 29; PL 32, p. 791.

59. Cf. *Confessiones* X, 20, 29; PL 32, p. 791 f.

60. *Vitam quaerere, vitam beatam quaerere* [Seeking life, seeking the happy life], not a *content;* accordingly, the *quaerere* has its own relational meaning, but in such a way that the actualization is decisive.

61. *Confessiones* X, 6, 8; PL 32, p. 782.

really strictly existential one.—*Beata vita* = *vera beata vita* [the true happy life] = *veritas* [truth] = God. How do I search for this? For this, somehow having *beata vita* according to its essence, according to its meaning. And how do I have it?)

According to what we determined about searching and finding, I "have" it only when I can say: Enough, here it is.[62] The *search* can now proceed "per recordationem [. . .] oblitumque me esse adhuc teneam" [by way of remembrance . . . remembering that I had forgotten it],[63] as if I had had it somehow but only lost it, but lost it in such a way that I still know about having lost it, thus also somehow knowing about what I lost. Or I never had it at all and I search for it "per appetitum discendi incognitam" [by way of an appetite to learn something unknown].[64] ("searching for life," "concern for life.")

"Nimirum ["in truth," "without a doubt"] habemus eam nescio quomodo" [Certainly ("in truth," "without a doubt") we have it, but in what way I do not know].[65] "To desire life"—*vita beata:* it is such a thing that "omnes volunt, et omnino qui nolit nemo est" [all desire, and which no one fails to desire].[66] But the manner of having is different. Some are only *beati* [happy] when they fully possess it (really "having" it), while others possess it already in *hoping* for it; they have it in hope. The latter is *inferiore modo,* a less valuable level of having, or of *beatus esse* [being happy], but still higher than the manner of those who "nec re nec spe beati sunt" [are neither happy in actuality nor in hope].[67] Certainly they, too, wish to be happy and they can be happy only if they intend, in some way, the *beata vita* at all. How is it there, and as what *beata vita* is had by such as these—this is what Augustine untiringly labors to find out. At this point, Augustine does not want to determine how all of us received it, or how we lost it; he only wants to determine whether it is in the *memoria.* If it is there, then the next question follows, in what manner the *beata vita* is there, in what manner it is experienced. (Does Augustine seek this radically? No, he remains at the same time within the classifying consideration of frameworks, and in a correspondingly dominant relational sense.— Greek [. . .],* "Catholic."—The manner of grounding by means of referring to widespread occurrence, and this according to guesswork and also in *attitudinal* orientation! Knowledge of the object!)

We saw above that, no matter how differently perfect the ways may be in which the *beata vita* is had, everyone *volunt* [desires it] ("widespread occur-

---

62. That is, by measuring it at the same time against that which I know in anticipation, *ubi oportet ut dicam* [but then I ought to say how].
63. *Confessiones* X, 20, 29; PL 32, p. 792.
64. Ibid.
65. Ibid.
66. Ibid.
67. Ibid.
*[One word is illegible here.]

rence," "everyone" has it), and we desire it because we love it; and we can love it only by somehow knowing about it. And however different the linguistic expressions of *beata vita* may be, everyone understands, beyond these differences, an identical meaning and admits that they desire it. This would not be possible if that for which we strive were not in the *memoria* in some way. (Understanding the word, the speech. Existential sense. *That* it is universally there, and *how* it is there.)

Is *beata vita* present to us *in the same way* as the city Carthage is, as long as somebody who once saw it in person now remembers it? Obviously not.[68] For Carthage was perceived sensuously. That does not hold for *beata vita;* it is not a material thing which has sensuous perception as its corresponding, genuine mode of access. Thus, *beata vita* is not sensuous but something non-sensuous. For example, "numbers" are of this kind, too. Is *beata vita* present in the way numbers are had? No, numbers themselves are present; we do not first strive to attain them. By contrast: "vitam [. . .] beatam habemus in notitia, ideoque amamus eam, et tamen adhuc adipisci eam volumus ut beati simus" [the happy life we have in our knowledge, and so we love it, and yet we desire to attain it so that we may be happy].[69] (What the happy life is in accordance with the established mode of access and mode of having is to be established at the same time, and by way of, the explication of the How of having. The primacy of the relational sense, or of the sense of enactment, is remarkable.—What it is: this question leads to the *How* of having it. The *situation* of enactment, authentic existence.—Appropriate the "having" such that the having becomes a "being.")

Thus, it is present in such a way that we have "knowledge" of it, but that we, precisely because of this knowledge, now really want to have it. And yet, it is the same with eloquence, for instance. We know what it is; and those who do not have it want to possess it. But here we attained *notitia* [knowledge] in such a way that we who possess it, perceived it sensuously and took delight in it. Again, knowledge was attained through the senses and from other people. Both things do not apply to the *beata vita.* Augustine opens a remarkable parentheses here: "quamquam nisi ex interiore notitia [Er. et Lov. habent, *in exteriore notitia*] non delectarentur, neque hoc esse vellent nisi delectarentur" [however, if it were not on the basis of inward knowledge (Er. et. Lov. had, *in exterior knowledge*), they could not have been delighted nor wished to be eloquent unless they were delighted].[70] Although they gain the delight only from an exterior knowledge, they would not want it unless they were delighted to some extent. (That is to say, this example only tells that and how we

---

68. The problematic of content and of relation are mixed up without distinction.
69. *Confessiones* X, 21, 30; PL 32, p. 792.
70. Ibid.—Editor's note: According to the Oscar Becker manuscript, Heidegger preferred the reading of the Leuven edition (Lov.).

experience a determinate What in which we take delight. But the being-delighted itself? Radical reference to the self, authentic facticity.—Something which cannot be taken over from others at all.)

Thus, the desire to take delight (or the desire to avoid pain) is the real motive: having delight. Do we then have the *beata vita* in the *memoria* like a delight? *Fortasse ita* [Perhaps this is the case]. For in this consideration, we have to say: I have never seen, heard, smelled, tasted, or touched my delight sensuously, "sed expertus sum in animo meo quando laetatus sum" [but I experienced it in my soul when I was joyful].[71,72] (Is *beata vita* present in wanting to take delight? In the manner of delight? Is the desire to take delight the motive for one's effort and for one's bustling activity? The manner in which *beata vita* is always somehow present: *delectatio finis cura* [delight is the end of concern].[73])

And further, delight is such that I can have it present to myself even when I am sad. That is, when *beata vita* is represented in this way, I do not need to be *beatus* but can have it as "*miser*" [miserable]; I can have it in (existential) misery: "tristis gaudium pristinum recolo" [I am sad as I recall former joy].[74,75] (What now is joy? A condition of the soul, thus *beata vita* a psychic being!? Cf. chapter 25!)

Now, when and where did I experience *beata vita* so that I can represent it to myself, and have it present to myself, only in the manner of a joy in order to love it and to strive for it? Augustine has the answer: "Nec ego tantum, aut cum paucis, sed beati prorsus omnes esse volumus. Quod nisi certa notitia nossemus, non tam certa voluntate vellemus." [Nor is it my desire alone, or of some few besides, but everyone wishes to be entirely happy. If we did not know this with certain knowledge, we would not desire it with a certain will.][76] Since it is indeed certain that all of us want it, we must have certain knowledge of it.

That this wanting is certain is demonstrated also by the most extreme case in which one person wants the opposite of what the other wants. For one and the same reason, one person wants to "serve" (*militare*), another not: "si autem ab eis quaeratur, utrum beati esse velint, fieri possit ut uterque statim se sine ulla dubitatione dicat optare; [. . .] Nam forte quoniam alius hinc, alius inde gaudet; [. . .] Quod etsi alius hinc, alius illinc assequitur, unum est tamen quo pervenire omnes nituntur ut gaudeant." [but if they were asked whether they would like to be happy, both would without all doubting say that they

---

71. *Confessiones* X, 21, 30; PL 32, p. 793.
72. To experience existence "non-sensuously," and with *my* being.
73. Cf. En. in Ps. VII 9; PL 36, p. 103.
74. *Confessiones* X, 21, 30; PL 32, p. 793.
75. Joy and the about-which of joy, that which is joyful! Explicate more precisely later on (cf. *tentatio* [temptation]).
76. *Confessiones* X, 21, 30; PL 32, p. 793.

would choose it; . . . Is it then that one person rejoices in this, and another in that? . . . Though one person obtains it in one way, and another in another way, yet there is one thing which all strive to attain, namely that they rejoice.]⁷⁷ "Atque ipsum gaudium vitam beatam vocant." [This very joy they call the happy life.]⁷⁸ Thus, no one can say that he never experienced something like this; thus, he has some knowledge of it. (Initially, the concrete factical motives are different and opposed; but it really is the same. *"Ut quisque gaudeant"* [that each rejoice] is decisive!)

And now, Augustine, before God, expels from himself the opinion that already every experienced joy is the true one, the *beata vita.* "Est enim gaudium quod [. . .] datur [. . .] eis qui te gratis [voluntarily] colunt [. . .]. Et ipsa est beata vita gaudere ad te, de te, propter te [toward you, by your side, and because of you]; ipsa est, et non est altera. Qui autem aliam putant esse, aliud sectantur gaudium, neque ipsum verum. Ab aliqua tamen imagine gaudii voluntas eorum non avertitur." [For there is a joy which . . . is granted . . . to those who worship you voluntarily. . . . And this is the happy life, to rejoice toward you, by your side, and because of you; this is the happy life, and there is no other. As for those who think there is another, they pursue another joy, not the true one. However, their will is not utterly turned away from some image of joy.]⁷⁹

Accordingly, it is not so very established that *everyone* strives for the *authentic beata vita.* Rather: "cadunt in id quod valent, eoque contenti sunt" [they fall back upon what they have the strength to do, resting content with that].⁸⁰ They fall back upon what is in their power to do, what is at their disposal in the moment, what is conveniently attainable for them of the surrounding-worldly and other significances of the world and of the self. (Formally indicated, the *beata vita* as such, and in relation to the how of its existence, is one. It really concerns the individual, *how* he appropriates it. There is *one* true one, and especially this, in turn, is for the individual. Cf. the path of the following explications.)

What, by contrast, is not at their disposal in the same way—what is not lying around, ready to be grasped, "non tantum volunt, quantum sat est ut valeant" [they do not will so much as is sufficient to give them the strength],⁸¹—they do not want as much, they do not will it to the same degree. They do not project this from out of themselves toward themselves as "possibility," in such a way that it would suffice to take possession [*bemächtigen*] of themselves in the first place. The concern for it is lacking to such an extent

77. Ibid.
78. Ibid.
79. *Confessiones* X, 22, 32; PL 32, p. 793.
80. *Confessiones* X, 23, 33; PL 32, p. 793.
81. Ibid.

that it is not really present, precisely because it becomes an object [*gegen-ständlich wird*] in its genuine manner only in such concern. (Thus it is something which is only present in an authentic complex of enactment. It has to be broken into—existentially—not in the attitudinal handling of content, but in the determinately articulated, factical historical complex of enactment.)

b) The *gaudium de veritate* [joy of truth]

For example, in a certain sense everyone wants the truth; they prefer *veritas* [truth] to *falsitas* [falsehood] (error), and this happens as easily and without inhibition as they want *beata vita*. (There is a connection to the general *velle gaudere—gaudium de veritate* [wanting to rejoice—joy of truth]. "Universality," generality—to be grasped historical-factically, on a determinate level of factical life. "Universality" is genuine, but its meaning has been contorted [*umgebogen*] through Greek philosophy—must be taken back into the existential-historical unity.)

"Beata quippe vita est gaudium de veritate." [A happy life is the joy of truth.][82] They experienced this joy where they somehow encountered truth in their lives. And where, in what manner, do they encounter the truth? Precisely where they do not want to be deceived. Although many people intend to deceive others, they do not want to be deceived themselves. In this wish not to be deceived, in this effort to escape deceit, they are guided by a sense of truth. For they would not and could not love truth, they could not rejoice in it; "nisi esset aliqua notitia ejus in memoria eorum" [unless there were some knowledge of it in their memory].[83] (In refusing and not wanting deceit, they are holding on to *veritas,* that is, the rejection itself takes place in the *delectatio veritatis* [delight of truth]. "Amant enim et ipsam, quia falli nolunt." [For they love the truth because they do not want to be deceived.][84]—*Veritas* is *vera beata vita* [true, happy life]: "*veritas.*")

c) *Veritas* in the Direction of Falling

So they are somehow rejoicing in, and making an effort toward, the truth. But why are they nonetheless not in the *beata vita,* in the genuine one, which you, God ("*veritas*"), are yourself? "Cur ergo non de illa gaudent?" [Why then do they not rejoice in this?][85] Why does the joy which corresponds to such *veritas* not live in them? "Quia fortius occupantur in aliis." [Because they are more

82. Ibid.
83. *Confessiones* X, 23, 33; PL 32, p. 794.
84. Ibid.
85. Ibid.

strongly occupied by other things.][86] The bustling activity in which they are absorbed, the cheap tricks to which they abandon themselves, rather makes them even more miserable ("potius miseros" [rather miserable]: makes them more and more lose the *beata vita*) than that what is *tenuiter* [tenuously][87] present in *memoria,* the "somehow" of truth, could make them into *beati* [happy ones]. "Adhuc enim modicum lumen est in hominibus" [For among men there is a little light],[88] there is still a modicum of "light." (*Lumen* has here a very determinate, existential sense of enactment in self-worldly, factical experience, and is not to be understood in a reifying-metaphysical way [*dinglich-metaphysisch*].)

But now, why is it that, while it seems that the effort at truth is effortless, since it is there by itself (naturally), the *real* truth is not being loved, but rather hated? "Cur autem veritas parit odium, et inimicus eis factus est homo tuus verum praedicans [. . .]?" [But why does truth instigate hatred, and your man become the enemy of those to whom he preaches what is true . . . ?][89]

In factical life, human beings somehow intimate something right, live in it and for it as something significant. Inasmuch as this "living" and experiencing is already an absorption in factical life, an abandoning oneself over to it, it is, and will become, at the same time that which fulfills the effort toward truth. "Hoc quod amant velint esse veritatem" [what they love they want to be the truth][90]—what is loved at the moment, a loving into which one grows through tradition, fashion, convenience, the anxiety of disquiet, the anxiety of suddenly standing in vacuity; precisely this becomes the "truth" itself, in and with this falling enactment. The truth and its meaning are taken even into this modification—that is, one does not only retreat from the vacuity, but even more, and primarily, from the "movement" toward it. (*Veritas*[91] in the direction of falling, but here, there is still the "genuine" remainder of securing; it does not have to harden into a "shell" [*Gehäuse*]; this is only an aspect of the content and does not belong to what is decisive. I can live in the "shell" without having one; even more, if I transform the building and tearing down of a shell into a process, I have secured the end in a shell-like way. "Shell"—a relational sense, a sense of enactment.—Jaspers cannot speak of the "whole" and of "life" and "process"—of what he intends by these, in whatever terms.)

In this situation, they do not want to let themselves be startled, because

---

86. Ibid.
87. That which resounds only slightly, hardly audible in the inner noise of bustling activity, with the overly noisy speech of that which wants to have its way. Cf. the inner speaking with *confiteri* [confessing], chapters 1–5!
88. *Confessiones* X, 23, 33; PL 32, p. 794.
89. *Confessiones* X, 23, 34; PL 32, p. 794.
90. Ibid.
91. *veritas* and *beata vita:* existential truth.

they are motivated—in a certain sense, genuinely, for them—to not want to be deceived; that is, they do not want to be, as it were, taken away from what they possess as truth. "Nolunt convinci quod falsi sint" [They do not want to be convinced that they are deceived],[92] they resist exposure of their error. An attempt toward truth—an attempt which, however, is not genuine and not radically appropriated (fall!)—keeps them in error. (How little depends on the What of the content; everything depends on the How.)

"Amant eam lucentem, oderunt eam redarguentem." [They love the truth when it enlightens them, but hate it when it reprehends them.][93] They love it,[94] when it encounters them as glitzy,[95] in order to enjoy it aesthetically, in all convenience, just as they enjoy every glamour that, in captivating, relaxes them. But they hate it when it presses them forcefully. When it concerns them themselves, and when it shakes them up and questions their own facticity and existence, then it is better to close one's eyes just in time, in order to be enthused by the choir's litanies which one has staged before oneself.[96]

Thus, human beings do wish that the "truth" reveals itself to them, that nothing is closed off to them (aesthetic), but they themselves close themselves off against it: "ab ea manifestari nolunt" [they do not want to be discovered by it].[97]

But what does a human being attain in this way? That the truth remains concealed to him, although he does not remain concealed before it. But what should have become clear here: even in this closing-himself-off against the truth, he loves the truth more than error, and thus makes an effort at the *beata vita.*

He who loves the *veritas sola* [only truth]—"per quam vera sunt omnia" [by which all things else are true][98]—*sine interpellante molestia* [without any discomfort interfering],[99] without any burden, without that which pulls him back, without an inauthentic [*unechte*], convenient, self-concealing willfulness—will probably have the authentic *beata vita.*

Beata vita is *gaudium,* more closely, *gaudium de veritate* [joy of truth], understood as existentially *related* to the *vita beata.* (By way of *veritas,* however, we have, at the same time, the invasion of Greek philosophy.)

---

92. *Confessiones* X, 23, 34; PL 32, p. 794.
93. Ibid.
94. if one can let oneself go for this
95. when it captures them and "lifts them up" [*"aufhebt"*] as and through "glamour"
96. Editor's note: manuscript of Schalk: to be enthused in one's own glamour
97. *Confessiones* X, 23, 34; PL 32, p. 794.
98. Ibid.
99. Cf. 142, below.

§ 11. The How of Questioning and Hearing
Chapters 24–27

In searching for what he loves when he loves God, he has not found anything *extra memoriam* [outside of memory]. ("Extra" in a double sense: 1. in that searching and finding in general are in the *memoria;* 2. in that *beata vita* is itself not an "extra" as an object.—But God is also not something *psychic.*)

And what he has found of him (truth, somehow), that is something *in* the *memoria* which he represents to himself in it, *ex quo didicit* [since he first learned (of You)], from that point, since he *didicit* [learned (of You)].[100] "Ubi enim inveni veritatem, ibi inveni Deum meum ipsam veritatem." [For where I found the truth, there I found my God, truth itself.][101] Thus, insofar as truth is something which I have in the *memoria,* which is accessible as such therein, I find God there, "cum reminiscor tui et delector in te" [when I recall You and take delight in You],[102] when I am mindful of You and enjoy myself toward You. (With this, God is somehow already there, if only *tenuiter* [tenuously].[103]) You, God, bestow this honor upon the *memoria* by living in it. But "in qua ejus parte maneas, hoc considero" [in what part of it, I now consider].[104] I have not found You in the representations of material things and not "ubi commendavi affectiones animi mei" [where I had committed the affections of my soul],[105] where I entrusted my experienced conditions and moods. And you were also not there where the soul has itself, "quoniam sui quoque meminit animus" [as the soul also remembers itself].[106] You Yourself are not an "affectio viventis, qualis est cum laetamur, contristamur, cupimus, metuimus, meminimus, obliviscimur, et quidquid hujusmodi est; ita nec ipse animus es, quia Dominus Deus animi tu es" [affection of a living person, such as when we rejoice or are sad, or when we desire, fear, remember, forget, or anything of that kind; nor are You the soul itself, for You are the Lord God of the soul].[107] (*Dominus Deus animi* [Lord God of the soul]: thus, nor simply a special object. Augustine renounces the regional characterization of the meaning of *Dominus.*[108])

"Et commutantur haec omnia, tu autem incommutabilis manes super omnia"

---

100. where and since then truth accessible, a relation to it—since *cura de vita beata* [concern for the happy life], thus on the way to God.

101. *Confessiones* X, 24, 35; PL 32, p. 794.

102. Ibid.

103. Modes of access: in *delectari, gaudium de veritate; reminisci tui—delectari in te* [taking delight, joy of truth; remembering you—taking delight in you].—In analogy to the interest in rhetoric: "seeking and having-God is circumscribed by—motivated in."

104. *Confessiones* X, 25, 36; PL 32, p. 794.

105. *Confessiones* X, 25, 36; PL 32, p. 795.

106. Ibid.

107. Ibid.

108. and yet *incommutabilis* [unchangeable]

[All these things are changed, but you remain unchangeable above all things].[109] You are not something like the soul, but You "habitas certe in ea" [certainly dwell in it],[110] even if, in the soul, there is no such thing as place and space, thus making it senseless to ask "where?" (As itself an experience, an experiential complex, this object cannot be God; it does not have the sense of Being of the *summum bonum* [greatest good]. Cf. *delectatio* [delight].)

But I must have experienced You somewhere, somewhere You must have gotten into *memoria:* "inveni te [. . .] in te supra me" [I found You . . . far above myself].[111]

Ubique, veritas [everywhere, truth]: in every experience, whatever is experienced, and *who*ever experiences. You are queried by many, who ask You different things, and You respond. (You are there for everyone, everyone can speak with You, can stand *before* You.)

"Liquide tu respondes, sed non liquide [clearly, unobscured, purely, genuinely] omnes audiunt [audire: "to understand," that is, mode of enactment]" [You respond clearly, but not all understand you clearly (clearly, unobscured, purely, genuinely)].[112] Or that one makes You, in cheap blasphemies, into an object of essential insights—which is even a few degrees worse than the proofs of God's existence which one criticizes haughtily—and that one plays the role of religious renewal at Your expense. Thus everything depends upon the authentic hearing, upon the *How* of the questioning posture, of the wanting-to-hear. Not only do some speculate about You in a convenient curiosity. Everyone gets counsel—*from whom* they want something—but they do not always *hear* what they really want. They take the current object of their efforts as the most important thing; that is, they want to hear something *regarding* that; they are fundamentally incapable of hearing, of *remaining open.* They are only curious to hear what "suits" them, and they are not capable of transforming what they hear into what precisely should concern [*bekümmern*] them, though it may not "suit" them. (The question *where* I find God has turned into a discussion of the conditions of experiencing God, and that comes to a head in the problem of what I am myself—such that, in the end, the same question still stands, but in a different form of enactment.) So the "questioning" and "hearing" does not suffice unless their How has been appropriated genuinely. And Augustine himself confesses: "Sero te amavi" [Late have I loved You],[113] late did I get to the level of factical life where I put myself in the position to love You. ("Amavi"—a complex of the sense of *enactment:* "Nemo quippe vivit in quacumque vita, sine tribus istis animae

---

109. Ibid.
110. Ibid.
111. *Confessiones* X, 26, 37; PL 32, p. 795.
112. Ibid.
113. *Confessiones* X, 27, 38; PL 32, p. 795.

affectionibus, credendi [grasping trustingly, somehow fixing an end] sperandi [awaiting, keeping oneself open for] amandi [loving devotion, appreciating]" [However, no one, in any walk of life, lives without his soul experiencing these three things—believing (grasping trustingly, somehow fixing an end), hoping (awaiting, keeping oneself open for), loving (loving devotion, appreciating)].[114]) "Et in ista formosa quae fecisti, deformis irruebam" [and in my deformed state, I rushed into those beautiful things which You made],[115] although I plunged headlong into the world and things as *formosa,* beautifully formed, impressive and announcing something significant, so that they captured me; and my desire to know made an effort at it—but *deformis irruebam,* I myself was not in *the* form, I did not have *the* Being, which is the genuine Being of a self. "Tetigisti me, et exarsi in pacem tuam" [You touched me, and I am burning for Your peace].[116]

§ 12. The curare *(Being Concerned) as the Basic Character of Factical Life* Chapters 28 and 29

a) The Dispersion of Life

My life is "deformis" [deformed].—Not in order to excuse himself, but indeed to push himself away from himself recklessly, and to gain himself from this severe distance, Augustine now makes it clear to himself, that "life" is no cakewalk [*Spaziergang*] and is precisely the most inopportune moment to assume an air of importance. "Oneri mihi sum" [I am a burden to myself].[117] It is such that the (constitutively existential) sense of enactment of the awaiting setting-out, the keeping-oneself-open-for, can only be "tota spes [. . .] non nisi in magna valde misericordia [Dei]" [all hope . . . is nowhere but in (God's) very great mercy].[118] (Hope from despair!) And this mercy [*Erbarmen*] precisely corresponds to the misery [*Erbärmlichkeit*] of this life: it is a *iubere—iubes continentiam* [commanding—You command continence]. (*iubere: "directio" cordis, cogitationes, delectationis—finis curae!* [commanding: the "direction" of the heart, of thoughts, of delight—end of concern!] Cf.: "Et diriges justum, scrutans corda et renes Deus" [And You direct the just, the searcher of hearts and guts is God].[119]

For "in multa defluximus" [we are scattered into the many],[120] we are dis-

---

114. *Sermones* CXCVIII 2; PL 38, p. 1024.
115. *Confessiones* X, 27, 38; PL 32, p. 795.
116. Ibid.
117. *Confessiones* X, 28, 39; PL 32, p. 795.
118. *Confessiones* X, 29, 40; PL 32, p. 796.
119. *Enarrationes in Psalmos* VII 9 (V.10); PL 36, p. 103.
120. *Confessiones* X, 29, 40; PL 32, p. 796.

solving into the manifold and are absorbed in the dispersion. You demand counter-movement against the dispersion, against the falling apart of life. "Per continentiam quippe colligimur et redigimur in unum [necessarium—Deum?]" [By continence we are gathered together and brought into the One (the necessary One—God?)].[121]

In this decisive hoping, the genuine effort at *continentia* is alive, an effort which does not reach its end. (Not "abstinence" which loses precisely the positive sense, but "containment," pulling back from *defluxio,* standing against it full of mistrust.) Those who are really *continens* "cogitet quid sibi desit, non quid adsit" [think what they desire, not what they are close to].[122] And there will always be something *quid desit* [which they desire]. For life is really nothing but a constant temptation. "Numquid non tentatio est vita humana super terram sine ullo interstitio?" [Is not human life on earth a trial without intermission?][123] It is necessary to grasp more sharply this fundamental character in which Augustine experiences factical life—the *tentatio* [trial, temptation]—in order to understand accordingly to what extent the one who lives in such saintliness, and on such a level of enactment, is necessarily a burden to himself.

"Tolerari iubes": "molestias et difficultates" [You command to endure: troubles and difficulties],[124] not just to carry the troubles (G) and difficulties (V) with us, but to tackle them as such. This does not mean, however, that we should love them—that is, basically turn the difficulties into a delight,[125] give oneself over to them—but confront them *in such a way* that the *tolerare* [enduring] remains decisive. "Nemo quod tolerat [really G.] amat, etsi tolerare amat." [No one loves what he endures, even if he loves to endure.][126] The *tolerare* circumscribes a peculiar complex of enactment which is not operative in isolation, but which moves in a characteristic and fundamental direction of factical life. In this direction, the *tentatio* also finds its sense and motivation, and in it becomes clear to what extent there are [*es "gibt"*] *molestiae* and *difficultates.*

b) The Conflict of Life

The "*in multa defluere*" [scattered, dissolution into the many] is an oriented being-pulled by and in *delectatio;* the life of the world in its manifold significance—*multum* has to be understood in this way—appeals to us. (Cf.

---

121. Ibid.
122. *Sermones* CCCLIV 5, 5; PL 39, p. 1565.
123. *Confessiones* X, 28, 39; PL 32, p. 796.
124. *Confessiones* X, 28, 39; PL 32, p. 795.
125. *delectari* as taking it easy
126. *Confessiones* X 28, 39; PL 32, p. 796.

above, p. 144: *"cadunt"* and the existential counter-movement.—*Multum:* the manifold, *unum:* the authentic [*das Eigentliche*]; cf. Aristotle: οὐσία—τόδε τι.)

In the *defluxus,* factical life forms out of itself, and for itself, a very determinate direction of its possible situations, which are themselves awaited in the *defluxus: delectatio finis curae* [delight is the end of concern]. Now, this *curare* [to care, to be concerned] has a relational sense which changes in the historical-factical complex of life.[127] It is enacted as *timere* and *desiderare,* as fearing (retreating from) and desiring (taking into oneself, giving oneself over to). The *multum* is the manifold, the many significances in which I live. These significances are sometimes *prospera* (supportive, conducive, appealing; that is, carrying over and supporting in the direction of significance), at other times *adversa* (impeding, countering that for which I strive). When I now[128] experience *adversa,* this experience is not simply a registering, a taking-note-of things, but "prospera in adversis desidero" [in adversity I desire prosperity].[129] This desiring which is also present indicates how the experience of *adversa* is itself placed in its own factically concrete *horizon of awaiting.* It is enacted, in a determinate sense, historically.[130] This co-presence is not adhered onto, but co-determines, the sense of the phenomenon of the experience of *adversa* (insofar as the experience is *cura* and has *aliquid delectationis* [something delightful]. I experience the counter-movement only insofar as I myself live in a *delectatio, cura prosperorum* [delight, prosperous concern].)

And: "adversa in prosperis timeo" [in prosperity I fear adversity].[131] In taking up and appropriating what is supportive, the fearing of impediments is, in turn, present.[132] Again, factical life is in the historical. The self—even if often only in a "weak" manner—is taken into a historical experiencing.— Basic motif: the historical in *cura* [concern] itself.

If we call this peculiar commingling of the various senses of the relation of concern in the factical experience of life (or its bustling activity) a "conflict" [*Zwiespältigkeit*], then this remains an objectively characterizing concept, which is useful as long as it does not claim to render the real sense of the phenomenon.

A "first" conflicted co-presence of *timor* [fear] and *desiderium* [desire] (*cupiditas*[lust])[133] carries new conflicts within itself; and this would be the given

---

127. Phenomenological connection between *curare* as concern [*Bekümmerung*] (*vox media* [middle voice]) and *uti* [to use, enjoy, possess] as dealing-with (in concern)

128. To steal oneself away from something! To approach something stealthily!—and when "anxiety" is genuinely close by.

129. *Confessiones* X 28, 39; PL 32, p. 796.

130. In the paraphrasing report here, do not yet emphasize the "historical"; characterize objectively as "dynamic" and "conflicted nature."

131. *Confessiones* X 28, 39; PL 32, p. 796.

132. Only inasmuch as the other one is also alive at the moment (what does that mean factically-existentially?) can I live in one of these.

133. *tentatori ianuae duae* [tempting the two doors]

ground for dialectical antitheses, that is, for a playful dealing with matters which do not tolerate such treatment.

Now, these experiences of concern are not simply there, in a psychic stream, as it were, but they themselves are had in the experiencing—(this having-had is their "being").[134] They are had not as a mere theoretical taking-note and registering, but themselves as a concern:[135] as *flendum* [weeping, sorrowful] or *laetandum*[rejoicing], as *malum*[bad] or *bonum*[good]—thus in such a way that not only the co-presence of *timor* and *desiderium* carries a conflict with it, but that the sides of the conflict are themselves, in turn, experienced in a conflicted manner—the *desiderium* as *flendum* or *bonum, maeror* [lament] as *laetandum* or *malum*. And the question is precisely in what *manner of concern* these experiences of concern are to be enacted. These experiences of concern are pulled together into a determinate manner of enactment according to their own sense—the sense of *finis curae delectatio*. There is not only the insecurity, but the danger to give in to the "pull" and to fall into what is not genuine [*das Unechte*].

Thus the enactment of experience is always insecure about itself. In the complex of experience, there is no *medius locus* [middle ground] where there are not also counter-possibilities. Thus, Augustine has to say: "ex qua parte stet victoria nescio" [which side has the victory I do not know][136] (toward what direction one's own life will incline in the end).[137] In experiencing, a devilish being-torn-apart has been uncovered. "Ecce vulnera mea non abscondo,"[138] look, I do not conceal my "wounds." And following Sap. 8, 21, Augustine already considers it a valuable insight to understand that the *continentia* is, by itself, a hopelessness, and that it must be given, if it is to be "had" somehow.

However, one does not yet see clearly what the connection is between this being-torn and the phenomenon of *tentatio,* to what extent *vita est tota tentatio sine ullo interstitio* [life is all trial without intermission]. And does Augustine treat only this question in the following chapters until the end? But it is becoming more and more difficult for him. His considerations are slowing down, are becoming more severe, and Augustine requires the most lithe dialectic in order to grasp those elements of the background that he, by relentless

---

134. That is, this (seen objectively) two-leveled, really primary conflict brings the "expression" closer.—Seen retrospectively, interpretively, this complex of enactment is the starting point of an existential expression. Exi[stent]ial.—Problem.

135. The possible question here concerning the "regressus" is a mistaken one. Mistaken attitude!

136. *Confessiones* X 28, 39; PL 32, p. 795.

137. Cf. chapter 21, 30. *Quaestio mihi factus sum.* [I have become a question to myself.] This "quaestio" is not an accidental consideration in the mood of a hangover! *Vita: ego—quaestio. Oneri [moles] mihi sum.* [Life: I—question. I have become a (heavy) burden to myself.]

138. *Confessiones* X 28, 39; PL 32, p. 795.

and understanding questioning, brings to light from the darkness of the soul, in order to grasp them in such a way that they flow in the fundamental direction of his *Confessiones,* and of Book X in particular.

One views the considerations that follow too easily as mere hair-splitting reflections of a pedantic "moralizer"; or one gets lost in isolated, surprising psychological analyses. In both cases, one has lost the real direction of understanding. It is necessary to view these chapters, in particular, in connection to the real question—searching for God—or to illuminate this question from the start on the basis of these chapters. But this also poses enough difficulties, and the interpretation—even on the real level of enactment—presented as such in a communal world has the purpose only of letting us encounter the difficulties. But even here, there is an essential limitation, inasmuch as the interpretation is phenomenological rather than theological. The difference and context of this interpretation is to be determined, not with a view toward a theory of science, but "historically."

Augustine himself sees quite clearly that his considerations cannot be understood without further ado: "Ecce ubi sum: flete mecum, et pro me flete, qui aliquid boni vobiscum intus agitis unde facta procedunt. Nam qui non agitis, non vos haec movent." [See where I am: weep with me and weep for me, You who are driven by something good within Yourselves from which the deeds proceed. As for those who do not have this drive, You are not moved by this.][139] Question: *Numquid non tentatio est vita humana?* [Is not human life a trial?][140]

§ 13. The First Form of tentatio: concupiscentia carnis *[desire of the flesh]* Chapters 30–34

a) The Three Directions of the Possibility of Defluxion

The special conditions for the proper understanding of the following chapters are clear to Augustine: *Nam qui non intus agitis aliquid boni, non vos haec movent.* [As for You who are not driven by something good within Yourselves, You are not moved by this.] Insofar as you do not have *agitis* for yourself—everyone for himself, in whatever manner of enactment, concerning himself with the good—and insofar as you do not only have it in an imagined tendency and as a wish, but make an effort at it in the concrete self-assertion, you will not be moved by this, it will not concern you, you will not understand it. This

---

139. *Confessiones* X 33, 50; PL 32, p. 800.
140. Anticipating the interpretation, advance the directions of meaning of *vita* and *tentatio.* *(Molestia)* facticity.

express emphasis upon an essential condition of understanding is, without emphasis and explicit mention, already operative in the presentation of the widespread generality of the *delectari* and the striving for the *vita beata*.[141] The point is not to plant it first of all, as it were, but only to encounter it, and to emphasize and seize it authentically in an enactmental manner.

The *iubere* is *iubere continentiam et iustitiam* [commanding continence and justice]. *Duces iustum.* [You lead the just.]—The concept of *iustitia* and its genuine conception is to be left aside, the difficulties of St. Paul and Luther, and on this basis even more new problems, that is, at the same time real existential problems.—Here, we only pursue that to which *continentia* refers and what concerns it. Three directions of the *defluere*, of the possibility of defluxion and the danger. ("Danger" here not objective.) Viewed from the outside, it looks as if Augustine only gave a convenient classification of the different directions of *concupiscentia*, of "desire" [*Begierlichkeit*]. *Concupiscere:* desiring-together, a concentration as well, but one where that which concentrates is precisely the "objectively" secular into which the self is pulled. According to its sense, a classification is, by itself, not a manner of grasping the phenomena of the *concupiscentia*. And we will see that it looks like an entertaining unraveling of psychic backgrounds. It is not probable that Augustine would have ever had the "time" for such an activity during the years in question.

Augustine conducts the "division," as we will say preliminarily, following 1 John 2:15–17:

Μὴ ἀγαπᾶτε τὸν κόσμον μηδὲ τὰ ἐν τῷ κόσμῳ. ἐάν τις ἀγαπᾷ τὸν κόσμον, οὐκ ἔστιν ἡ ἀγάπη τοῦ πατρὸς ἐν αὐτῷ. ὅτι πᾶν τὸ ἐν τῷ κόσμῳ, ἡ ἐπιθυμία τῆς σαρκὸς καὶ ἡ ἐπιθυμία τῶν ὀφθαλμῶν καὶ ἡ ἀλαζονεία τοῦ βίου, οὐκ ἔστιν ἐκ τοῦ πατρός, ἀλλὰ ἐκ τοῦ κόσμου ἐστίν. καὶ ὁ κόσμος παράγεται καὶ ἡ ἐπιθυμία αὐτοῦ· ὁ δὲ ποιῶν τὸ θέλημα τοῦ θεοῦ μένει εἰς τὸν αιῶνα.

[Do not love the world, neither the things that are in the world. If anyone loves the world, the Father's love is not in him. For all that is in the world, the desire of the flesh, the desire of the eyes, and the secular ambition, is not the Father's, but is the world's. The world is passing away with its desires, but he who does God's will remains forever.][142]

(1) *concupiscentia carnis* [desire of the flesh], (2) *concupiscentia oculorum* [desire of the eyes], (3) *ambitio saeculi* [secular ambition]. Augustine does not merely characterize these phenomena objectively, as somehow existing, but his presentation is always in the fundamental posture of the *confessio;*

141. In this an unhistorical thingly, life-thingly basic aspect is operative.
142. World: Nature—not divine; secular—not spiritual [*geistig*]; *terrena*—*Dei* [earth—God]; "world" in the phenomenological sense.—"World-view": helplessness and a sign of disorientation, a phenomenon of falling [*Verfallsphänomen*].

that is, he confesses how temptations grow on him through these phenomena and in this posture, and how he relates, or tries to relate, to them. (*Confiteri:* interpretation, here in a very determinate How!)[143]

b) The Problem of the "I am"

Augustine now considers sensual lust in a more restricted sense, the life of sexual drives, not in a biological-psychological and theoretical attitude, but according to the characteristics of how he has factically experienced it and still experiences it—that is, how and when he encounters it: *malitiae diei et noctis* [the evils of the day and the night] ("dayliness"). To be sure, he followed the demand of God—that is, he gave up *concubitus* [copulation]; even more, he followed the advice and chose abstinence from marriage. "Sed adhuc vivunt in memoria mea, de qua multa locutus sum, talium rerum imagines, quas ibi consuetudo mea fixit; et occursant mihi vigilanti quidem carentes viribus" [But in my memory of which I have spoken so much, there still live images of those things which were fixed there by my habit; and they occur to me even while I am awake though they lack strength].[144] But in my sleep and in my dreams, they gain power over me. "Numquid tunc ego non sum [. . .]?" [Am I not myself at that time . . . ?][145] How about my being? (The problem is the "I am." That is: what about it, what is it really? *Vita—quaestio* [Life—a question].—By contrast, while I am awake, when they have no power, "I am." My "being" is determined, somehow, by the sense of the circumvention and the coping.—*Sum* = I am—existence—; existence is pulled into a being and a change of being, so that precisely with this difference [*Unter-schied*], it could modify itself and yet does not have to.)

While I am awake I am able to stand firm, even and especially when the temptations attack my body, when I have to deal with it. By contrast, I do fall for them while asleep and dreaming, although only the "images" are there. Is *ratio,* the possibility of deciding freely, of evaluating, taking a stand, and choosing, closed with the eyes as well? But how then does it occur that we retain in dreams, too, the directions of stance and choice that we seized, and that we stand firm in the face of what lures us?

"Et tamen tantum interest inter meipsum et meipsum, intra momentum quo hinc ad soporem transeo, vel huc inde retranseo!" [And yet there is so much difference between myself and myself, in that moment wherein I pass from waking to sleeping, or return from sleeping to waking!][146] There is a differ-

---

143. The true interpretation from the viewpoint of the end; now, according to the paraphrasing and indicating attitude, only emphasis in the earlier chapters!
144. *Confessiones* X 30, 41; PL 32, p. 796.
145. Ibid.
146. Ibid.

ence, a distance between the transitions. (And yet in all those "betweens" there is somehow the "same"; *transire—retransire—"sum"* [to pass—to return—"I am"], this uncovers: "facticity.") However, this difference is not only the difference that "I" behave differently in different situations, but precisely through this difference I experience that I behaved in such and such a way— for example, in dreams—that I myself was not really there, so that: "evigilantes ad conscientiae requiem redeamus; ipsaque distantia reperiamus nos non fecisse, quod tamen in nobis quoquo modo factum esse doleamus" [when we wake up we return to peace of conscience; by the distance discovering that we did not do what, however, we regret that it has somehow been done in us].[147] Especially in the "transition" we have a noteworthy experience with ourselves, namely, that there is something *quod nos non fecimus* [that we have not made], which is not enacted *by us, quod in nobis factum est* [(but) which is made in us], but which nonetheless occurs and proceeds with us and in us, so that we are somehow sad about it, something that is in us, something that we "are" ourselves and yet, that we are not.—Concept of the *molestia* [trouble].—It is to be noted in what complexes of experience this difference inflates [?] itself, and to which ones it belongs accordingly ("in conscience"). We can already see from what has been experienced: no juxtaposition. Nothing is said of duality and being split and so forth, but how *me ipsum,* my being myself, is determined in its full facticity on this basis. That means that it is necessary not to take the experiences, and experiences of dreams, as "occurrences," but to take them in their full factical How, in which I have the world and my life and in which I am. One has to leave aside all theoretically formulated divisions like body and soul, sensuality and reason, body and mind, and so forth. Primarily, the decisive sense of the phenomena is not here at all.

c) *Voluptas* [Pleasure]

The *languores animae* [exhaustions of the soul] are placed in the hope of the *misericordia Dei* [God's mercy], "ad pacem plenariam, quam tecum habebunt interiora et exteriora mea" [until the full peace which I shall have with you in me and outside of me].[148] In this hope is a certain ideal—whose origin and ideal being—(*die quies* [quiet day]).

"Est alia malitia diei." [There is another evil of the day.][149] It is very obvious here how Augustine sees these experiences: as troubles of his day. This dayliness (day and night) includes meals and relaxations. "Reficimus enim quotidianas ruinas corporis edendo et bibendo." [For we restore the daily decay

---

147. *Confessiones* X 30, 41; PL 32, p. 796 f.
148. *Confessiones* X 30, 42; PL 32, p. 797.
149. *Confessiones* X 31, 43; PL 32, p. 797.

of the body by eating and drinking.][150] So we bear with us an *indigentia* [need]. We are a *corruptibile* [corruptible (body)] and carry this heavy burden. "Nunc autem suavis est mihi necessitas." [But now, this necessity is sweet to me.][151] I turn the "necessity"—the burdensome necessity which indicates a need (always to be seen in this full significance of experience)—into a pleasure. The needing and demanding is agreeable to me. And *fames et sitis* [hunger and thirst] are indeed, and can be, pains, "urunt, et sicut febris necant" [which burn, and kill like a fever],[152] but "voluptate pelluntur" [they are expelled by pleasure].[153] And since we can heal the pains from what is at our disposal: "calamitas deliciae vocantur" [a calamity is called a delight].[154] So something is turned upside down, *molestiae* [troubles] and *malitiae* [evils] are *deliciae* [delights]. Food and drink are supposed to be only *medicamenta* [medicines] to sustain "me." ("*Ruina*" [decay], philosophically-Christian: passing away, perishing—in view of immortality; the objective Greek-theoretical aspect of the concept of facticity; being-dependent-upon, urgency, which is present over against me and in me.)

"Sed dum ad quietem satietatis ex indigentiae molestia transeo, in ipso transitu mihi insidiatur laqueus concupiscentiae." [But while I pass from the trouble of need to the quiet of satisfaction, in the very passing lies an insidious trap of desire.][155] Another "*transeo*" [I pass] is to be noted here. "Ipse enim transitus voluptas est, et non est alius qua transeatur quo transire cogit necessitas." [For that passage is itself a pleasure, and there is no other way to pass by but the passage forced upon us by necessity.][156] The need, and that one should preserve oneself, demand according to their own sense this *transitus,* but it in turn is a *voluptas;* "adjungit se [...] periculosa jucunditas, et plerumque praeire conatur" [a dangerous pleasantness joins in ... and often tries to go before it].[157] (The transition itself becomes important to me; a significance in which I live and which then absorbs the *necessitas* as the proper thing, letting us merely "see" and experience meals.) The *voluptas* and the pursuance of *iucunditas* contain a possibility of movement within themselves, such that this possibility pushes itself in between and in first place as the proper τέλῶς. "Nec idem modus utriusque est: nam quod saluti satis est, delectationi parum est. Et saepe incertum fit utrum adhuc necessaria corporis cura subsidium petat, an voluptaria cupiditatis fallacia ministerium suppetat. Ad hoc incertum hilarescit infelix anima [pursues joyfully, takes it up, appro-

---

150. Ibid.
151. Ibid.
152. Ibid.
153. Ibid.
154. Ibid.
155. *Confessiones* X 31, 44; PL 32, p. 797.
156. Ibid.
157. Ibid.

priates it as valuable, conducive, convenient], et in eo praeparat excusationis
patrocinium." [They do not have the same measure: for what is enough for
health is too little for delight. And often there is uncertainty whether the
necessary concern of the body seeks sustenance, or whether the deceptive
desire for pleasure demands service. In this uncertainty, the unhappy soul
rejoices (pursues joyfully, takes it up, appropriates it as valuable, conducive,
comfortable), and in this has a ready-made excuse for its protection.][158] (One's
own uncertainty is exploited for the sake of comfort.—It is the facticity in
which I maintain myself and give [myself] "existence" which pushes itself
into *my* "authentic" existing. Uncertainty, danger, possibility: *ad quod hilarescit infelix anima* [in which the unhappy soul rejoices]. Mode of significance, of the claiming of the enactment. "Conflict." Uncertainty of the decision, "consilium [certain decision] mihi de hac re nondum stat" [I have not
yet made a certain decision on this matter].[159])

   "Non ego immunditiam obsonii timeo, sed immuniditiam cupiditatis." [It is
not the uncleanness of the meat which I fear but the uncleanness of my lust.][160]
"In his ergo tentationibus positus, certo quotidie adversus concupiscentiam
manducandi et bibendi" [Therefore, placed in these temptations, I struggle
every day against the desire of eating and drinking],[161] against the determinate
direction, against a determinate *How* of this concrete dealing-with. "Non enim
est quod semel praecidere [cut off, throw off] et ulterius non attingere decer-
nam, sicut de concubitu potui." [For it is not such that I could cut myself off
(cut off, throw off) from it once and for all, and decide to never touch it again,
as I was able to do with carnal copulation.][162,163] (*Concubitus* [copulation]: a
certain situation which I can leave behind, but I do not get rid of myself in
this way.)

   Again, a characteristic meditation intervenes and urges toward what is decisive.

d) *Illecebra odorum* [The allurement of smell]

Regarding the *illecebra odorum*, I appear to myself as if they could not reach
me. They do not come near me, as it were, so that I would have to labor with
them. "Ita mihi videor; fortasse fallor." [That is how I see myself; but perhaps
I am mistaken.][164] At first sight, when I view myself from above as a thing
fixed in the *now*, and of such and such a constitution, it seems like that to

---

158. *Confessiones* X 31, 44; PL 32, p. 797 f.
159. *Confessiones* X 31, 44; PL 32, p. 798.
160. Ibid.
161. *Confessiones* X 31, 46; PL 32, p. 799.
162. Ibid.
163. Again and again, "necessarily present" *ad reficiendam ruinam* [until the restoring decay].
164. *Confessiones* X 32, 48; PL 32, p. 799.

me. But I have to weep at myself in my misery, not only insofar as I see that I am situated in uncertainties, but "et istae plangendae tenebrae, in quibus me latet facultas mea quae in me est: [. . .] plerumque occultum est" [there is the deplorable darkness in which the faculty which is in me is hidden from me: . . . often it is concealed].[165] The knowledge of the uncertainty[166] itself lies in darkness. I cannot just look at myself to see myself lying open before me. I am concealed to myself, "nisi experientia manifestetur" [unless experience reveals it],[167] if the complex of experience, that is, the historical experiencing in its "expansion" [Erstreckung] (the experience oriented toward the self, existential experience), does not expose it. I can never appeal to a moment that is shut down, as it were, in which I supposedly penetrate myself. Already the next moment can make me fall, and expose me as someone entirely different. For this reason, insofar as the having-myself can be enacted at all, it is always in the pull away from and toward this life, a to and fro.[168] "Et nemo securus esse debet in ista vita, quae tota tentatio nominatur (Job. VII, 1), utrum qui fieri potuit ex deteriore melior, non fiat etiam ex meliore deterior." [No one should be secure in this life, which is called a total temptation (Job. VII, 1); anyone who could be made better from worse could also be made worse from the better.][169] The "fieri potuit"—the past, what became possible and what I am in this having-become—stands in a "fiat":[170] the becoming which could still occur. Thus, the self is to be sought originally in this direction of experience. In this direction, and only in this direction, does the tentatio encounter us. That is, inasmuch as it is there, life, the ista vita, has to be experienced in this way[171]—understanding the self in this in its full facticity of experience. (How little I have myself in this way, and if I have myself—toward the future—then in significant calculations.)

e) Voluptas aurium [The pleasure of the ear]

This "aspect" of the factical is clearly also the basis for the consideration of the voluptates aurium [pleasures of the ear]:[172] "omnes affectus spiritus nostri pro sui diversitate habere proprios modos in voce atque cantu, quorum nescio qua occulta familiaritate excitentur" [all the diverse affects of our spirit have

---

165. Ibid.
166. of myself
167. Confessiones X 32, 48; PL 32, p. 799.
168. The past is no less indifferent than the "from where."
169. Confessiones X 32, 48; PL 32, p. 799.
170. meum fiat—"it can"—is only there in the experiential enactment of the "can." What structure of sense does this enactment have?
171. inasmuch as a temptation is experienced, I attain this situation. But what is "experiencing temptation"?
172. Cf. above, p. 150.

their various corresponding modes in voice and chants, and are stirred up by a mysterious association].[173] Thus, inasmuch as this *familiaritas* exists and inasmuch as the sounds and *cantus* [chants] trigger a *delectatio* [delight] which can turn into a *frui* [enjoyment]—*quibus non est fruendum* [which is not to be enjoyed]—life in *affectus spiritus* [the affects of the spirit] will always, at the same time, stand in the uncertainty of its factical enactment. Because of this close association, the sounds and chants carry their own danger within them, a danger which can also be conducive, in that precisely through them, in the co-experience of the sounds, the *affectus spiritus* are becoming even more "alive." (Thus, what is decisive here is the sense of function of hearing or of what becomes accessible in it for the *affectus spiritus.*—Hearing to be regarded from this perspective.)

The factical, unreflected experience—placed at the service of, in view of, holding itself in the ordering-toward—the *summum bonum* [greatest good] or the relation of the self to it. The same holds for the theoretical consideration of the sounds.

f) *Voluptas oculorum* [The pleasure of the eye]

"Restat voluptas oculorum istorum carnis meae [caro—not what is spiritual]" [There remains the pleasure of these eyes of my flesh (the flesh—not what is spiritual)].[174] Correspondingly, the *seeing* is not related to purely sensuous objects; it is a "how" of *dealing-with* ("*in carne*" [in the flesh], in an orientation that is separated, non-divine, non-spiritual, and not concerned existentially, not authentically concerned, in a self-worldly manner, for the *beata vita*). Similarly, and in general, in the consideration of the "senses" in the context of the *tentationes,* that *which* they bring to the fore of experience stands in a peculiar, characteristic sense, full of content, a sense which is perhaps precisely the genuine, existentially decisive one. What is crucial is not a new determination of the content, the material What, regionally, but "opening up possibility"—but this in such a way that the temptation lies precisely in setting aside the possibilities, and in settling oneself[175] in the *real,* in what is significant—as "being accompanied by a possible fall."

And the emphasis on the *voluptas istorum oculorum* is on the "amant oculi" [what the eyes love], what they are looking for at the moment: "pulchras formas et varias, nitidos et amoenos colores" [beautiful and varied forms, glowing and pleasant colors][176]—*lux* [light]. The devotion is such that this possession becomes entirely familiar and is taken for granted. Form and color

173. *Confessiones* X 33, 49; PL 32, p. 800.
174. *Confessiones* X 34, 51; PL 32, p. 800.
175. allowing oneself to slide into the *calculation of significance.*
176. *Confessiones* X 34, 51; PL 32, p. 800.

are there *totis diebus* [the whole day]. *Lux, regina colorum,* "multimodo al-lapsu blanditur" [Light, the queen of colors, "gliding by in many forms, en-ticing me"].[177] "Insinuat autem se ita vehementur, ut si repente subtrahatur, cum desiderio requiratur; et si diu absit, contristat animum" [For it insinuates itself so forcibly, if it is withdrawn suddenly, it is sought with longing; and if long absent, it makes the soul sad].[178] (*Transitus* [transition]! Cf.: "Non autem sentio sine quo esse aut aequo animo, aut aegre possim, nisi cum abfuerit" [For I cannot know whether my soul can be balanced or upset to be without something, unless it is absent].[179]—How I conduct myself in having, in dealing-with . . . , how, and to what extent, it concerns me; how, and to what extent, I am interwoven and involved.)

Factical experience has fixed itself in *that* direction, such that it is concerned to add something, to increase the significances—that is, to multiply the man-ifold and the alteration of what is at its disposal, "the new." (This increase and alteration shows how important this is taken to be, and how it can fill a life.[180])

g) *Operatores et sectatores pulchritudinum exteriorum* [The artists and followers of external beauty]

Homines: "foras sequentes quod faciunt" (*cadunt in ea quod valent*) [Humans: "outwardly they follow what they make"[181] (they fall into that which they are able to do)], they settle themselves and follow that which they can accomplish. "Quam innumerabilia [. . .] addiderunt homines ad illecebras oculorum" [In-numerable things . . . have men made to entice their eyes],[182] those *operatores et sectatores pulchritudinum exteriorum* [the "producers of bustling activity"] *usum necessarium atque moderatum longe transgredientes* [artists and follow-ers of external beauty (the "producers of bustling activity"), far exceeding necessary and moderate use]: pursuing, continuing, seeking new fulfillment in falling, endlessly. What is significant is experienced in such a way that it suffices for itself, by itself and by its continuation. (It assumes the role of endowing facticity with meaning.)

To be sure, they "ab illa pulchritudine [. . .], quae super animas est [per quas pulchra trajecta in manus artificiosas—Plotinus], [. . .] approbandi modum, non autem inde trahunt utendi modum" [derive the manner of ap-

177. *Confessiones* X 34, 51; PL 32, p. 800.
178. Ibid.
179. *Confessiones* X 37, 60; PL 32, p. 805.
180. A peculiar situational transition in factical life. The direction lies in the significance itself. The situational character has almost been absorbed. The sense of "real" is located in such significance.
181. *Confessiones* X 34, 53; PL 32, p. 801.
182. Ibid.

proval (. . .) from that beauty (. . .) which is above the soul (through the beautiful things delivered by skilled hands—Plotinus), but they do not draw from there the manner of using them].[183] When it is a matter of measuring the factical significance and the corresponding esteemability and one's own performance, a calling upon a superordinate meaning and value comes alive. But in this, the superordinate meaning itself is placed at the service of bustling activity. (This increase is then merely a hidden calculation of the same sense of enactment after all, or it has not been radically and thoroughly clarified. The cultural-philosophical extension and peak of this: the idea of culture, the progress of culture, the rise of the human spirit, and whatever else these utopias name themselves.—One is not content with mere enjoyment and connoisseurship, but at the same time one adds a great world-view theory, a—however mythical—"deepening," in order to achieve an even greater expansion by calling upon this deepening. But the attitude toward that from which one derives the calling, and in which one grounds it, is an attitude *in carne* [in the flesh]—also understood in the sense of comfort. In order not to be disturbed, one closes one's eyes before the possibility of such a selfly [*selbstlich*] relevant attitude.)

Sectatores pulchritudinum exteriorum: fortitudinem suam non ad te custodiant [. . .] eam spargant in deliciosas lassitudines [The followers of external beauty: they do not guard their strength for You; they dissipate their strength in exhausting delights].[184] They do not preserve the security and liveliness of the enactment of concern and of engagement for themselves in their relation to You, but they dissipate it and spend it easily in an amusing slackness and a delightful laziness. It is no longer at their disposal for an authentic decision. They fail while giving themselves, in a communal world, a borrowed significance and posture as the *enjoyers and connoisseurs* of these things, pretending to be familiar and intimate with the meaning of the world and the secrets of life. (Decisive is the How and the enactment of the direction of *fortitudo* [strength].—The selfly [*selbstliche*] competence: the ability, the power, what is disposable of the possibilities of enactment of selfly existing.)

"Istis pulchris gressum innecto" [I entangle my steps in beautiful things][185]—everywhere and all the time, I entangle myself in these beautiful, alluring things, as possible situations and possibilities of continuation, of enjoyment and activity factically force themselves upon life. These characteristics of what is experienced in the How of experiencing *in carne.* "Ego capior miserabiliter" [I am miserably captured],[186] I am being drawn into it miserably. "Haereo in ubique sparsis insidiis" [I become stuck in the snares laid every-

183. Ibid.
184. Cf. ibid.
185. Ibid.
186. Ibid.

where][187] and thus lose the genuine and authentic orientation toward the *lux vera, illa pulchritudo* "cui suspirat anima mea die ac nocte," *deus decus meum* [true light, that beauty "after which my soul sighs day and night,"][188] my God and beauty].

"O lux quam videbat Tobias, cum clausis oculis istis filium docebat vitae viam, [. . .] Aut quam videbat Isaac [. . .], cum filios non agnoscendo benedicere, sed benedicendo agnoscere meruit" [O light which Tobit saw when, with his eyes closed, he taught his son the way of life (. . .) Or that light which Isaac saw (. . .) blessing his sons without recognizing them, but in blessing them, deserving to recognize them].[189] (The *benedicere* [blessing] endows one with sight in the authentic sense.)—"Erigo ad te invisibiles oculos" (*amantes!*) [I lift up to you invisible eyes (lovingly!)].[190]—"Ipsa est lux, una est, et unum omnes qui vident et amant eam" [This is the light, it is one, and one are all those who see it and love it].[191] (Cf. in Joh. Ev. Tract. I, no. 18, 19.)

§ 14. The Second Form of tentatio: concupiscentia oculorum
[desire of the eye]
Chapter 35

a) *Videre in carne* [seeing in the flesh] and *videre per carnem* [seeing through the flesh]

Alia forma tentationis: "concupiscentia oculorum," "curiositas supervacanea cognoscendi" [A different form of temptation: "the desire of the eye," "the superfluous curiosity of knowing"].[192] To what extent is there a different form of *tentatio* here? Does it concern one of the different manners of experience, discussed above, and to what extent is it different? Not only different in the way seeing is different from hearing, and hearing from tasting, but in another way. (Factical life: in what sense perspective? Since one is not clear about the sense of such divisions, as they plainly exist terminologically, and instead "separates" faculties and regions, one arrives at puzzles [*Vexierfragen*].—Sensuousness is a How of *full* experiencing.)

In all experience as *curare* [concern], the basic tendency of *delectatio (uti—frui)* [delight (use—enjoyment)], a *curare* characterized in different ways, is

187. *Confessiones* X 34, 52; PL 32, p. 801.
188. *Confessiones* X 34, 53; PL 32, p. 801.
189. *Confessiones* X 34, 52; PL 32, p. 801.
190. Ibid.
191. Ibid.
192. Cf. *Confessiones* X 37, 60; PL 32, p. 804.

co-present, thus co-present is always a certain *appetitus* [appetite], a striving for something (formal—otherwise ambiguous, dangerous). In the aforementioned possibilities of temptation, the *appetitus* is directed toward an *oblectari* [entertaining]: being entertained by something to pass the time, dealing with the content of what becomes accessible at the moment through the senses themselves (emotionally). A *cupiditas se oblectandi* in carne [lust of entertainment *in the flesh*] itself. The *delectatio* follows the How of the relational sense of sensuousness, a relational sense which remains in the content as such, and indeed in the manner of a thorough and savoring enjoyment, a being-pulled in it and by it. In this, what is "seen" and "heard" has the sense content of seeing as that which is enjoyed.

But now, there is *per eosdem sensus* [through the same sense] a different *cupiditas* [lust]: "non se oblectandi in carne, sed experiendi per carnem" [not an entertainment in the flesh, but an experiencing through the flesh].[193] Sensuousness now has a different function: *per carnem* [through the flesh]. This concerns sensuousness in such a way that it enters, according to its full sense, into the sense-character of access and the performance of access (only this is dominant now, and indeed in such a way that the access stands in the *appetitus* of *experiendi* [experiencing]. *Haec concupiscentia est* "in appetitu noscendi" [This desire is "in the appetite of knowing"],[194] of the experience that takes cognizance of, and gets to know, something. It is the appetite of *looking-about-oneself* (not of dealing-with) in the various regions and fields, "what is going on there." *Curiositas,* curiosity as the greedy desire for the new [*Neugier*], "cupiditas, nomine cognitionis et scientiae palliata" [the lust, hidden under the title of knowledge and science][195] ("pallium": probably Greek scholar and philosopher), assuming the cover of profundity and of the absolute cultural necessity of special achievements. (The seeing and hearing that enjoys is the factical seeing and hearing; as enjoyment, it is so natural that we do not even "see" it any longer, or it is covered up and hidden insofar as one deceives oneself.—Seeing and hearing lend the content, the experienced significance, its basic *articulation*.)

Voluptas [or] cupiditas oblectandi *sectatur pulchra, canora, suavia, sapida, lenia* [Pleasure (or) *lust of entertainment* pursues beautiful objects, sounds, smells, tastes, and tactile experiences]. *Curiositas* [or] cupiditas experiendi *sectatur etiam his contraria (noscendi libidine—non ad subeundam molestiam)* [Curiosity (or) *the lust of experience* even pursues the contraries of these pleasures (out of lust for knowing—not for the trouble they bring)].[196] That is, for these the dealing-with . . . is not primarily in question. Even that which

---

193. *Confessiones* X 35, 54; PL 32, p. 802.
194. Ibid.
195. Ibid.
196. Cf. *Confessiones* X 35, 55; PL 32, p. 802.

does *not* yield positive enlightenment to the worldly, factical enjoyment, even the opposite of that, is intended, because the intention is such that it renders the content of the What accessible in such a way that it cannot trouble it, and keeps it at bay. But precisely in this, the intention looks at the content—and only looks at it—, and a letting-oneself-be-moved is possibly sought only on the basis of this keeping-at-bay. And what is crucial is not really the content but the "relation," and indeed the mere enactment of the relation as such.

b) The Curious Looking-about-Oneself in the World

The dominant sense is the *mere desire to see,* the naked curiosity, in particular if the experience is enacted with emotional emphasis: fear, terror, horror. The expressions of this basic disposition toward the objects are multiple (cinema).

"Hinc etiam, si quid eodem perversae scientiae fine per artes magicas quaeritur" [Hence also, if with the same end of perverted science, the magical arts are used to inquire].[197] In this curiosity (in a certain emphasis upon one possibility of experience, and in a certain enactment of it) lies also the falling into, and the dealing with, magic, mysticism, and theosophy. *Finis delectationis* [the end of delight] is *perversa scientia* [a perverse science] which has already, from the beginning, given up any criticism about its own sense of enactment.

"Hinc etiam in ipsa religione Deus tentatur, cum signa et prodigia flagitantur, non ad aliquam salutem, sed ad solam experientiam desiderata" [Hence also in religion itself God is tempted by demands for signs and wonders, not desired for any saving end, but only for the sake of experience].[198] (God has to endure becoming a factor in human experiments. He has to respond to an inquisitive, pompous, and pseudo-prophetic curiosity, that is, a curious looking-about-oneself in regard to Him, which does *not* submit [*fügt*] to His sense of objecthood, that is, which is non-sense [*Un-fug*].)

Why is this *concupiscentia* understood and designated as *concupiscentia oculorum*? "Oculi autem sunt ad cognoscendum in sensibus principes, [. . .] Ad oculos enim proprie videre pertinet" [For knowing the eyes are the principal senses, . . . For to see pertains properly to the eyes."[199] (Insofar as sensuousness involves a cognizing sense of achievement, *seeing* has to be accorded first place among its different ways.) "Utimur autem hoc verbo etiam in caeteris sensibus, cum eos ad cognoscendum intendimus" [Yet we also apply this word to other senses, when we use them toward knowing],[200] when we give to sensuousness the full sense-direction and sense-function of knowl-

197. Ibid.
198. Ibid.
199. *Confessiones* X 35, 54; PL 32, p. 802.
200. Ibid.

edge, which it does not have without further ado, or always and primarily as such.

"Cum aliquid cognitionis explorant" [When they explore other knowledge],[201] when the senses are supposed to explore and render accessible something on the order of knowledge, an object of knowledge as such, then we call its relational sense—and accordingly the full sense—a *seeing*. For *caeteri sensus [videndi officium] sibi [. . .] usurpant* [usurp, accord themselves], *in quo [officio videndi] primatum oculi tenent* [the other senses usurp onto themselves (accord themselves) (the faculty of seeing), in which (faculty of seeing) the eyes hold first place].[202,203] (To see means to first give an object as object.)

If we want to ascertain something in the manner of cognition, if we want to refer to something as present-at-hand—as existing and in the manner of its existing—in the regions of what becomes accessible through the senses in *their* manner of the relational sense (which is no manner of *experiri* [experiencing]): "Neque enim dicimus, Audi quid rutilet; aut, Olfac quam niteat; aut, Gusta quam splendeat; aut, Palpa quam fulgeat" [For we do not say, hear how red it is; or smell how bright that is; or taste how that shines; or feel how that gleams].[204] (Here the determinations are referred to *lux* [light], for "*lux*" is that which is seen, what is objective *qua* what is merely objective.)

"Videri enim dicuntur haec omnia" [For all these are said to be seen],[205] that is, what becomes accessible in seeing (in a seeing not concretely emphasized), is never, in regard to the cognizing, relational manner of grasping, designated other than as seeing. The other relational senses are not functionalized for the achievement of access, but, inversely, seeing has the meaning of rendering accessible (what is objective), in the emphasized sense of the mere taking-cognizance-of. By contrast, we say: "Vide quid sonet; vide quid oleat; vide quid sapiat; vide quam durum sit" [See what it sounds like, see what it smells like, see what it tastes like, see how hard it is].[206] (Here we are dealing with a manifold of what is not really visible, that is, of what is objective as such [*des Gegenständlichen als solchen*], but it becomes objective only in the seeing; it receives its relational or content modification in the "seeing," in the co-enactment.) According to its meaning, the "seeing" is: only looking at, considering, bringing to one's cognizing givenness, letting something become an object for oneself as the object of mere taking-cognizance-of. ("Generalis experientia sensuum" [the general experience of the senses],[207] the cognizing experience in sensuousness in general: "seeing.")

"Seeing" has the primacy in *officio videndi* or *cognoscendi* (the faculty of

---

201. Ibid.
202. Cf. ibid.
203. do not really have this sense of achievement?!
204. *Confessiones* X 35, 54; PL 32, p. 802.
205. Ibid.
206. Ibid.
207. Ibid.

seeing or knowing). Thus, wherever the concrete factical experiencing is according to its sense, and where it intends an emphasized taking-cognizance-of (which in turn has different purposes), the *delectatio videndi* [delight of seeing], which can be a *concupiscentia,* is alive. To what extent? The relational sense as such is self-willed, and the full sense of *videre* is then self-willed and primary; it determines all factical experiences, including the decisive and the final ones. (The self-willed relational sense goes beyond the immanent, selfly enactmental interpretation [*selbstliche Vollzugsinterpretation*] of its existential relevance. The relational sense does not only not care about it, but itself directs all life.—Now, with Augustine the self-willing toward what and away from what?)

This *forma tentationis* [form of temptation] contains *multiplicius periculosa* [multiple dangers]. "Quando audeo dicere nulla re tali me intentum fieri ad spectandum, et vana cura capiendum?" [When dare I say that nothing of the sort provokes me to go and look at it, and that I am not caught by a vain concern?][208] (In curiosity, in this relational direction, everything is in principle accessible, without restraint.)

"Cum enim hujuscemodi rerum conceptaculum fit cor nostrum, et portat copiosae vanitatis catervas" [When our heart becomes the receptacle of such things, and carries a plethora of vanities][209]: caves, hideaways for the reception and carrying-within-oneself of godless vanities.[210] (One principal way, and one "existing" opportunity, of dispersion! "In life," intercourse of the human being with God: what does [not] happen here!—Interjections of curiosity are interspersed throughout factical experience.)

§ 15. The Third Form of tentatio: ambitio saeculi *[secular ambition]*
Chapters 36–38

a) A Comparison of the First Two Forms of Temptation

"Tertium tentationis genus cessavit a me, aut cessare in hac tota vita potest?" [The third kind of temptation has not ceased for me, or can it cease in this

---

208. *Confessiones* X 35, 56; PL 32, p. 802.
209. *Confessiones* X 35, 57; PL 32, p. 803.
210. "Aut aliquid nos reducet in spem, nisi tota misericordia tua, quoniam coepisti mutare nos?" [Or will nothing lead us back to hope but your whole mercy, since you have begun to change us?] (*Confessiones* X 36, 58; PL 32, p. 803). An important address! *Misericordia* [mercy]! Trust. Even our praying is something which we really "inter contemnenda deputabimus" [have to count among the condemnable things] (ibid.).—"Me primitus sanas a libidine vindicandi me" [You cure me first of all of the lust for self-justification] (ibid.). Self-righteousness!—"Compressisti a timore tuo superbiam meam, et mansuefecisti jugo tuo cervicem meam. Et nunc porto illud, et lene est mihi [. . .] et nesciebam quando id subire metuebam" [You have curbed my pride with your fear, and tied my neck to your yoke. And now I bear that yoke, and it is light for me . . . and I did not know it when I feared to submit to it.] (ibid.).— In *superbia* [pride] and self-love.

whole life?][211] The experiential relations that determine the situation are, in the first two forms of *tentatio,* the following: 1. the *dealing-with* that enjoys; 2. the curious *looking-about-oneself* that only wishes to get to know. These experiential relations aim at something that has to do essentially with the surrounding world, and not with the self [*Selbstliches*]. For even where, in (1) as well as in (2), something communal-worldly [*Mitweltliches*]—these or other human beings in this or other situations—is the object of dealing-with, or primarily the object of looking-about-oneself, of the curious wanting-to-get-to-know, being-allowed-to-be-familiar-with, knowing-about-it, even here this dealing-with and looking-about-oneself remain in an essentially surrounding-worldly character of the *object* (significance): that is precisely what is characteristic of their corresponding experiential relations. (And this so "objectively," that they precisely accomplish and enable the absorption.)

All communal-worldly relations that turn up are taken into the determining experiential relation of the dealing-with or looking-about. In regard to the How of the self-worldly or even selfly "being-among" [*Dabeisein*], this means that the self *qua* self does not articulate itself enactmentally in the experiential enactment.[212] In (1), the self is absorbed in dealing-with or in that with which it deals ("absorption": a phenomenon of its own!). In (2), the self, admittedly, is not absorbed, but it does not come to itself just the same. What is peculiar to the phenomenon is here precisely that it is neither an absorption, as in (1), nor a having-oneself, such that it basically is "not there."[213] (The *Dasein,* the self, the being-real of life, is an absorption. The self is being lived by the world, and all the more strongly so if it in fact thinks that it lives authentically in such existence [*Dasein*]. This "being-lived" is a special How of facticity, and can only be explicated on the basis of the authentic sense of existence [*vom eigentlichen Existenzsinn her*].)

In the third form of *tentatio,* the self articulates itself enactmentally in a certain way, insofar as this form explicitly revolves around the self itself. The self is supposed to be taken as important in an authentic sense; it is "with" it [*dabei*], that is, the *self-significance* becomes *finis delectationis* [the end of delight].[214] At issue is the *self-validation* in factical experiencing, that is, in the communal-worldly contexts of life, but finally also in the self-worldly contexts. The relation to the world is, here, the communal-worldly one, the self-like worldly one in general.

---

211. *Confessiones* X 36, 58; PL 32, p. 804.
212. an articulation of the self that does not enact—the modes of "being-among"
213. an absorption in looking-about-oneself.
214. Cf.: "Sermo autem ore procedens, et facta quae innotescunt hominibus, habent tentationem periculosissimam ab amore laudis" [But the word proceeding from the mouth, and the actions that become known to men, carry the most dangerous temptation in the love of praise] (*Confessiones* X 38, 63; PL 32, p. 806).

b) *Timeri velle* [wishing to be feared] and *amari velle* [wishing to be loved]

Augustine begins the consideration with the "timeri et amari velle ab hominibus" [wishing to be feared and loved by men].[215] Further, he calls the "humana lingua" [human language] the "quotidiana fornax nostra" (*horum tentationum*) [our daily furnace (the tempting hour)].[216] These two determinations clearly refer to the communal-worldly context of experience. The *curare* of this experiencing is at work [*geschäftig*] in gaining a certain position for the one who experiences in relation to the communal world. It is a *velle:* wanting, striving for, consciously organizing one's life such that one is feared or loved by others. One's own world ("world" phenomenologically: that in which I live)—that is, the world of one's own acting and achieving, the *self-world* (not the self in its authentic sense)—pushes itself into the foreground; it emphasizes itself. In this *velle,* experience views itself in the eyes, the claims, judgments, tastes, or inabilities, fickleness, and stupidity of others. In the *timeri et amari velle,* the self-world puts on airs in a communal-worldly situation it views in a special way. It is about the being-in-communal-worldly-validity. In the *timeri velle,* one views oneself as the superior one, and makes an effort at such communal-worldly assertion. In the *amari velle,* one takes oneself to stand out as the valuable one who deserves the esteem of others.— Both *velle* can be the expression of a certain inner vehemence of existence, but they are just as much, and mostly, motivated by cowardly weakness and insecurity, the dependence upon models, a need of being allowed to go along, or by the concealing prevention, and pushing away, of confrontation. (In giving in to this *tentatio,* the self is lost for itself in its ownmost way. Correspondingly, here is the gaining and finding, the possibility of knowing oneself and getting clear about oneself.)

The characterization of language—more precisely, of speaking, of communicating oneself and hearing, as the source of this form of *tentatio*—leads the communal-worldly context of experience back to the decisive manner of the *enactment* of communal-worldly experiencing. At the same time, this indicates how particularly great, according to their own sense, the possibilities of hiding oneself, of playacting, etc., are in this manner of enactment.

Augustine calls a *misera vita,* a miserable life, and a *foeda iactantia,* a shameful arrogance, a life in which these communal-worldly contexts of experience are thoroughly dominated by such a *curare.*[217]

Now, as with the other forms of temptation, the direction of possibilities of temptation—the communal-worldly direction, and indeed this particular one

---

215. *Confessiones* X 36, 59; PL 32, p. 804.
216. *Confessiones* X 37, 60; PL 32, p. 804.
217. Cf. p. 181 ff.

that is about loving and fearing, or about being loved and being feared—is here co-"present" in the facticity of *Dasein*.[218] According to its sense, it is the being-adjusted of the experiential relations to the significances of what can be experienced in the communal-world: "propter quaedam humanae societatis officia necessarium est amari et timeri ab hominibus" [because certain offices in human society make it necessary to be loved and feared by people].[219] Thus, we have encountered a new mode of the sense-motivation of the *molestia* [trouble] in facticity. ("*Necessarium,*" the sense of facticity: always (?) "present" in factical life—"inescapably," that is, the seriousness of existence must "necessarily," from its own full possibility of enactment, be directed toward being concerned with it. A direction of concern, and indeed a direction co-given with the experience of "world.")

Let us briefly consider together the different senses of *molestia* that belong to, and really determine, the forms of *tentatio*.[220] The selfly *Dasein*, the existence, bears in different ways a *molestia*, is attached to it, and thus determines itself in its facticity. The being-attached of selfly *Dasein* to a *molestia* is an object-like characterization. For the radical conception of the phenomenal complexes encountered here, it is decisive to deal with the problem sensibly [*sinnmäßig*] from the beginning.

For reasons that will not be investigated further here, Augustine did not approach the problem in this way, even if precisely the problem of *tentatio* yields valuable indications, if one has seen the problem.

The *molestia* is not a piece of object—a region of being, present in some sense of the theoretical objectification of nature—but designates a *How* of experiencing. And precisely as such a How, it characterizes the How of factical experiencing, insofar as we now consider it in aligning it to our special task, at least from different perspectives, that is, from the full sense of facticity, that which is full of sense. How we can experience it ourselves in today's situation is not determined by this. What is perhaps missing in the explicit articulation of the problem is precisely the authentic determination of sense, the historical.

The modes of factical experiencing indicated in the different senses of *molestia* are not an ordering juxtaposition. Rather, their formal relation is itself, in turn, only a How of experiencing and articulating of *facticity,* the expression in enactment of facticity.

Now, we only want to indicate, by taking them together, the explicative directions of the phenomenon of facticity, under the following qualifications: (1) in limiting ourselves to what we find in Augustine; (2) above all, with the

218. a *necessitas*
219. *Confessiones* X 36, 59; PL 32, p. 804.
220. facticity, *molestia;*—situation and determination of the origin of the respective explication.

qualification that we do not discuss the problem of the starting point of the explication, a problem which represents an essential part of the explication, and which precisely co-expresses the peculiar sense of facticity; and (3) the problem of the connection between these modes of factical experiencing and the authentic original sense and final sense of enactment of a facticity, of factical existence. With these three qualifications we at the same time indicate three fields of investigation of facticity and the problematic of existence.

(The "Hows" of one's "own" selfly full being. Factical life: occurrence, being-present, existence [*Dasein*], "situation" or care of the situation—this "or" also with the others—being-among [*Dabeisein*], existing; neither strata nor levels; to be articulated in no particular order at all. The difficulty lies in the otherness of genuine articulation, and in a phenomenologically radical uncovering of the problem-complex; but therein also lies the decisive sense which can only be interpreted enactment-historically in each case.—Insofar as this problem finds its origin of sense in existence—which is itself enactment-historical, factical—all explicates of sense to be uncovered in this problem are *existentiale* [*Existenzialien*], that is, "categories" formally viewed, and indeed *enactment-historically hermeneutic* categories, not attitudinal categories of order. Formal sense of category: λέγειν.—Each of the "Hows" above—set apart attitudinally, and considered genuinely in its material—results in its own field of *objectities* [*Objektitäten*] of different senses; important for the "construction" [*Aufbau*] of the objective-historical objectity.)

c) *Amor laudis* [love of praise]

The desire to validate oneself is motivated, and maintained in its enactment, by a certain *self-importance* [*Selbstwichtignahme*]: "ab amore laudis, qui ad privatam quamdam excellentiam contrahit emendicata suffragia" [from the love of praise which collects the votes it begged for to advance a certain private excellency].[221,222] And this self-importance has its effects in worldly experience as the bustling activity (*cura*) to gain praise: not only an esteem of value, but a certain explicit declaration of value before others or for oneself, thus an explicit placing-in-validity and bringing-into-validity within the communal world and within factical achievement and ability. That explains the preponderance of *laudare* [to praise], *laudari* [to be praised], and *laudatio* [praise] in the following considerations.

This bustling activity for the sake of praise, for a communal-worldly standing of validity, is a *cura* [concern] for being liked or being pleasing [*Gefallen*]. That is, those who extend liking toward us, those who maintain us in our

---

221. *Confessiones* X 38, 63; PL 32, p. 806.
222. Standing out—being presumptuous?

experience in their own communal world, themselves now become important: "Divitiae [riches, significances] vero quae ob hoc expetuntur, ut [ambitioni] [. . .] serviant" [As for riches which are sought for this, that they may serve (ambitions) . . .].[223] *Homo movetur laudibus humanis* [human beings are moved by human praise], that is, the real source of motivation for one's own life concentrates itself fully on one's standing of validity in the communal world. (The special complex of achievement of life receives its direction from the effort at attaining concrete possibilities of setting oneself up in validation and maintaining oneself therein.) Here too—only in a more hidden and more dangerous manner—one is praised instead of praising oneself; but precisely one's own life is viewed in this as if it were eminently important and deserved for its own achievement.

Giving into temptation is now explicated—in an *axiologizing* manner—as a shifting of the direction of *placere* [liking, being pleased]. *Foeda iactantia* [shameful arrogance]. "Hinc fit vel maxime non amare te, nec caste timere te" [Hence especially it comes that men do not love you nor fear you in purity].[224] Love of God, fear. God himself is not taken to be decisively important anymore; the *amplius placet* [what is more pleasing] has become different. (Shifting the *cura* from its direction toward *summum bonum* [the highest good]; *amor maximus* [the greatest love] and *timor castus* [pure fear] are not enacted.)

"Et a veritate tua gaudium nostrum deponamus, atque in hominum fallacia ponamus" [And we give up our joy in your truth, and place it in the deceitfulness of human beings].[225] (Important for the correct grasp of the *veritas Dei* [truth of God].) *Deponere:* shifting the direction of *cura,* or the esteem and the positing of the *finis* [end], and *ponere:* moving it toward the opinions of human beings, making an effort in regard to "how they think of us," how, and as what, we are held in validation by them, settling oneself there with one's aspirations of factical life.

"Libeatque nos amari et timeri, non propter se, sed pro te" [It becomes our pleasure to be loved and feared not for your sake, but instead of you].[226] We find it more pleasing, and like it more, and prefer to be loved and esteemed instead of You, in Your place. You are pushed back and set aside. (Not for Your sake, so that every *bonum* [good] in us is really and only esteemed and praised as *bonum tuum* [Your good].)—In all of this "instat adversarius verae beatitudinis nostrae" [the adversary of our true happiness threatens us][227] with

---

223. *Confessiones* X 37, 60; PL 32, p. 805.
224. *Confessiones* X 36, 59; PL 32, p. 804.
225. Ibid.
226. Ibid.
227. Ibid.

the possibility of a *falsa beatitudo* [false happiness]; the *tentatio* always revolves around this.

d) The Genuine Direction of *placere*

What, now, is the connection between this preferring and setting-aside, and
the *laudari* as the manner considered here of the really existing (existential)
being-in-communal-worldly-validity? *Peccator (homo!) non* "laudatur in de-
sideriis animae suae, [. . .] laudatur homo propter aliquod donum quod dedisti
ei" [No sinner (human!) "is praised for the desires of his soul (. . .) a human
being is praised for some gift which you gave him"].[228] Thus, insofar as a
human being is praised at all, and is seen and declared as important and
valuable, this happens neither on the basis of, nor with regard to, his ownmost
concerns and resolutions. He has nothing which he could ever bring forth as
deserving of praise, and if he does have it, he has received it: the *donum,* gift,
endowment. The significance in relation to oneself, of which one can dispose,
is a *donum Dei* [gift of God].[229] (A special enactment of experience, cannot
be viewed merely objectively.)

Thus it comes about that before God, it is rather that *melior est* "ille qui
laudavit, quam iste qui laudatus est" [better is "he who praised, than he who
is praised"],[230] for *illi (qui laudavit)* "placuit in homine donum Dei" [he (who
praised) "is pleased by God's gift to the human being"].[231] He has the genuine
direction of the *placere,* the genuine mode of preferring; he performs the
praising in view of the *donum* as the *donum Dei*—that is, he really refers the
laudare to God, the *summum bonum.*

By contrast, "huic [qui laudatus est] amplius placuit donum hominis quam
Dei" [the other (who is praised) is better pleased with the gift of human beings
than of God].[232] The *donum hominis* [gift of human beings] is the *laudare,*
the *laudatio* itself (as stemming from human beings). Augustine interprets this
more closely: "at ille plus gaudet sibi laudari se, quam ipsum donum habere
unde laudatur" [but he finds more joy in being praised than in having that gift
for which he is praised].[233] Finding joy in being praised as such is a taking-
oneself-to-be-important, and in the context of *tentatio,* it is a falling, since the
human being, according to its significance, is a "nothingness" before God.
Life in the communal world—that is, here in the possibility of being praised—

228. Ibid.
229. "gratia" [gratitude], cf. p. 176 ("iustitia" [justice])!
230. *Confessiones* X 36, 59; PL 32, p. 804.
231. Ibid.
232. Ibid.
233. Ibid.

contains in itself the danger of an unexpected taking-oneself-to-be-important. (Finding joy in the *donum* is the highest duty and by no means convenient!)

How, then, does Augustine himself stand in relation to this *tentatio*? What does he have to confess? "Quid, nisi delectari me laudibus?" [What, but that I am delighted with praise?"][234] I am open to it, I find joy in it, but "amplius ipsa veritate quam laudibus" [with the truth more than with the praise].[235] *Video quid eligam*, I see, I am clear about, what I choose and prefer if I have the choice: "utrum malim furens [passionate, having let go, unbridled, releasing the *voluptates* (pleasures)], aut in omnibus rebus errans, ab omnibus hominibus laudari; an constans [keeping to oneself, secure], et in veritate certissimus, ab omnibus vituperari" [of being praised by all human beings, though wrong and mad (passionate, having let go, unbridled, releasing the pleasures), or erring in everything; or of being reproached by all, though steadfast (keeping to oneself, secure) and most certain in having the truth].[236] (*Veritas* [truth]: (1) Security, steadfastness; (2) absolute validity existing in itself, directly a being; both things do not have to go together; (3) priority of the foundation.)

In veritate certissimus constans [steadfast in most certain truth] is a *bonum* [good]. "Verum tamen nollem ut vel augeret mihi gaudium cujuslibet boni mei suffragatio oris alieni" [Yet I truly do not want the vote born of another to increase my joy for whatever is good in me],[237] that is, I see the full value of truth, and that this *bonum* is a *donum Dei,* and that it does not need help from applause, privilege, and admiration from others. And I do not want it, because this *laudatio* does not increase the *gaudium* [joy], but only deforms it. *Verum tamen nollem, sed auget, fateor* [I truly do not want it, but, I admit, it increases], and yet, I have to admit, at the heart of it I do enjoy it more, that is, I let myself be drawn away from genuine, concerned joy.

The *vituperatio* [reproach] is a sign for my not being able to maintain myself in the pure enactment of joy, in its genuine sense. "Vituperatio minuit" [reproach diminishes it],[238] (assails my joy, that is, attending to the reproach, taking it—and thus myself, the one in question—to be important, I experience a diminishing of the joy, which would not be possible if I lived in the pure enactment of this joy). The reproach, after all, makes me stagger, and makes me look to others. I do not keep purely to the genuine joy; "ista miseria ma perturbor" [this my misery disturbs me],[239] and so I am confused. I am no longer sure of myself and fall into the communal world. "Subintrat mihi ex-

234. *Confessiones* X 37, 61; PL 32, p. 805.
235. Ibid.
236. Ibid.
237. Ibid.
238. Ibid.
239. Ibid.

cusatio" [Excuses enter me subliminally],[240] and an excuse sneaks its way into me then, and pushes itself in. I seek to rescue and justify myself by saying that it is not really my fault that I am falling: "human beings simply are like that," it is "nature" and things like that. "Quae qualis sit, tu scis, Deus; nam me incertum facit" [How good the excuse is, you know, God; for it makes me uncertain].[241]

So what is the authentic conduct in the communal-worldly life context, in what is experienced, in being praised? One ought not to see oneself as the one who is praised, but as the one who praises, and indeed how one praises! To rejoice in one's genuine ability to praise; then, that he is so far along as to see, value, and thus validate, a genuine *donum (Dei)* [gift (of God)]; in this joy I am myself co-concerned only for the *bonum* [good] as such; *de profectu delectari* or *de malo* (in the *vituperatio*) *contristari* [to take delight in progress or to be saddened by the failure (in the reproach)].

In this *tentatio,* the direction of overcoming is precisely a genuine giving-oneself-over to the communal world, but a giving enacted from the clear position of one's own in the facticity of one's own life; such giving can never be proven in—even the most radical—mere giving-over to the objective in every sense.

In the *continentia* [continence]—which, in the experience of *tentatio,* represents the mode and direction of the overcoming and the halting of the fall—we do not only find the *cohibere amorem ab aliqua* [refraining from love of things]. Rather, what is also demanded is the *iustitia* [justice], the *collatio, positio amoris quo* [bringing-together, positioning of love toward], love's bringing-toward, leading-toward, and genuine direction of concern. *Iustitia* is the authentically and originally sense-like directedness ("piety"; cf. Luther's understanding of *iustitia*), in its entirety, of the factical experience of significance. (This original sense of enactment and of existence of *iustitia* has to be separated even more and entirely from the axiologization.—The How of the enactment of the endurance of *tentatio.* It is a *certamen* [competition] between two directions of loving.)

The direction of pleasing points toward the communal world; before it itself, a taking-oneself-to-be-important is enacted in regard to a *bonum* which one supposedly is and has in oneself.

Now, this *placere aliis* [pleasing others] may be lacking, and also such a *communal-worldly* validation of oneself may even be repressed and explicitly kept at bay. (Toward the outside, in the communal world, overcoming *amor laudis* [love of praise]; but it can have settled itself all the more tenaciously,

240. Ibid.
241. Ibid.

primarily determining one's own existence [*Eigendasein*] and the sense thereof.)

§ 16. Self-importance
Chapter 39

"Etiam [yet] intus est aliud in eodem genere tentationis malum, quo inanescunt qui placent sibi de se" [Yet, within us is another evil, in the same kind of temptation by which those who please themselves in themselves become vain].[242] In this kind of temptation, there is the possibility of a falling which is such that the self—and with it, the *Dasein* of the individual in general—becomes vain and dissipates into the void and into nothingness. *Sibi placens* [pleasing oneself]: validating oneself to oneself, taking oneself to be important to oneself, ascribing a *bonum* [good] to oneself; the *gaudium (delectatio)* [joy (delight)] is directed toward the self-world; in making an effort at *beata vita* [the happy life], the self-world is taken to be important.

Here, the enactment of experience is such that—always in the concrete form of an enacted past of one's own—one's own *self-world* (that is, the sphere of one's action, one's occupation, the possibilities and abilities of accomplishment) is presented to oneself (this is already in itself a mode of self-importance) in order to explicitly take oneself to be important in one's presented self-world.

In this, a number of different possibilities result, possibilities which in themselves always indicate a certain mode of one's own *Dasein,* insofar as these modes are seized as, in each case, the decisive How of the enactment of experience. "Different possibilities" as different modes of the *gaudere* [rejoicing] to oneself (pleasing oneself, thus taking oneself as important, thus rejoicing in a *bonum* or a quasi-*bonum*):

1. "De non bonis quasi bonis" [In not-good things, as if they were good][243]: thus one takes as important what one "has done," what one "does" but what cannot really be seen as a genuine good. Not only does one take goods, especially selfly directed ones, as important, but one advances the tendency of this self-importance to the point at which one, first of all, marks a non-good a good. One is *conceited* [*bildet sich etwas ein*]. (With the "*bonum*," of course, we are always dealing here with a *bonum* as the endowment of the self *qua* self, thus not with, for instance, the disposing and possessing of worldly objective goods which the self also "has." "Existence." Self—as this

---

242. *Confessiones* X 39, 64; PL 32, p. 806.
243. Ibid.

singular self which I myself am, and not according to the general What of objective properties as such an object, but the *How* of "am.")

2. "Verum etiam de bonis tuis quasi suis" [But also taking your goods as if they were one's own],[244] or now: even if genuine insight into the character of the good exists, and if a genuine good belongs to the self ("being good": authentic existing!)—which, as such, can only be from God—it is, to oneself, taken as self-appropriated, as having been given to the self by itself (*Dasein*— existence), having elevated oneself to this position and this level of existence.

3. "Aut etiam sicut de tuis, sed tanquam ex meritis suis" [Or as if your goods, but as given to oneself for one's own merits]:[245] even if this self-importance is given up to the extent that the "good" (existence) is recognized as not appropriated by oneself, as not created and worked for by the self, one's own self is still taken as important. For the self is, and takes itself for, such a self that has elevated itself to the position, not in order to give itself the good, but to be worthy of the gift, and somehow to *deserve* the *bonum* and its ascription to oneself.

4. "Aut etiam sicut ex tua gratia, non tamen socialiter gaudentes, sed aliis invidentes ea" [Or as if from your grace, and yet not rejoicing in it socially, but grudging it to others]:[246] but even if the self does not ascribe the desert to itself, and confesses to possess the good without deserving it—*ex gratia* [from grace]—the *gaudium boni* [joy of the good] may be such that the self finds joy not in sharing it with others, in co-rejoicing with others about oneself—in which case the self is had, as it were, objectively, separated from having itself—but in having this undeserved good enviously for oneself, keeping it locked up and not wishing it for others. (Con-ceit [*Ein-bildung*], *superbia, amor sui, peccatum* [pride, self-love, sin]!)

(In the end, the self-world becomes a communal world, as in (1) and (2), self-absorption in world, likewise of the communal world in world, possible connections of enactment among (1), (2), (3).—We are dealing with phenomena which the axiologization, in its most exaggerated form, precisely overlooks, although here they are still grasped mostly in an axiologizing manner.— The direction of the *placere* and the *gaudium* is moved into the self, but precisely in such a way that the self-world here becomes the still dominant communal world. Precisely in this "worldly" positioning—holding before oneself [*Vor-halt*]—the self is lost.—The meaning of the authentic fall from the self: this losing or never gaining and [. . .].* On the other hand, precisely the overcoming of the *tentatio* can lead to insight and self-revelation. For what is

244. Ibid.
245. Ibid.
246. Ibid.
*[An illegible word.]

overcoming? A genuine enacting or understanding of enactment. Explicatively: *tentatio* as an existential complex of expression.)

It is a peculiarity of these four modes of self-importance that a genuine appreciation of the *bonum* is indeed enacted "more and more"—the *bonum* not only as such, but in its "Whence" and "How" and "Why" of being given as a gift—but that the self always sees itself before itself, positing [*vor-setzt*] its own self-world to itself, and taking it to be decisively important, even if only in *such* a way that it is the *one in* which and *before* which grace realizes itself. But this means that it is precisely in that mode in which the self no longer attributes any achievements to itself, that everything is released in rejoicing before God. For, ultimately and first of all, the concern leaps off precisely here in a self-importance, and indeed in such a way that the enactment of concern becomes novel: a positing of this in itself genuine experience or existence *to* one's own self-world. Indeed, this occurs in such a way that through this hidden "movement" everything falls into the void, *inanescit* [becomes vain or void], and everything is invalidated in regard to the *summum bonum* (before God). In the last and most decisive and purest concern for oneself lurks the possibility of the most groundless dive [*abgründigsten Sturzes*], and of authentically losing oneself. ("Groundless," because the dive has no longer any hold, and it cannot be enacted before anything, so that one could finally turn it into a secular importance after all. Here lies what is really satanic in temptation! There is no alien control here, no assistance, and the falling itself is something which could be turned into a big thing.—The self-concern appears easy and convenient, interesting and superior as "egoism," at the same time destructive of the "general good," a dangerous individualism. Really: self-concern is precisely the most difficult, taking oneself to be less and less important by engaging oneself all the more; positing to oneself precisely an "objectity" in the face of which that of the "generality" is mere playfulness, a convenient getting-done of the things themselves and of the beings and their connections.)

Augustine clearly sees the difficulty and the ultimately "anxiety-producing character" of *Dasein* in such having-of-oneself (in full facticity). "In his omnibus atque hujusmodi periculis et laboribus vides tremorem cordis mei; et vulnera mea magis subinde a te sanari, quam mihi non infligi sentio" [In all these and other similar perils and toils, You see the trembling of my heart; and I often feel my wounds to be healed by You, rather than inflicted upon me].[247]

---

247. Ibid.

§ 17. Molestia *[Trouble]*—the Facticity of Life

a) The How of the Being of Life

Without indicating explicitly the interpretory-methodical context, and without pointing out explicitly how the object is determined more closely *in principle* according to its How, we now want to predelineate the direction of interpretation with regard to the phenomenal connections indicated by *molestia* and *exploratio*. The interpretation as a whole "runs" in such a way that it now takes the return route, and indeed in such a way that the explication becomes visibly more original. (*Tota vita—tentatio* [The whole life—temptation[248]]: "Non ut ipse discat, sed ut quod in homine latet aperiat (for the human being itself, having oneself) [We do not learn for ourselves, but so that what hides in humans becomes apparent (for the human being itself, having oneself)].[249] "In tentatione apparet, qualis sit homo" [In temptation appears what kind of a human being one is].[250]— "Nescit se homo, nisi in tentatione discat se" [You do not know a human being unless you have gotten to know him in temptation].[251])

Molestia: a burden of life, something which pulls life down; and what is peculiar to the burden lies precisely in the fact that *molestia* can pull down. In this, the "can" is formed by the enactment that belongs to each experience itself. Thus: this possibility "grows" *the more life lives;* this possibility grows, *the more life comes to itself.*

These two determinations belong together; not only insofar as a certain *How of the being of life* has been posited here from which talk of *molestia* is meaningful at all;—in the end, a radical self-concern before God. (Leading to the objects in strictly phenomenological explication!)

Thus, a certain *How* of the being of life—what it means here: life, *my* life "is"—gives direction to the complexes of sense. But the two determinations belong together more concretely in this way (The belonging-together of *esse, nosse, amare* [to be, to know, to love]—the real prestructuring [*Prästruktion*], preforming basic experience—is precisely what is decisive. Worldly objectity as such, also already significance, also *nosse* [to know] as such, likewise *amare* [to love]; all [three of them]—as self-willed—constitute the possibilities of *tentatio*. But they also constitute, at the same time, the world as that in which I live in this or that way at all.):

248. Editor's note: This probably refers to *Epistulae* XCV 2; PL 33, p. 353: "Ecce unde vita humana super terram tota tentatio est" [See, from this, human life on earth is all temptation].

249. Editor's note: The *Index Generalis* (PL 46, p. 627) refers thus to *Sermones* II 2–3; PL 38, p. 28 and 29.

250. Editor's note: The *Index Generalis* (PL 46, p. 628) refers thus to *Tractatus in Joannis evangelium* XLVI 10; PL 35, p. 1730.

251. *Sermones* II 3, 3; PL 38, p. 29.

1. The *"the more life lives"* means: the more fully the *directions* of experience of facticity are enacted. In the first instance, this does not so much concern the fullness of *what* is experienced, but the directions of experience as such—the surrounding-wordly, communal-worldly, and self-worldly directions—; the more *these* as such are full (that is, the more they surrender to themselves their complex of enactment, or the complex of enactment proper to their facticity), the more the full sense is explained historically factically. [This means:] The more the *curare* engages itself in every direction and pulls alongside itself the others according to their sense of experience in the respective engagement.—This "more" isolates: it seems to be an objective quantification, but not in the genuine connection with (2). (This pre-separation belonging-together is no objective belonging-together, but an enactment-like, historical one, an "it can"—horizon, passage of time—in the most radical sense, *the* happening of enactment which has to form itself, and especially itself, and which is only in the enactmental self-formation.)

2. The *"the more life comes to itself"* is the second determination and indicates that the *being* of life somehow also consists in the fact that it is had: the more life experiences that it is itself, its *being,* that is at stake in its full self-enactment. (The categorial sense-structure of this being is the problem for which the executed interpretation should provide a certain cultural-historical, phenomenal situation. Regarding the concept of "life," cf. the critique of Jaspers in the lecture "Phenomenology of Intuition and of Expression."[252])

Now the life in which something like *molestia* can be experienced at all, in which—as the life growing in itself, coming to itself—the possibilities of *molestia* grow, is a life whose being is *grounded* in a radical having-of-oneself. It is a having-of-oneself that takes effect only in enactment, and fully only in *its* historical facticity.

b) *Molestia*—the Endangerment of Having-of-Oneself

In this tendency toward a radical factical historical having-of-oneself in its specific self-clarity, the concrete "worldly" experiential complex of enactment first of all becomes fully visible (cf. *tentatio*). The directions of experience as directions of experience, their possibilities as possibilities of this factical experience in its own enactment, and that means the sense of *molestia,* are determined by the authentic How of life itself.

Insofar as *molestia* is experienced in its own sense, it is not something like

---

252. Martin Heidegger, *Phänomenologie der Anschauung und des Ausdrucks. Theorie der philosophischen Begriffsbildung* Early Freiburg Lecture Summer Semester 1920. *Gesamtausgabe* vol. 59, ed. Claudius Strube. Frankfurt, Klostermann, 1993, p. 10.

an objective equipment of human being, an objective quality in an existing something, which one should cut off and throw away. All Greek pagan ascesis views human beings like this, and so does every Christian ascesis which remains entangled in Greek antiquity, according to the cultural-historical situations.

Molestia: a How of experiencing, a burden to, and an endangering of, having-of-oneself—in full facticity. This having-of-oneself is, as factical, such that it enacts this endangering itself and forms it [*sich ein-bildet*]. In the concrete and genuine enactment of experience, it gives itself the possibility of falling, but in its ownmost radical self-concern, it gives itself at the same time the full, concrete, factical "opportunity" to arrive at the *being* of its ownmost life.

Thus, what is decisive is the factical having-of-oneself in forming-out [*Ausbilden*] and forming [*Ein-bilden*] of the possibility as the "opportunity" to pass the test of *tentatio,* [. . .]* and of the enactment [. . .],** grasping the authentic direction of concern of one's own factical *Dasein.*

Thus, *molestia* determines itself according to the How of having-oneself in the How of the factical enactment of experience. (How "life" has itself, how it *can* have itself, historically factically.)

1. Having-of-oneself—enacted, intended in that of "life"—is the concern for the *being* of itself. The self is crucial, it is important. Hidden in this thus lies the self-importance. *Molestia* goes along. In self-concern, the self forms—in the How of its ownmost being—the radical possibility of falling, but at the same time the "opportunity" to win itself. Thus, our life must somehow *concern* [*angehen*] us ourselves. (Fore-having, having in "life."—The How of "being," being of facticity.—*Quaestionem fieri sibi* [I have made a question of myself]. Fore-question, a questioning oneself that does not stand out.)

2. "Propter quaedem humanae societatis officia necessarium est amari et timeri ab hominibus" [Because certain offices in human society make it necessary to be loved and feared by people].253 Thus, the communal-worldly enactment of experience, the co-experiencing in and for the communal world, aims in itself at a certain standing-in-validity. As such, it in turn carries with itself, and forms, the *molestia,* the possibility of the communal-worldly desire to be validated.

3. Factical experiencing, the worldly one, a mode of taking-cognizance-of, a looking-about-oneself, the formation of the possibility of the self-willed mere looking-about-oneself precisely in the seriousness of the radical effort at confronting and desiring-to-know the world. (The How of having-of-

*[An indecipherable abbreviation.]
**[Several illegible words.]
253. *Confessiones* X 36, 59; PL 32, p. 804.

oneself.—Subjectivism, relativism are very mistaken categories. They argue from a position that does not even see the phenomena about which it speaks.— These Hows "are there," not objectively like things, but "historically" there: in historical enactment of the object, cultural-historically, in historical enactment.)

4. Factical experiencing, dealing-with, use, enjoyment, care for daily life, *reficere ruinam* [to restore the decay], procreation, preservation. In the radical effort lurks the bustling activity.

(The fore-giving of phenomena [*Phänomenvorgabe*] is always a factical interpretation motivated in enactment.—The question is not such that we orient ourselves toward a "How" that accidentally [came] to stand out and is formed-out in itself. Rather, it is asked which "can"—grounded in the facticity of a genuine enactment of a possible cultural history—is present for us factically and historically. The "can" comprises in itself the objectity (an objectity rooted in something altogether different) of the existential in the direction of its ownmost sense [?]!)

What am I? *Quaestio mihi factus sum. Quid amo?* [I have become a question to myself. What do I love?] "Questionable" in the experiential directions, in experiencing and having myself. "Life"—a How of having, and indeed an experiencing of *tentationes*. It is a *tentatio*, it forms the possibility of losing and of winning oneself. "Life": a How of a being of a determinate structure and categorial expression. (The having-oneself of life, having oneself, *exploratio, quaestio mihi factus sum*, "what and how I *am*."—Dependence of the possibility of explication upon the historical, cultural-historical, and enactment-historical level and foreconception of interpretation.)

The having and fore-having that does not stand out, in the factical experience of life, in a certain historically objective, factical situation and possibility. Life finds itself in such a way, without it being necessary that the historical How and Where and Whither of its own facticity is also found as already explicitly standing out and demarcated.

The complex of motifs of the standing-out of life's having-of-oneself against the factical experience of life. [We are] by no means close to the self yet. In a radical sense, it is not really necessary that it ever comes to that.

This standing-out and the articulation of the foreconception, the determinateness of the foreconceptions and the changing foreconception from the surrounding world and the communal world—not standing out. The breakthrough of the historical and the first self-aspect of life that stands out!

APPENDIX I

Notes and Sketches for the Lecture Course

Augustine, "Confessiones"—"confiteri," "interpretari"
[on § 7 b]

"Interpretation" as a determinately characterized interpretation of oneself, in such a way that that *in front of* which one becomes familiar to "oneself" is not only the empty "in-front-of," but leads the authentic interpreting, making it precisely something special. "Special"—[that means here:]

—concretely naming possible stages of the interpretations in formal indication;

—then showing how the *confiteri* [confessing] is motivated in its basic starting point: *quaestio mihi factus sum* [I have become a question to myself].

Grasping the theological-philosophical "writings"—*Sermones, Epistolae* [sermons, letters], polemical pieces, and so forth—from this viewpoint as what has been interpreted determinately in *communal-worldly* complexes of experience and in the *surrounding-worldly* state of knowledge.

To what extent a new lead [*Duktus*] enters the theological concepts, to what extent this tendency succumbs not only to the Church, but to Greek antiquity!

On the Destruction of Confessiones X
[on § 7 b]

Memoria not radically, existentially, as enactment, but Greek, falling in regard to the *content,* not how "it was" with him and how it "is" in a "was," but separately, what is present in itself, that truth has its "standing" [*Bestand*] unchanged, toward which he then throws himself away and into which he orders himself. But in this, always radically existential movements.

Enactmental Complex of the Question
[on § 8 b]

How the self wins its existence, and in what existence consists, already through the *searching:* placing oneself somehow before God or *vita beata* [the happy life]. In searching, it places itself in the absolute distance, and tries to win the distance. Explicated phenomenologically?

"The criterion for the self is always: that directly before which it is a self; but that in turn is the definition of 'criterion.' "[1]

"The greater the conception of God, the more self there is; the more self, the greater the conception of God."[2]

Tentatio *[Temptation]*
[on § 12 a]

[The *tentatio* is] no event, but an existential sense of enactment, a How of experiencing. What is it about? The sense in which experiencing is encountered. Not such that it is present self-sufficiently, significantly, not in absorption, but that a "possibility" is experienced, that *significance* refers, in terms of content, toward something else, cf. "conflict." Experiencing possibility, living in the open, keeping open, opening authentically. Prestruction [*Praestruktion*]—"intentionality."

The How of the breaking apart of *tentatio.* "Authentically" forming. For whom is it truly present in the enactmental renewal? For those who radically become "questions" to themselves. An opening in relation to oneself. *Possibility* is the true "burden." *Difficult! Vita = tentatio* [Life = temptation]. (Experiencing *tentatio*—"passing," "falling"—does not simply happen, but is experienced. What I do with it! Whether I appropriate it in such a way that it opens up only possibilities? The falling, the ability to fall and the future of falling, increase the anxiety and reveal: *disco* [I learn]!)

In this context, how is Augustine's "classification" and sequence of stages to be explicated? Increase? of *"possibilities,"* of "burden" (phenomenon of the *"transitus"* [transition]). In how far? Insofar as *solid reality* disappears and *freedom*—in terms of content—becomes more one's own. That is, the modes of *tentatio* in which it becomes accessible.

Experiencing *possibility,* which means viewing oneself fully in enactment in misery, that it "is" stronger, and that existing means to live radically in possibility, and also "objectively": *"being left open"* [dahin *"gestellt sein"*]. *Receiving existence!*

Significances of the surrounding world, communal world, self-world—"limits of life"—negligible in the face of anxiety, of possibility.

I. *Being honest in the face of possibility.*

II. *Administering, in an orderly manner, the discoveries of honesty.*

1. S. Kierkegaard, *Sickness unto Death,* p. 79.
2. Ibid., p. 80.

[Oneri mihi sum *(I am a burden to myself)*]
[on § 12 a]

"Cum inhaesero tibi ex omni me [. . .] et viva erit vita mea" [When I will have adhered to you with my whole self . . . and my life shall be truly alive].[3] My life is *authentic life,* I exist. When I adhere to you, with the last part of myself, when I put everything radically onto you—*vita erit tota plena te* [my entire life will be full of you]—all relations of life, the whole facticity permeated by you, enacted in such a way that all *enactment* is enacted *before* you.

Since that is not the case, "oneri mihi sum,"[4] I am a burden to myself, fall back, *non sublevas* [not lifted up]. I fall away from there and am unable to authentically search. (How this is connected to what came before.)

The "burden" lies in the "strife" [*Widerstreit*] in which I live, *contendunt* [in strife]: *laetitia flendae—maerores laetandi* [regrettable joys—joyful sorrows].[5] Do I not live in joys about which I should weep, and sorrows about which I should rejoice; they are at strife.[6] "Et ex qua parte stet victoria nescio" [And on which side is the victory, I do not know].[7]

"Contendunt maerores mei mali cum gaudiis bonis" [My sorrows over my evil and my good joys are in strife with one another].[8] Sinful sorrow, despair—optimistic joy.[9]—*Vulnera non abscondo* [I do not hide the wounds]: being torn apart.

Numquid non tentatio est vita humana—sine ullo interstitio? [Is not human life all temptation—without intermission?] Finding oneself between these possibilities that impose themselves, and over which one does not reign.—The comfortable ones do not see this; rather, one is the replacement of the other; they let themselves be borne in an unemphasized light-heartedness and tepidness. But those who experience it *seek* to fix the end, to gain a stand.

Certamen: in multa defluximus [Strife: scattered into the many]. Hopeless.—Thus, *iubes continentiam. Tota spes mea non nisi in magna valde continentia tua* [You command continence. All my hope is nowhere but in Your very great continence].[10]

Out of the *dispersion.* And this dispersion is founded in like manner in the basic tendency of *timere* [fearing] and *desiderare* [desiring]. Both lie in the *concern* for the *secular;* and that is one's own *irruere—defluere* [rushing into—being scattered]: gliding down, sinking down, in the sense of slackening.

---

3. *Confessiones* X 28, 39; PL 32, p. 795.
4. Ibid.
5. Burden: the falling apart, splintering. No continuity, existence.
6. and this concerns: *gaudium/maeror (vita)* [joy/sorrow (life)]
7. *Confessiones* X 28, 39; PL 32, p. 795.
8. Ibid.
9. and these are not superficial moods.
10. Editor's note: The original has *"misericordia"* instead of *"continentia."*

In the *defluxus,* I give myself, and create for myself, a situation that is, in a determinate sense, closed, a situation that carries a possibility in itself, but its tendency is directed toward *delectatio* [delight], bustling activity; only insofar as it is present does *timere* and *desiderare* emerge.

"Prospera in adversis desidero, adversa in prosperis timeo" [In adversity I desire prosperity, in prosperity I fear adversity].[11] Because in experience I have a certain knowledge of how things always go (according to what came before), and because I somehow always stand within experiences, a fallen *historical* knowledge in tending toward *delectatio.*

Experience is somehow always co-present in *desiderium, situs anima* (as *vox) media* [desire, lying in the middle of the soul (as voice)]. There is no *medius locus,*[12] *ubi non sit tentatio* [middle place, where there is no temptation]. In how far? What is this? *Nescio in qua parte stet victoria* [I do not know on which side is the victory].

Maerores laetandi—laetitia flendae—maerores mei mali cum gaudiis bonis [joyful sorrows—regrettable joys—my sorrows over my evil and my good joys]—and, in addition: *nescio* [I do not know].

1. Conflict within factical life itself—in the *defluere*—the unrest—being thrown.

2. Conflict within oneself again easy[?]. (*Timor—maeror laetandus* [Fear— joyful sorrow]. Or is it *maeror malus* [evil sorrow]? Do I have it such that I ought to rejoice in it? *Laetitia flendae* [regrettable joys] or *gaudium bonum* [good joys]? Is it a joy about which I ought to weep?)

3. *Nescio* [I do not know], where victory is; I do not know what *will be* and what the outcome will be. (*Tentatio* and the historical. How the historical raises itself to the *nescio*—how I experience myself—*quastio factus sum* [I have become a question].—"Conflict" objective, it is [. . .],* which [. . .]** historical horizon—existential intentionality. The taking-a-stance itself, the How of appropriation, of the taking-along in *timere* and *desiderare* is conflictual, and these in turn are in conflict among themselves.

[on § 13 a]

Reaching back to *iubere continentiam (et iustitiam)* [commanding continence (and justice)][13]—related to the *concupiscentia* that turns in three directions

---

11. *Confessiones* X 28, 39; PL 32, p. 796.
12. No *medius locus* between opposites.
*[Two words illegible.]
**[One word illegible.]
13. "Genuine" positing of value! *Decus iustum* [just virtue]. "Nam qui non [intus] agitis [aliquid bona], non vos haec movent" [As for you who are not driven by (something good within yourselves), you are not moved by this] (*Confessiones* X, chapter 33, 50). Condition of understanding!

(following 1 John 2:15, 16, 17): 1. *concupiscentia carnis* [desire of the flesh], 2. *concupiscentia oculorum* [desire of the eyes], 3. *ambitio saeculi* [secular ambition].

Malitiae diei [the evils of the day]. They are present and tempting as *deliciae* [delights] and *suavitates* [loveliness], and one turns them into enjoyments, whereas they are really *the* danger for me. What is base pulls down, turns the will into a servant, and has it confirm the falling as what is authentic. What does this complex of movements mean factically, historically, existentially? (What happens and occurs; and what I enact.—No juxtaposition, but existential-phenomenologically[?] the authentic *facticity,* not biologically, objectively isolated, but concrete life, "marriage"[?]—eating, drinking, meals, "teatime"—concrete, surrounding-worldly significance.

Temptation *lurks* precisely in what belongs to my facticity, what is with me and in which I am. "Temptation is *historically* present."

Vita = tentatio tota [Life = all temptation]. In the factical, I slide into possible self-individuations.

Against the opening up of possibilities, against the genuine self-possession and being of *vita, delectatio* [life, delight]. (Chapter 32: experience as historical; *tentatio* belongs here, to be interpreted, contrarily, on the basis of *tentatio* toward the historical. *Experience*—opening up *tentatio,* but *nescio* [I do not know] what will be.—Existential motivation of the destruction [. . .]* from the basic experience of being-hidden-from-oneself and concealing oneself again in life—the blocking off.)

This increases more and more so that the *most uncanny power* of *tentatio* opens [itself] precisely in the most radical, genuine self-concern, so that only here has the most radical situation of self-experience been won, in a direction of consideration in which the self knows neither in nor out—*quaestio mihi factus sum* [I have become a question to myself]. Cf. end of chapter 40! (In the end, "what I am," my "facticity" is the *strongest temptation* and the counter-attack on my existence and existing; it is the self-projection toward oneself of the genuine possibilities—that is, more precisely, the *concern for this complex of enactment;* in it, I move in a somehow falling manner.)

Tentatio
[on § 13 a, b]

Concupiscentia: a direction in itself, directions of concrete, factical experience, of the full self-facticity of life.

The *direction of experiencing* indicates: something possible, *opens up pos-*

---

*[One word illegible.]

sibilities; but only if they are experienced as directions, that is, if the facticity of life itself lives in a directed enactment—as directed. The "as directed" may be illuminated in different ways; as always, in the "as directed," that is = "directed *thus,*" it is a to-ward and an away-from. The "away-from" is itself co-experienced, and with it so is the "away-from-*what.*" (*The possession— one which understands radically—of the "as" in the* quaestio sibi fieri [being made a question]: a *sense-genetically,* factically enacted connection between the "as" in a merely objective, absolute taking-cognizance-of—somehow also possessing it carelessly, but pushing it away at the same time—and the authentic approach to the "as," that is, to one-self.)

The tempting or the being-tempted is an experiencing in which an experiential direction, *as thus* directed in itself—by virtue of its full sense in this full facticity—*tempts* this facticity and addresses while attracting it, searchingly *pre*ferring it in the self-direction, and indeed in such a way that the authentic *cura* [concern] is lost in this. (This *curare* in every *concupiscentia* into which the individual *"lets himself enter"* [*"ein-läßt"*][14]—letting oneself go and enter—leads into the significance of the world, delightful, curious self-significance. In this, the "wherein," whereinto, itself has a pull [*fortziehend*]. The letting-go is now itself led; it only keeps alive the direction in general— "further," "more"—but it leads into the *world,* and indeed into the historical facticity; therewith, the latter undergoes a shrinking and "finally opens up" [*"geht letztlich auf"*].)

The authentic *cura* [concern] is factically somehow present in the "away-from" and the "away-from-what," for life, which is in general *so far advanced* that it stands at all in temptation, that is, a life that somehow searches its facticity and that has a clarity of its own.

Two principally different interpretations of molestia [trouble]: they are connected to the possibility of seeing the occurring phenomena at all.

1. *Molestia* as a characteristic [*Beschaffenheit*] or objective equipment, as objective burden, standing there and operating as a thing. (A hardening [?] of oneself in this: making disappear through objective means—casting off and removing—one's own being itself a *condition* [*Zustand*], an objective characteristic.)

2. *Molestia* as "opportunity" of seriousness, an opportunity with oneself, pre-forming it *as* such first of all, rendering it experienceable to *myself as* facticity, grasping it *existentially,* possessing life in memory and experiencing in this way, increasing the seriousness. (Bringing oneself to encounter, and forming out, the *existential* possibility as the authentic one.)

14. T[erm]

It is entirely lop-sided to represent the radical self-possession as a hyper-reflected solipsism, or something like it. The self "is" the self of the full historical facticity, the self in its world, with that in which it lives; thus, the "possessing" in conformity to its relational multiplicity and its multiplicity of enactment—not only multiplicity, but historical factical connection; and the "possession" is no temporary, quietistic and leisurely one, but is enactment-historical.

Only in this "opportunity" formed in the existential enactment: "opportunity" is a *character of enactment,* [. . .].* The giving of existential sense also for the "*existentially full* objectivity" (fate, predestination, etc.) that has been experienced for *existence.*

The authentic concept of "*facticity*" cannot be determined on the basis of an objectivity that has been posited in advance and that is grasped attitudinally, but in the existentially enacted interpretation of a How of "being" from the existentially experienced content.

The Phenomenon of tentatio
[on § 13 c]

[The *tentatio*] arises (The How of arising belongs to it, as an experiencing viewed phenomenologically; not objectively, [as] material, biological emergence, which has no tentative meaning.) from experiences that open up into significances whose following and enactment of appropriation belong themselves to historical factical existence; they also make up existence. Thus they are really placed in the genuine enactment of existence which stands in the possibility of falling so that of the seemingly authentic enactments of existence—*deliciae, hilaritas* [delights, hilarity], one's own choosing and deciding—the factical [. . .]** *molestiae* [troubles] are turned, through seemingly genuine enactments of existence, into *false,* non-genuine significances.

The significance can be placed away in different ways, for example, being unmarried; as the opposite: not eating or drinking.

Still, it is decisive for its meaning that it can be experienced as such: being firmly attached to a certain *apprehension* of value.

The danger of the axiologization of the connections of phenomena is as fateful as the theoretical-regional forming-out—by the way, these two go together.

In how far the *tentatio* is a genuine *existential.*

---

*[One word illegible.]
**[One word illegible.]

Light

[on § 13 f]

"Multimodo allapsu blanditur mihi aliud agenti, et eam non advertenti. Insinuat autem se ita vehementur, ut si repente subtrahatur [transitus!], cum desiderio requiratur; et si diu absit, contristat animum." [Gliding by in many
forms, enticing me while I am busy with something else, taking no notice of
it. For it insinuates itself so forcibly, if it is withdrawn suddenly (transition!),
it is sought with longing; and if it is absent for long, it makes the soul sad.][15]
Falling, significant possession. ("Non autem sentio sine quo esse aut aequo
animo, aut aegre possim, nisi cum abfuerit." [For I cannot know whether my
soul can be balanced or upset to be without something, unless it is absent.][16])

"Ipsa est lux, una est, et unum omnes qui vident et amant eam." [This is
the light, it is one, and one are all those who see it and love it.][17]

"Foras sequentes [homines] quod faciunt." [Outwardly (humans) follow
what they make.][18]

"Quem invenirem qui me reconciliaret tibi?" [Who could be found to reconcile me to You?][19] Depravity—far from God.

Molestia. "Hic esse valeo, nec volo; illic volo, nec valeo; miser utrobique."
[Here I am able to stay, but I do not wish it; there I wish to be, but I am not
able—miserable in both places.][20] That, being by myself, I move away from
You further and further.

Anxiety before one's ownmost deceiver within oneself.

Weaning oneself from the calculations of significance!

In Augustine, not everything breaks through clearly! Because he attached
himself too temptingly in *frui* [enjoyment], but within it!

"Guilt is a more concrete conception, which becomes more and more possible in the relation of possibility to freedom."[21] "But whoever becomes guilty
also becomes guilty of that which occasioned the guilt. For guilt never has an
external occasion, and whoever yields to temptation is himself guilty of the
temptation."[22]

15. *Confessiones* X 34, 51; PL 32, p. 800 f.
16. *Confessiones* X 37, 60; PL 32, p. 805.
17. *Confessiones* X 34, 52; PL 32, p. 801.
18. *Confessiones* X 34, 53; PL 32, p. 801.
19. *Confessiones* X 42, 67; PL 32, p. 807.
20. *Confessiones* X 40, 65; PL 32, p. 807.
21. S. Kierkegaard, *The Concept of Anxiety,* trans. Reidar Thomte. Princeton, N.J.: Princeton
University Press, 1980, p. 109.
22. Ibid.

Deus lux
[on § 13 g]

Deus lux [God the light]: highest object and highest self-brightness—"knowledge."

Deus dilectio [God the love]: authentic existing.

Deus summum bonum [God the highest good]: the highest good; object of valuing.

Deus incommutabilis substantia [God the unchangeable substance]: cognizing search for subsistence! Subsisting in itself, derived sense of substance.

Deus summa pulchritudo [God the highest beauty]: highest beauty of joyful contemplation.

In every determination, a different point of departure, of access, of determining within the access. The "whence" of the means of determination, the How of forming-out.

Here in the old conceptual framework, there frameworks used in novel ways and re-formed, now new points of departure.

Since the basic tendency is still Greek—as is philosophy up to the present day—there is no destruction. Mere so-called critique of knowledge does not help here.

Problem: U[nity] and m[ultiplicity] of the connections of the access enactment. Origin—their facticity authentically, meaningfully enacted. Less psychologically, classification in general. Regional schemata of order, transcendental ideas are not only insufficient, but obstruct the problematic.

The *tentatio* in our interpretation—but an opportunity to lead toward decisive phenomena—*molestia.*

(*Formae—concupiscentia carnis, oculorum* [forms—desire of the flesh, of the eye]—not according to capacity, III especially shows.)

Tentatio: in carne—per carnem *[Temptation: in the flesh—through the flesh]*
[on § 14 a]

I. The *temptation* of *uti* [use], of the dealing-with, in the *cupiditas oblectandi (in carne)* [lust of entertainment (in the flesh)], taking-delight-in, comfort, calculation of significance, pretending-to-oneself, more precisely: pretending one significance before the other one and, in this, wriggling oneself out of the noose. (Direction: letting the significance force itself upon oneself.) Saving oneself in the uncovering and ascertaining of one possibility of delight, even if that were one's own neediness and uncertainty.

II. The *temptation* of knowledge (curiosity)—*per carnem:* leading is a selfly intention. Ideas inventive[?].

(I) in a certain sense—mediating—cannot be gotten rid of. Palpable *molestia.* But easier precisely because of this, for they can be found more easily in the singular as falling.

The others conceal themselves more, to the extent that in the end, I discover in myself the most difficult *tentatio.*

[A Comparison of the Three Forms of tentatio]
[on § 15 a]

Explicating on the basis of the three *formae* [forms].

Tentatio: What for[23]—away from what. How is the *falling* conceived, and what does it mean existentially? To what extent objective, constative, normative (theoretizingly, attitudinally)? To what extent factical, selfly, existential, in the manner of enactment?

The different modes of *molestia* attach[?] to "necessity," levels of sense of facticity. To what extent a connection between the "what for"? To what extent an "increase"? Whither, in what direction?

In I. and II., each time an attitude![24] In III., self-concern, but self-concern viewed from attitude and from what has been accomplished for the world in attitude!

The transference of the *tentatio*-like significance from the specially experienced *content* (I) to the relation, or in the direction of the relation (needs[?] the peculiar concealment [...].*) The *relation* as such is the *source* of enjoyment, of the falling (III).

Axiologization
[on § 15 b–d]

The giving-in (sin).

The getting-lost.

Not-giving-in: Overcoming (faith). Cf. Luther, *de tripl.* and *de dupl.,* 1518; *iustitia* [justice]: F[...]** *teutonice. Factical* complex of enactment: "for the sake of God," "from" love of God, that is (phenomenologically), existence

---

23. Whither: to *amor sui, superbia* [love of oneself, pride], loss of existence (objective). Because existence is what?—The Augustinian and a basic sense.

24. *Securitas* [security]—no *timor* [fear]!

*[Two words illegible.]

**[One word illegible.]

"wanting"-God, that is, wanting to gain the authentic enactment as existential. Decisive is here not a preference of values, the axiologized separation is a th[eoretical] misinterpretation of the real phenomenon, but: existential concern (enactment of existence).

Faith:(1) genuine, radical self-love (absolute egoism)

        (2) genuine, absolute love of God (absolute "surrender")

In this authentic existence, the most radical fear is constitutive of concern.

But the being-"absolute" is not to be dissolved in being-"universal," in the law, but radical, concrete, historical being-the-individual.

The orientation toward the axiologized *summum bonum* [highest good], etc., turns the whole conduct into a near-aestheticism in yet another sense: not only as attitude, but as *delectatio* [delight].

By contrast, the historical problematic of enactment: gaining the terrible, the difficult, the questionable (quaestio), or what is to be indicated in the communication[?]. In giving in, one steals away from this, and axiologization as attitude is a concealed giving-in.

Cf. Augustine, *Confessiones* X c. [. . .]* on dispersion in prayer (monstrosity—however, not the most radical execution in Augustine—consideration of *misericordia* [mercy].)

[Agnosce ordinem]
[on § 15 c]

"Agnosce ordinem, quaere pacem. Tu Deo, tibi caro. Quid justius? quid pulchrius? Tu majori, minor tibi: servi tu ei qui fecit te, ut tibi serviat quod factum est propter te. Non enim hunc ordinem novimus, neque hunc ordinem commendamus. Tibi caro et tu Deo; sed, Tu Deo, et tibi caro. Si autem contemnis Tu Deo, nunquam efficies ut Tibi caro. [. . .] Primo ergo te subdas Deo; deinde illo docente te et adjuvante praeliris." [Observe order, seek peace. You belong to God, your flesh to you. What more just, what more beautiful? You to Him that is greater, he that is less to you: serve Him who made you, so that that which was made for you may serve you. For we do not know nor commend this order. "Your flesh to you, and you to God," but "you to God, and your flesh to you." For if you despise "You to God," you will never bring about "your flesh to you." (. . .) First, then, submit yourself to God; then, with Him to teach you and encourage you, fight.][25]

An order of value-ranks, and a correspondingly axiologized forming-out, fails here entirely in regard to the authentic interpretation.

---

*[Reference missing.]

25. *Enarrationes in Psalmos* CLXIII 6; PL 37, p. 1860.

It becomes clearer and clearer how the *tentatio* and the modes of enactment of coping [*Fertigwerdens*], on the one hand, aim at a certain direction and mode of enactment of selfly experiences, on the other, on a higher level of an interpretation given by Augustine himself, how they aim at determinately regulated modes of *making decisions.*

Tentatio: meaning on the basis of an order—order of value-ranks—("modern")—Augustine apparently the question about this, whether genuine or not. Greek. Theorization directed in a certain way (being interwoven [with the] Greek-Platonic).

Axiologization directed in a certain way (*incommutabile* [unchangeable] and *summum bonum* [highest good]; and the whole order on the basis of this), which can become even more fateful because it also pays attention to precisely those *phenomena* that are crucial in a certain regard.

These orders present in Augustine, explicitly—cf. *De doctrina christiana.*

For the interpretation of the *Confessiones,* however, do not move forward in this direction, but stay with the way in which they are secured there; the existential predelineation is to be grasped from there, and attempt to depart the destruction already here.

In this, however, the axiological view in Augustine is not only attached, but holds sway throughout all considerations. Cf. *De doctrina christiana.*

[on § 15 c]

Having validity in the communal world: being loved and feared in order to enjoy this for oneself, that is, one takes oneself to be important firstly as the one who is "superior," and secondly, as the one who is so valuable that he is esteemed by others.

One views *oneself* in this entirely in the eyes and tendencies of the others. One takes *oneself apart,* elevates oneself.

But that is *misera vita* [the miserable life].—"Hinc fit vel maxime non amare te, nec caste timere te." [Hence especially it comes that men do not love You nor fear You in purity].[26] Through this, the authentic and highest love, directed at You, is impaired. Through this, the *pure fear,* directed at You, is endangered.

"Tu superbis resistis." [You resist the proud.][27] You resist, because they do not really stand by You but run away from You and, in fear, prefer something else to You.

To prefer: axiologizing, transferring everything to one plane—objects of

26. *Confessiones* X 36, 59; PL 32, p. 804.
27. Ibid.

value. Precisely the decisive complexes of enactment are covered up, and especially the transitions.

Through the axiologization, the character of calculation, leveling, and ordering posits itself in the self-conception, interpretation, and conceptuality (*placing* in a direction: ordering), that is, the authentic concern is disfigured and viewed as concealed calculation[?]. The emphasis of meaning and the origin of explication do not lie in the authentic and historical enactment.

"Propter quaedam humanae societatis officia necessarium est amari et timeri ab hominibus." [Because certain offices in human society make it necessary to be loved and feared by people.][28] The obligations, services, and relations in human society, however, render these communal-worldly relations necessary. But: "instat adversarius verae beatitudinis nostrae" [the adversary of our true happiness threatens us].[29] Possibility of a *falsa beatitudo* [false happiness]! "Libeatque nos amari et timeri, non propter se, sed pro te" [It becomes our pleasure to be loved and feared not for Your sake, but instead of You].[30] (Facticity of having an attitude that is *significant* in the communal world. "Not for oneself alone" in a different sense.)

"Quotidiana fornax nostra est humana lingua." [Our daily furnace is the human language.][31] Language as the manner of enactment of communal-worldly (concrete factical) experiencing. "Et multum timeo occulta mea (Ps. XVIII, 13), quae norunt oculi tui, mei autem non. Est enim qualiscumque in aliis generibus tentationum mihi facultas explorandi me; in hoc pene nulla est." [And I much fear my secrets (Ps. 18:13), which your eyes know, but mine do not. For in other kinds of temptations, I have the capacity for self-examination, but in this matter almost none.][32]

Every kind of temptation has a certain, corresponding How of *explorare* [examining]. According to each "level" and significance in which the *tentatio* is possessed in its full sense, the grasping and interpretation is *easier* or more difficult: easier, if it is even more objectifiable; more difficult, if we are dealing with the self-interpretation, and the *self-possession* can cover itself up more and more temptingly, and can move in surrogates. (Through this, the *tentatio* even more dangerous.)

[Four Groups of Problems]

1. *Tentatio:*[33] problematic of enactment with regard to the self. Basic sense of the self as historical.

28. Ibid.
29. Ibid.
30. Ibid.
31. *Confessiones* X 37, 60; PL 32, p. 804.
32. Ibid.
33. The How is decisive, but in the concretion.

2. *Defluere:*[34] *multum—unum* [Flowing down, scattering: many—one]. *Molestia*—facticity.

3. *Quaestio mihi factus sum* [I have become a question to myself]: insecurity, conflict, becoming questionable, authentic manner of becoming a question to oneself. What this expresses? "Possibility." (Decisive is the How: The phenomena push themselves increasingly into the complexes of the enactment of sense. All the *content* receives its sense from there.—Problem: how I experience myself insofar as I experience *tentatio*. What kind of concern for *facticity*! Can be [. . .],* accidental, objective, objective measure of value—axiologization, cf. Augustine himself!)

4. *Tentatio*—basic orientation in a certain, axiological forming-out.

Moving away from God, increasing the distance. In the question of possessing God: The more he advances toward the authentic conditions of enactment, the more dangerous these conditions turn out to be, in hostility to themselves.

Discussion of Rom. 1:20: basic structure delineated, that is, this passage in particular for the vestibule [*Vorbau*] of Greek philosophy (theoretical and practical). Yet it did not remain there, but precisely in Augustine the following is decided: (1) total ignorance of Augustine himself (casting off of the Plotinian, of the historical era), (2) misunderstanding of the Christian—reaching back to Augustine.

There where every serious attempt at a radical appropriation of the soil—cultural history—is lacking, there is not the slightest right to even start uncovering the essential views.

Today's unhealthy, non-genuine religious fraud (here metaphysical curiosity—with the gesture of inwardness): it is revealing that it falls into the trap of surrogate appearances.

Only indicate scientifically the cultural-historical connections, no apologies for Christianity.

Sin

What is base has its power in pulling toward itself, in blocking *authentic* understanding and in obscuring it.

Understanding passes on to the side of the will, follows the falling inclination and even confirms that this is what is authentic.

Christian complex of motivation:

34. Concrete facticity.
*[One word illegible.]

1. Not understanding what is right,
2. Not wanting to understand,
3. Not *wanting.*

The human being[?] [. . .]* what is not genuine, although he understood what is right, has the authentic defiance.

"Therefore, interpreted Christianly, sin has its roots in willing, not in knowing, and this corruption of willing embraces the individual's consciousness."[35]

That the sin is *before* God is precisely what is positive about it.

The category of sin is the category of individuality.

Axiologization
[on § 17]

In understanding facticity, its *questionability* and the *enactment of questionability,* what surfaces is the fatefulness, and inappropriateness for existence, of the axiologization. (And very strongly present in Augustine in particular. Precisely that which Scheler retains must be eliminated, that is, he does not understand the problem radically enough.)

Preferring—spurning—being indifferent.

This is basically bustling activity *with God,* which takes the easy path; and one only has to follow essential *insights.*

But here there is no trace at all of the authentic sense of the enactment of love.

What is precisely crucial is to constantly have a radical confrontation with the factical, and not to flee. In order to attain existence, I precisely *must* have *it.*

This *having* precisely means *living in it,* but not giving in, not even overcoming it comfortably and axiologically.

The sense of existential overcoming. The sense of facticity.

Holding on to, appropriating, in a genuinely factical manner, the *worldly* or the experiential relation and enactment. This means neither "valuing positively," since this is not at issue and is a misinterpretation ("Luther" and misunderstanding), nor "making compromises," which likewise is now merely an inferior bustling activity (Catholicism!).

Trying to gain *that* facticity that "forms" existence.

---

*[One word illegible.]
35. S. Kierkegaard, *Sickness unto Death,* p. 95.

Correspondingly, "*molestia*" is to be determined existentially: not "burden"—ascetically-Greek, but opportunity of seriousness. I precisely must only pre-form the *molestia* itself in the first place, not falsely overcome it.

[Molestia]
[on § 17]

Being the singular one—being under the ownmost, strictest "observation."

The *molestia*—"radically forming" mine as *molestia*—determinate complex of enactment.

To *appropriate,* in the manner of enactment, the *moles* [burden] as *what is pulling down* [*Abziehendes*], not letting it stand as a thing and as "nature," but grasping the *sense of facticity* and enacting it *existentially* and understanding it thus *historically* in memory and expectation. Giving life *this* existential facticity and brightness, that is, increasing the seriousness!

[Exploratio]

The How and the possibilities of the enactment of the *exploratio* are different also in the How in which the *tentationes* are encountered. They can be massively emphasized and become clear. They can be entirely hidden and protect themselves by means of the enactment of experience itself in which they lie.

Explorare: simultaneously concerns and comprises within itself the "seeing" of:[36] "quantum assecutus sim posse refrenare animum meum" [how much I have succeeded in being able to refrain my soul].[37] That I see, that is, the *exploratio* is easier if and insofar as this *tentatio:*[38] "cum eis rebus careo, vel voluntate, vel cum absunt" [when I do without those things, either willingly of when they are absent].[39] *Res* [things]: the contents of the *tentatio.*[40] In being free of that: "Tunc enim me interrogo, quam magis minusve mihi molestum sit non habere" [Then I ask myself how troublesome it is to me not to have them].[41]

36. Dealing with, but not falling into! Without compromises!—No remaining habit, objectively acquired property, but only in anxiety—carrying *possibility* before oneself.—Possibility of doing without.

37. *Confessiones* X 37, 60; PL 32, p. 804.

38. According to what moments of sense including within themselves the possibility of *Non-*[. . .]* sense. *[One syllable illegible.]

39. *Confessiones* X 37, 60; PL 32, p. 804 f.

40. But what does this mean here: experiencing the factical? Situational character—I am not always attached to them in the same sense. Whence the change in the "always"?

41. *Confessiones* X 37, 60; PL 32, p. 805.

"Divitiae vero quae ob hoc expetuntur, ut [serviant] alicui trium istarum cupiditatum [. . .], si persentiscere non potest animus utrum eas habens contemnat, possunt et dimitti, ut se probet" [As for riches which are sought for this, that they may (serve) one in one of those three lusts (. . .), if the soul cannot discern whether it condemns having them, that can be tested by giving them away].[42]

Possibility of seeing the *being free,* the overcoming and the having overcome, the understanding of who I "am" and what I "can."

But when it comes to "praise," how may the possibility of doing without it be tested? *Quid in carendo laudis possum explorandum male vivendum est.* "At si bonae vitae bonorumque operum comes et solet et debet esse laudatio, tam comitatum ejus, quam ipsam bonam vitam deseri non oportet." [What is explored in being able to do without praise is an ill life. "If praise is the usual and proper companion of a good life and of good works, we ought to renounce it as little as we ought to renounce the good life itself."][43]

The *danger* of *tentatio* and the prevention of the (genuine) exploration must precisely be enacted.—The *laus* [praise] as *comes* [companion]—*libido carnis, voluptas* [lust of the flesh, pleasure] [. . .]*—also *comes?*—but how?

The *abesse* [being absent] of *laus* can only be accomplished by living without disgrace, opening ourselves to disgrace and scorn. For we are supposed to strive for *bonam vitam* [the good life], in *bonum* [. . .].** *Non autem sentio* [But I do not know]—the possibility of doing without—, *nisi cum* (somehow) *abfuerit* [unless it will (somehow) have been absent.]

[Anxiety]

Letting the *corresponding* possibilities encounter! Corresponding to *that* which I experience in a *worldly* manner!

(*Delectatio—gaudere velle.* [Delight—wanting to enjoy.] What is other. Something is missing. With this, already placed in possibility, even if entirely in worldly falling. But even here, there is still something of the genuine existential movement—in the twitching, as it were.)

"Attacks of anxiety"

42. Ibid.
43. Ibid.
*[One word illegible.]
**[Two words illegible.]

"historically"—enacted—preserving the earlier ones
to *open*—possibilities—itself *historically*. "Anxiety discovers fate."[44]

The experience of *directionless* anxiety: No direction from the authentic self. Anxiety itself directs.

The *selfly* directed anxiety: direction. Free of the preference for worldly significances. In *anxiety*, "fearing them" is driven out.

T[erm]: "anxiety" not better the directionless fear of significance! "Fear" [*Furcht*] the real anxiety: *reverence* [*Ehrfurcht*].

[The Counter-Expected? (Wider-wärtige), the Temptation, the Appeal (Anfechtung)]

The counter-expected, "counter to the *expectation*": the relation posited from significance to significance within the falling direction of experience.

The temptation (ethical): The "lowly" one lures, and seeks to pull down what is "higher." (*Being pulled away* in the factical direction of significance.)

The Appeal (religious): What is higher (jealously, as it were) limits the individual away from itself, increases with religiosity. The absolute's own resistance. (*Being pushed back* in concern already requires existing! How?— How does concern encounter us, and how is it characterized? What does being-pushed-back mean in enactment?)

On the Destruction of Plotinus

Since, in the end, factical existence is crucial, and in it, *destruction* is lived and has meaning, everything to be destructed is, in the end, to be explicated as to its How. That is, the task is: precisely to see the unspoken lead [*Duktus*] that one does not gain as long as one lives only in the "matter" itself, for example by discussing it (improving, re-forming, and the like).

One can only "see" the unspoken lead in an authentic (existential) foreconception itself. And what is crucial is precisely to observe the steps sharply and not let oneself be seduced by any convention in this.

44. S. Kierkegaard, *The Concept of Anxiety,* p. 159.

Appendix II

Supplements from the Notes of Oskar Becker

1. *Continentia*
[Supplement to § 12 a]

"*Jubes continentiam*" [you command continence]—the *iubere* [commanding] is a *directio cordis* [direction of the heart]. Cf. *Enarrationes in Psalmos* [*On the Psalms*] 7, V. 10: *iubere* is not oriented in the Church, in objective faith.

"Quomodo ergo justus dirigi potest, nisi in occulto." [For how can the just man be directed except in secret.][1] Through events at the beginning of the Christian age, the effectivity of God could indeed once be experienced objectively as a miracle. But now, when the name of Christians has grown to such heights, the *hypocrisis*—the hypocrisy of those who want to please people rather than God—grows as well. How else can the just one be led out of such *confusio simulationis* [confusion of simulation], if not by God's testing him in the heart and gut (*Cor,* heart = inner consideration; *ren,* gut = *delectatio in malam partem* [delight in the bad parts]. The *delectatio* is something base in life; that is why it is designated by a baser, lower organ.) Augustine now elaborates, in what this *scrutinium* [scrutiny] is enacted.—"Finis enim curae delectatio est" [For the end of concern is delight]:[2] For everyone strives in his concern and consideration for what is attainable by his own *delectatio,* but God himself speaks in our conscience, and he sees our concern and our goal; that which we are doing through actions and words may be known to a human being, "sed quo animo fiant" [but what we do in the soul],[3] and what we thus aim at, God alone knows.

Iubes continentiam is to be understood in this sense.

2. *Uti and* frui
[Supplement to § 12 b]

The *curare* (*the being-concerned*) is a basic characteristic of life, it is meant as *vox media in bonam et in malam partem* [the middle voice between the

1. *Enarrationes in Psalmos* VII 9 (V. 10); PL 36, p. 103.
2. Ibid.
3. Ibid., p. 104.

good and the bad parts]: there is genuine and non-genuine concern (the latter = "bustling activity").

Uti [use]: I "deal with" what life brings to me; this is a phenomenon within the *curare*.

Frui: "enjoying."—"Beatus est quippe qui fruitur summo bono." [Happy is he who indeed enjoys the highest good.][4] A certain basic *aesthetic* meaning lies in this; one notices the *Neo-Platonic influence: the beautiful belongs to the essence of being.*

And then we also say that a thing is a joy if it is such "quae nos non aliud referenda per se ipsa delectat" [that it gives us delight in itself, not by reference to something else].[5]

As *uti,* we grasp that way of pleasing in which we strive for something for the sake of something else ("uti vero ea re [dicimur], quam propter aliud quaerimus" [but (we are said) to use something we need for the sake of something else][6]).

In enjoyment, we are said to possess eternal and unchangeable things. The appropriate comportment to the other things is *uti,* since precisely through this, we will attain to the *frui* of what is genuine (cf. *De doctrina christiana,* lib. 1, cap. 22).

Only the *trinitas* [trinity] must be held in enjoyment, that is *the highest and unchangeable good.*

Fruendum est rebus invisibilibus. [To be enjoyed is the invisible thing.] "Frui enim est amore alicui rei inhaerere propter seipsam. Uti autem, quod in usum venerit ad id quod amas obtinendum referre, si tamen amandum est." [For to enjoy a thing is to stay in love for it for its own sake. To use, on the other hand, is to use whatever means are at one's disposal to obtain what one loves, if only it is loved.][7]

"Omnis itaque humana perversio est, [. . .], fruendis uti velle, atque utendis frui. Et rursus omnis ordinatio, quae virtus etiam nominatur, fruendis frui, et utendis uti." [However, all human perversion is (. . .) the will to use for the sake of enjoyment, and to enjoy for the sake of use. By contrast, all order which is to be called virtue demands that one enjoy for the sake of enjoyment, and use for the sake of use.] (*De diversis quaestionibus octoginta tribus, quaest. 30* [*83 Various Questions,* 30]; written soon after Augustine's conversion).[8]

Aesthetic basic meaning of *frui; fruendum est trinitate, rei intelligibilis pulchritudo* [?] (= νοητὸν κάλλῶς)[?]; *incommutabilis et ineffabilis pulchri-*

---

4. *De libero arbitrio* II 13, 36; PL 32, p. 1260.
5. *De civitate Dei, libri* XXII, recogn. B. Dombart, Leipzig, 1877. XI 25; vol. 1, p. 496.
6. Ibid.
7. *De doctrina christiana* I 4, 4; PL 34, p. 20.
8. *De diversis quaestionibus* XXX; PL 40, p. 19.

tudo = God [to be enjoyed is the trinity, the beauty of intelligible things (= νοητὸν κάλλῶς); unchangeable and ineffable beauty = God]. The *frui* is thus the basic characteristic of the Augustinian *basic posture toward life itself.* Its correlate is the *pulchritudo;* thus there is an *aesthetic* moment in it. Likewise in the *summum bonum.*—With this, a basic aspect of the medieval object of theology (and of the history of ideas in general) has been designated: it is the specifically *Greek* view. *The* "fruitio Dei" [enjoyment of God] *is a decisive concept in medieval theology;* this basic motif led to the formation of medieval *mysticism.*

However, the *"fruitio"* in Augustine is not the specifically Plotinian one, which culminates in intuition, but is rooted in the peculiarly Christian view of factical life.

In the end, the *fruitio Dei* is opposed to the possession of the self; they do not stem from the same root, but have grown together from without.

Connected to this is the fact that for Augustine, the goal of life is the *quies* [rest]. *Vita praesens:* "in re laboris, sed in spe quietis; in caren vetustatis, sed in fide novitatis" [Present life: "in actual labor, but in hope of rest; in the flesh of aging old life, but in faith of the new"].[9]—In the flesh (σάρξ in Paul not only sensual *libido,* but factical life in general) of decay (falling), in faith in the renewal.

"Quo praecedit spes vestra, sequatur vita vestra." [Whither your hope moves ahead, let your life follow.][10] Life is enacted in the direction of that toward which expectation runs ahead.

Schematic Overview of the Phenomena

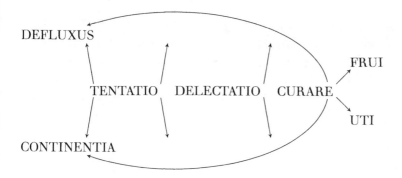

The *curare* [concern] consists of the *uti* and *frui.*—The basic direction of *vita:* the *delectatio.*—The *tentatio* lies in the *delectatio* itself. It has the possibilities

9. *Epistulae* LV 14, 26; PL 33, p. 217.
10. *Enarrationes in Psalmos* CXXXVI 22; PL 37, p. 1774.

of turning into the *defluxus* [flowing out, sliding down, scattering] and the *continentia* [continence].

3. Tentatio
[Supplement following § 12 b]

Tentatio (c. 28): Different meanings of *tentatio: tentatio deceptionis* [temptation of deception]: with the tendency to bring-to-a-fall; 2. *tentatio probationis* [temptation of probation]: with the t[endency] to test. In the first sense, only the devil (*diabolus*) tempts, in the second, God tempts too.[11]

"*Diabolus*": in Augustine, there is here still vivid a belief in demons with concrete ideas, but this is not all: see Letter 146.

No human being is equipped with justice to such a degree that no appeal [*Anfechtung*] of confusion would be necessary for him.[12] This is the real *tentatio, the tentatio tribulationis,* so that the human being becomes a question to himself. It is necessary "vel ad perficiendam, vel ad confirmandam" [be it for perfection, be it for confirmation].[13]

"Nescit se homo, nisi in tentatione discat se" [You do not know a human being unless you have gotten to know him in temptation].[14] A human being does not know himself at all unless he gets to know himself in *tentatio*. One notices the historical basic meaning of *discere* [to learn, to get to know], which takes place in concrete, factical, historical self-experience. *Tentatio* is a specifically historical concept.

"Amores duo in hac vita secum in omni tentatione luctantur, amor saeculi, et amor Dei" [In all temptation, two kinds of love are struggling with one another in this life: love of the world, and love of God].[15] On the concept of *diabolus,* cf. *Enarrationes in Psalmos,* ad. Ps. 148.

Within us, the appeal [*Anfechtung*] and [. . .]* struggle daily, not always for [. . .],* for we also bear [. . .],* and there is a constant danger within us, so that he who is not awake will be conquered; but if we do not consent, we do indeed gain the upper hand; but in this too, there is a burden, *resistendo delectationibus* [resisting delight].[16]

---

11. Cf. *Epistulae* CCV, PL 33, p. 948.

12. "Nullus enim hominum est tanta justitia praeditus, cui non sit necessaria tentatio tribulationis" [For no human being is endowed with so great a justice that for him no temptation of tribulations would be necessary]. (*Contra Faustum Manichaeum* XXII 20; PL 42, p. 411).

13. Ibid.

14. *Sermones* II 3, 3; PL 38, p. 29.

15. *Sermones* CCCXLIV 1; PL 39, p. 1512.

*[Omissions in the lecture notes of Oskar Becker.]

16. [Editor's note: Due to the omissions in the notes, here is the Latin text of reference.] "Contendunt nobiscum quotidie tentationes, contendunt quotidie delectationes: etsi non consentiamus, tamen molestiam patimur, et contendimus, et magnum periculum est ne qui contendit

Paul, Gal. 5:17; "*Caro enim concupiscit adversus spiritum*" [For what the flesh desires is against the spirit]. You do not do what you want, and that is a struggle; and what makes it even more burdensome is the fact that it is an *inner* struggle.

"In quo bello si sit quisque victor, illos quos non videt inimicos, continuo superabit. Non enim tentat diabolus vel angeli ejus, nisi quod in te carnale dominatur [is alive in this real facticity]" [And in this war, each one who is victorious will straightaway overcome enemies whom he does not see. For the devils and his angels do not tempt, except the carnal part that rules in you (is alive in this real facticity)].[17]

And when the devil tempts someone in whatever manner, he always tempts the one who agrees with him, "non cogit invitum" [he does not force a person against that person's will]; he seizes only the one "quem invenerit ex aliqua parte jam similem sibi" [whom he finds to be in some part like himself], and thus, the gate is open for the entry of devilish suggestion (*iunua tentatione* [the gate of temptation]).[18]

The emergence of *tentatio* from factical life takes place on different levels. Division of phenomena: in concretely tangible temptations (for example, sexual ones), and not concretely tangible ones (mental ones, performed in *cogitatio* [thought]).

The *tentatio* has a twofold connection to the authentic experiences of the self.

In what basic direction of experience does it itself have its sense? We must go back to its authentic basis of enactment. Here is an opportunity to refer [to] a connection we have not seen so far, a connection between Augustine and Neo-Platonism!

Augustine assumes a concrete situation of temptation (in "*De doctrina Christiana*"): living-in-avarice (*avaritia*). What is decisive is the *dilectio* [esteem, love], the *amor pecuniae* [love of money]. What kind of *delectatio* [delight] is dominant will become decisive for one's comportment in the appeal [*Anfechtung*] and in coping with it.

From the outside, the devil suggests a gain, one which, however, requires fraud. He places before you what you have overcome internally. (That is, something significant that corresponds to the relational direction of the experience that is already alive in that human being.) If you defeat avarice, if

vincatur; si autem non consentiendo vincamus, molestiam tamen patimur resistendo delectationibus" [Daily temptations strive with us, daily delights: although we do not consent, yet we suffer troubles, and strive, and great is the danger lest he who strives be ·conquered; and even if by not consenting we conquer, yet we suffer troubles in resisting delights]. (*Enarrationes in Psalmos* CXLVIII 4; PL 37, p. 1940.)

17. *Enarrationes in Psalmos* CXLIII 5; PL 37, p. 1858.

18. *Sermones* XXXII 11; PL 38, p. 200.

it is internally dominated in you, the temptation will have been overcome. Everything depends on the dominant direction of *delectatio.* But an expectation always remains alive. Something else, however, may be placed before expectation, so that an inner struggle emerges. The human being is placed before a decision. "You are broken within yourself by sin." ("Etenim ex peccato divisus es adversum te" [For through sin are you divided against yourself].[19]) "Habes contra quod pugnes in te, habes quod expugnes in te" [You have within you that with which to fight, you have within you what to overcome].[20] Implied in this is the fact that, in considering the *tentatio,* what is crucial is not the objective situation that leads to the temptation, but the situation of self of he who experiences it. In each case, something different is required; when you are struggling, when you are victorious, when you rejoice, for instance, a gain is set before you, *delectationem habet* [it has delight]. "Suggeritur aliquod lucrum, delectat, habet fraudem, sed magnum est lucrum, delectat, non consentis" [Some gain is suggested to you, you take delight in it, it involves deceit, but great is the gain, and you take delight in it, yet you do not consent].[21] The persuasion and urging is still going on. Already considered. Already fallen. "Contempsit justitiam, ut fraudem faceret" [He has thought lightly of justice so that he may commit deceit],[22] or: *contempsit lucrum* [He has thought lightly of his gain] for the sake of justice. "Sed etiam ille qui vicit, numquid omnino egit in se" [But even he who was victorious, has he altogether achieved in himself][23] that money cannot trouble him any longer? "Aut nihil in eo excitet delectationes" [That it excites in him no delight]?[24] Although money no longer seems to him to be worth the struggle, "inest tamen aliqua delectationes titillatio" [yet there is in him a titillation of delight].[25] This titillation is present and remains in the human being, even if temptation is no longer present. (Here, Augustine comes to the problem of original sin.)

The role played by the setting-before and setting-after shows that a certain *ordo* [order] is the basis of the phenomenon. You belong to God, but the flesh belongs to you (the flesh refers to what is at one's disposal in factical life). You belong to what is higher in value, the lower value belongs to you. It is not the following order that we recognize and recommend: "Tibi caro et tu Deo; sed, Tu Deo, et tibi caro. Si autem contemnis Tu Deo, nunquam efficies ut Tibi caro. [. . .] Primo ergo te subdas Deo" ["Your flesh to you, and you

19. *Enarrationes in Psalmos* CXLIII 5; PL 37, p. 1859.
20. Ibid.
21. *Enarrationes in Psalmos* CXLIII 6; PL 37, p. 1859 f.
22. Ibid., p. 1860.
23. Ibid.
24. Ibid.
25. Ibid.

to God," but "you to God, and your flesh to you." For if you despise "You to
God," you will never bring about "your flesh to you." (. . .) First, then, submit
yourself to God; then, with Him to teach you and encourage you, fight],[26]
then you will struggle in his illumination and under his guidance. It does not
only depend on the relation to God, but on the How of the *ordo*. "Agnosce
ordinem" [Observe order],[27] put in modern terms: Observe the ranking order
of values.

For us, it is important: first, how this order of rank is the basis; second,
that the order is viewed in a certain conceptual form. It is not natural that that
which is experienced in the *delectatio* stands in a ranking order of value.
Rather, this is based on an "axiologization" which, in the end, is on the same
level as the "theorization." This ranking order of values is of Greek origin.
(In the whole manner of concept-formation, it stems ultimately from Plato.)
Proof of this is, among other things, the connection to the *incommutabile*
[unchangeable]. Thus, such a ranking order is already present in Augustine.
However, does this axiologization correspond to the explicated phenomena?

The axiologization is more difficult to grasp than the theorization, because
it actually deals with what is in question.

Chapters [. . .]* of Book X of the *Confessiones* show how Augustine indeed uses a ranking order as a basis, but it ultimately takes on an essentially
different meaning.

This ranking order dominates Augustine to a very large extent. However,
it is not grasped in a manner as removed as it is today (for example, in
Scheler); it is connected to his concrete metaphysics, and the conception of
reality (*res*) is tailored to it.

What does Augustine mean by "*res*" (reality)? The modes of concern, of
uti [use] and *frui* [enjoyment], in their relation to "*res*," result in the following
division into three kinds: "Res ergo aliae sunt quibus fruendum est, aliae
quibus utendum, aliae qua fruuntur et utuntur" [There are some things, then,
which are to be enjoyed, others which are to be used, others still which enjoy
and use].[28]

The *res* [things] are opposed to the *signa* (signs). "Proprie autem nunc res
appellavi, quae non ad significandum aliquid adhibentur, sicut est lignum,
lapis, pecus, atque hujusmodi caetera" [On the other hand, a thing, properly
speaking, is designated as that which is not employed to signify anything else,
such as wood, stone, cattle, and other things of that kind].[29] But this is not

26. Ibid.
27. Ibid.
*[Omission in the lecture notes.]
28. *De doctrina christiana* I 3, 3; PL 34, p. 20.
29. *De doctrina christiana* I 2, 2; PL 34, p. 19.

understood in the sense of the wood that Moses cast into the bitter waters, nor of the stone that Jacob put under his head, etc.—Opposition: *signum* = symbol. This is connected to the interpretation of Scripture and goes back to the Alexandrian school of exegetes (which, in turn, goes back to the school of philologists: problem of the interpretation of all texts). These latter things (Moses' wood, etc.) are signs of other things at the same time. But there are still other signs whose consistent and full use consists in designating itself (whereas the wood does not necessarily possess the character of indication). No one uses words for purposes other than designation. Every sign is a *res,* otherwise it would be nothing, but not every *res* is a *signum.* Thus, when looking at the *res,* we only pay attention to what they are (according to their content), not to what else they might indicate. And, vice versa, if I deal with a thing as a sign, I must pay attention not to what it is, but to the fact that it is a sign (such that I have to look away from them).[30]

What is the human being itself? Is he a *fruendum, utendum* [an object of enjoyment, of use], or both? We who *fruimur et utimur* [enjoy and use] are, somehow, a *res* [thing] ourselves. "Magna enim quaedam res est homo" [For man is a truly great thing],[31] because he has reason. "Itaque magna quaestio est utrum frui se homines debeant, an uti, an utrumque" [And so it is a great question whether human beings ought to enjoy, or use themselves, or do both].[32] There is the commandment of reciprocal love, but the question is whether one human being is loved by another as a human being (*propter se* [on account of himself]), or for the sake of something else. If a human being is loved for his own sake, *fruimur eo* [we enjoy him], if not, *utimor eo* [we use him]. However, it now seems that a human being must be loved for the sake of something else, for in that which is to be loved for its own sake, "in eo constituitur vita beata" [in this consists the happy life].[33] But we do not have the *res* from the *vita beata* (we do not have the latter as such), *sed spes* [but hope].

If you see clearly, the human being may not even be the object of *frui* for itself. "Si autem se propter se diligit" [If, however, he loves himself on account of himself],[34] he does not relate to God. If he is turned toward himself, he is not turned toward the unchangeable. And since that which he supposedly loves in himself is characterized by a defect (*defectus,* that is, transience), it is to be preferred that he is attached without defect to the *incommutabile* (unchangeable), rather than that he "ad seipsum relaxatur" [opens himself toward himself].[35]

30. Cf. ibid., p. 20.
31. *De doctrina christiana* I 22, 20; PL 34, p. 26.
32. Ibid.
33. Ibid.
34. *De doctrina christiana* I 22, 21; PL 34, p. 26.
35. Ibid., p. 27.

He "qui rerum integer aestimator est" [who estimates things without prej-udice],[36] that is, "qui ordinatam dilectionem habet" [who has ordinate love] lives in a holy way.[37]

The positioning [*Stellungnahme*] within the *tentatio* is enacted from this *ordo* [order]; from it, the basic comportment to things is decided.

This doctrine of value is already on a high level of *forming-out*. But one misperceives it if one isolates it and does not view it in its context. Then the problem emerges whether such ranking order of values is a meaningfully necessary one, or whether it does not merely rely on the role Greek philosophy plays in Augustine's thought.

More on the doctrine of value: "Non autem omnia quibus utendum est, diligenda sunt, sed ea sola quae aut nobiscum societate quadam referuntur in Deum [being related to God on the basis of a community with us]." [However, not all those things which are to be used, are to be loved, but only those which are in a community with us in relation to God (being related to God on the basis of a community with us).][38] (Here lies the origin of the thought of Christian solidarity).

Those things deserve an estimation of love that are related to us, but "be-neficio Dei per nos indigent, sicuti est corpus [the flesh as the seat of sin]" [they need the goodness of God through us, such as the body (the flesh as the seat of sin)].[39] Thus, there are four kinds of objects that are to be loved: (1) What is above us. (2) What we are ourselves. (3) What is next to us. (4) What is beneath us.

Regarding (2) and (4), no special reason is required to love them. However much a human being may fall from the truth, the self-esteem and the esteem of his body remains intact. "Nemo ergo se odit" [No man, then, hates him-self].[40] But because of self-love of a certain kind, commandments of a certain order are necessary. The human being has a certain posture in relation to himself, since his self-esteem is there by itself with the facticity of life. (This comprises a certain phenomenal complex of self-experience, which is to be explicated.)

He who is the *integer aestimator rerum* [unprejudiced estimator of things], who possesses the *ordinata dilectio* [ordinate love] loves in an authentic way, so that he does not either love what may not be loved at all, or love that more which may not be loved more, etc.[41] (A certain formalism lies in this strati-fication of the order of value.)

36. *De doctrina christiana* I 27, 28; PL 34, p. 29.
37. Ibid.
38. *De doctrina christiana* I 23, 22; PL 34, p. 27.
39. Ibid.
40. *De doctrina christiana* I 24, 24; PL 34, p. 27.
41. "Ne aut diligat quod non est diligendum, aut non diligat quod est diligendum, aut amplius diligat quod minus est diligendum, aut aeque diligat quod vel minus vel amplius diligendum est, aut minus vel amplius quod aeque diligendum est" [He neither loves what he ought not to

However, one may not remove this order of value-ranking from its cultural-historical context, from the peculiar entwinement of Greek philosophy (in particular, Platonism) with the Christian view of life.

In considering the following chapters of the "*Confessiones*" (lib. X, cap. 30 ff.), we will have to pay attention to the following four groups of problems:

1. The problem of "*tentatio.*" In this, the complex of enactment of my concrete full self-experience: how I decide.—From the problem of *tentatio*, we will get to the basic sense of self-experience as *historical.*

2. Connected to the *tentatio* is the "*defluxus in multum*" [flowing into the many] (into the multiplicity of the significances of factical life). The "*molestia*" (burden, trouble) proves to be constitutive for the concept of facticity.

3. The problem of the meaning of "*quaestio mihi factus sum*" [I have become a question to myself]. The becoming-a-question-to-oneself is meaningful only in the concrete context of self-experience. It is not a question of objective presence, but of authentic selfly existence.

4. The problem of the *basic orientation of* dilectio *in a determinate axiological system.*—It is to be decided to what extent this originates from one's own experience, and to what extent it can be demonstrated to have been determined by the cultural-historical situation of Augustine.

The problem of the universal theory of value is connected to Neo-Platonism and the doctrine of the *summum bonum,* in particular, to the conception of the way in which the *summum bonum* becomes accessible. The Pauline passage of the Letter to the Romans, chapter 1:20, is fundamental for the whole of Patristic "philosophy," for the orientation of the formation of Christian doctrine in Greek philosophy. The motif for the Greek underlying structure and re-structuring [*Unter- und Neubau*] of Christian dogmatism has been taken from this passage. However, this "pre-structure" [*Vor-bau*] was then structured into the basic patterns of the Christian thought of the dogmatism. For this reason, one cannot simply dismiss the Platonic in Augustine; and it is a misunderstanding to believe that in going back to Augustine, one can gain the authentically Christian.

Rom. 1:19 f. says: ὁ θεὸς γὰρ αὐτοῖς ἐφανέρωσεν. τὰ γὰρ ἀόρατα αὐοῦ ἀπὸ κτίδεως κόσμου τοῖς ποιήμασιν νοούμενα καθορᾶται, ἥ τε ἀΐδιος αὐτοῦ δύναμις καὶ θειότης . . . Since the estimation of the world, what is invisible in God is seen by thought in His works.

This proposition returns again and again in Patristic writings; it gives direction to the (Platonic) ascent from the sensible world to the supersensible world. It is (or is grasped as) the confirmation of Platonism, taken from Paul.

love, nor fails to love what he ought to love, nor loves that more which ought to be loved less, nor loves that equally which ought to be loved either less or more, nor loves that less or more which ought to be loved equally]. (*De doctrina christiana* I 27, 28; PL 34, p. 29.)

However, this is a misunderstanding of the passage from Paul. Only *Luther* really understood this passage for the first time. In his earliest works, Luther opened up a new understanding of primordial Christianity. Later on, he himself fell victim to the burden of tradition: then, the beginning of *Protestant scholasticism* sets in.

The insights of Luther's early period are decisive for the cultural [*geistigen*] connections of Christianity to culture. Today, this is misperceived in the concern for Christian-religious renewal.

Luther's view finds a clear expression in his 1518 Heidelberg Dissertation. In it, he defends forty theses: twenty-eight theological ones and twelve philosophical ones. For us, the theses 19, 21, and 22 are important here.

(19) "Non ille digne Theologus dicitur, qui invisibilia Dei per ea, quae facta sunt, intellecta conspicit" [The man who looks upon the invisible things of God as they are perceived in created things does not deserve to be called a theologian].[42] He who sees what is invisible of God in what has been created, is no theologian.—The presentation [*Vorgabe*] of the object of theology is not attained by way of a metaphysical consideration of the world.

(21) "Theologus gloriae dicit malum bonum et bonum malum, Theologus crucis dicit id quod res est" [The theologian of glory calls evil good and good evil, while the theologian of the cross says what a thing is].[43] The *theologus gloriae* who aesthetically takes delight in the wonders of the world, names what is sensible in God. The theologian of the cross says how things are.

(22) "Sapientia illa, quae invisibilia Dei ex operibus intellecta conspicit, omnino inflat, excaecat et indurat" [The wisdom that looks upon the invisible things of God from His works, inflates us, blinds us, and hardens our heart].[44] Your wisdom that sees what is invisible of God in His works, inflates, blinds us, and hardens us.

4. *The* confiteri *and the Concept of Sin*
[Supplement following § 13 b]

It is important that the *molestia* belongs to facticity, a belonging-together that arises in one's own experiencing, just as the continuous experiencing of, and self-confrontation with, *molestia* belongs to authentic life. Later on, the *molestia* is intellectualized [*vergeistigt*]; the *tentatio* is no longer sensuous-material, but more hidden and more dangerous. With this, the sense of factic-

42. M. Luther, *Disputatio Heidelbergae habita*. 1518. *D. Martin Luthers Werke* (critical edition), vol. 1, Weimar, 1883, p. 354.

43. Ibid.

44. Ibid.

ity, and the sense of the "*quaestio mihi factus sum*" [I have become a question to myself], increase.

Thus, we have treated four basic phenomena, which are important for the further discussion of the *Confessiones:*

(1) the *tentatio;* (2) the *defluxus in multum* [flowing into the many] and the *molestia;* (3) the "*quaestio mihi factus sum*"; (4) the question of the axiological forming-out.

In our further interpretation, we have to take into account two things:

1. That Augustine communicates all phenomena in the posture of the *confiteri* [to confess], standing within the task of searching and of having God. The reference to the authentic condition of the enactment of experiencing God is important. The condition is such that, if one takes it seriously, one (initially) moves away from God. With the "*quaestio mihi factus sum*," the distance to God increases.

2. That our possibility of interpretation has its limits, for the problem of *confiteri* arises from the consciousness of one's own sin. The tendency toward *vita beata* [the happy life]—not *in re* [in actuality] but *in spe* [in hope]— emerges only from out of the *remissio peccatorum* [remission of sins], the reconciliation with God. But we have to leave aside here these phenomena because they are very difficult and require conditions of understanding that cannot be achieved in this context. However, in our consideration, which is of the order of understanding, we will gain what is basic for the access to those phenomena of sin, grace, etc. However, the consciousness of sin—and the manner in which God is present in it—stands, in Augustine, in a peculiar interrelation to Neo-Platonism. (For this reason, his conception of sin cannot [. . .]* guide the phenomenological explication of the "genuine" phenomenon.)

In Augustine, the *concept of sin* has a threefold character:

1. A *theoretical* one: sin as *privatio boni* [privation of the good], oriented toward the *summum bonum* [highest good]. Sin is a lower measure of reality; for this reason, it bears within itself a higher measure of mortality so that it itself is death, so that death is given with it.—These are Plotinian ideas that connect to a certain conception of Paul's thoughts in the Letter to the Romans.

2. An *aesthetic* one: Cf. for this the beginning of *Confessiones* Bk. VIII, ch. 7.—After the narrative of Ponticianus about Saint Antony, it is said: "Tu autem, Domine, inter verba eius retorquebas me ad meipsum, auferens me a dorso meo ubi me posueram, dum nollem me attendere; et constituebas me ante faciem meam, ut viderem quam turpis essem, quam distortus et sordidus, maculosus et ulcerosus" [But while he spoke, You, my Lord, turned me around

---

*[One word illegible.]

toward myself, so that I no longer turned back on myself where I had placed myself while I was not willing to observe myself. And you showed me my face so that I might see how ugly I was, how disfigured and dirty, blemished and ulcerous].[45]

3. The character of an *enactment:* only he loses You who leaves You; he who leaves You, to where does he flee, if not from You as the merciful one to You as the wrathful one? This is the decisive conception.

5. Augustine's Position on Art *("De Musica")*
[Supplement following § 13 e]

Ch. 33. Important for Augustine's position on *art,* in particular, on *music.* One may not extract an analysis of art from Augustine. His basic motives are important. Art must be integrated into a higher complex. Likewise, *aesthetics.* It must explicate the aesthetic objects such that they are grasped as a path to absolute beauty (Neo-Platonic conception!).

For this, Augustine's statement in the *"Retractationes"* about his book *"De musica libri VI"* is characteristic.

Of the six books on music, the sixth one is the most crucial one, because it deals with its object in an authentic mode of knowledge, namely in the following way: it is shown how the transition is possible from the sensible and mental relations of numbers, which themselves are changeable, to the unchangeable relations of numbers, which themselves are in unchangeable truth.

"De musica" is Augustine's formal aesthetic; in this book, he delivers a theory of numbers and a doctrine of relations. He distinguishes five different species of "numbers" (*musica ars bene modulandi* [music is the art of playing well]):

1. *numeri "in ipso sono"* [numbers "in the sound"][46]

2. *numeri "in ipso sensu audientis"* [numbers "in the auditory sense itself"][47]

3. *numeri "in ipso actu pronuntiantis"* [numbers "in the act of pronunciation"][48]

4. *numeri "in ipsa memoria"* [numbers "in memory"][49] (as they are in consciousness)

---

45. *Confessiones* VIII, 7; PL 32, p. 756.
46. *De musica* VI 2; PL 32, p. 1163.
47. Ibid.
48. *De musica* VI 3; PL 32, p. 1164.
49. Ibid.

5. *numeri "in ipso naturali judicio sentiendi"* [numbers "in the natural judgment of the perceiving listener"],[50] or: *numer iudiciales* [numbers of judgment]. (In these "numbers in themselves" lies the motive of the transition toward the unchangeable.)

Augustine does not offer a psychological presentation, but the manner of comportment in listening.

Cf.in the *Enarrationes in Psalmos* (T) the frequent designation of the New Testament as *"canticus novus"* [new song].—"Cantare est res amantis" [Singing is the loving thing.]—The interpretation of art: taking art back into the wholeness of factical human life, albeit in such a way that it is not metaphysically formed-out, but has its determinate place on the basis of the order of value, from out of the *summum bonum.* However, these considerations may not be severed from the whole context, or else phenomena are overlooked.

Augustine's own words about *"De musica"* are characteristic for this: those who read these books will find that we are dealing with things in art not on the basis of taking an evasive stance in which we then dwell, but from out of the necessity to understand art itself as a path. ("Illos igitur libros qui leget, inveniet nos cum grammaticis et poeticis animis, non habitandi electione, sed itinerandi necessitate versatos" [And so, whoever reads the preceding books will find us dwelling with grammatical and poetical minds, not through choice of permanent company, but through necessity of wayfaring].[51])

Even if the way is base (*vilis via*), the goal does not have to be base.

These writings have been written for those who deal with worldly science and literature, and who are entangled in manifold errors, and who squander their good mental capacities on little things (*in nugis*) without seeing what is really valuable (*ibi delectat* [what is delightful there]) in the objects with which they are dealing.

The entire structure of *"De musica"* has to be understood in this context. The individual *"numeri"* and their order has to be understood on the basis of the basic orientation toward the *summum bonum.* This order stems from Neo-Platonic aesthetics.

6. Videre (lucem) Deum *[To See God (the light)]*
[Supplement following § 13 g]

"Decus meum" [my glory], said about God—a *Neo-Platonic* thought.

"Lux" [Light], determined through the Neo-Platonic tradition and the Gospel of John, both of which go back to Greek philosophy. John 1:4: ἐν αὐτῷ

---

50. *De musica* VI 4; PL 32, p. 1165.
51. *De musica* VI 1; PL 32, p. 1161 f.

[τῷ λόγῳ] ζωὴ ἦν τὸ φῶς τῶν ἀνθρώπων· καὶ τὸ φῶς ἐν τῇ σκοτίᾳ αὐτὸ οὐ κατέλαβεν. [In it (the word) was life, which was the light of men. The light shines in the darkness, and the darkness does not overcome it.]

Connection to the question of grasping God. Cf. Augustine's commentary on the Gospel of John (*Tractatus in Joannis Evangelium*) and Letter 146 ("*De videndo Deo*"); the older writings are frequently different.

Lux and *lumen* are to be distinguished. *Lux:* in an objective sense, what is present as the object of seeing (*regina colorum* [the queen of colors]). *Lumen:* brightness, always of the soul.

Cf. *Quaestionem Evangeliorum libri duo: "Si quod lumen est in te tenebrae sunt, ipsae tenebrae quantae (Matth. VI, 23)? Lumen* dicit bonam intentionem mentis, qua operamur: tenebras autem ipsa opera appellat, sive quia ignoratur ab aliis quo animo illa faciamus, sive quia eorum exitum etiam ipsi nescimus, id est, quomodo exeant atque proveniant eis quibus nos ea bono animo impendimus" [*If the light in you is darkness, how great is the darkness itself (Matt. 6:23)? Light* speaks of the good intention of the mind with which we labor: but darkness calls itself labor, be it because it does not know of another soul through which we may do things, or because we do not know their ruin even in itself, that is, how they go out and flourish through those things that we use in that good soul].[52] (The [. . .]* are those in whose direction we intended them, with good intentions.)

Tractatus de Joannis Evangelio I 18 (on John 1:4): "*Et vita erat lux hominum;* et ex ipsa vita [Verbi] homines illuminantur. Pecora non illuminantur, quia pecora non habent rationales mentes, quae possint videre sapientiam" [*And life was the light of men;* and through the life itself [of the word] men are illuminated. Animals are not illuminated because animals have no rational minds which are able to see wisdom].[53] (The truth of life; not theoretical.) 1:19: "Sed forte stulta corda adhuc capere istam lucem non possunt, quia peccatis suis aggravantur [. . .] Non ideo cogitent quasi absentem esse lucem, [. . .]: ipsi enim propter peccata tenebrae sunt" [But perhaps foolish hearts cannot grasp that light because they are weighed down by their own sins (. . .) But they should not think, therefore, that the light is absent (. . .): for they are darkness themselves because of their sins].[54] "Quomodo homo positus in sole caecus, praesens est illi sol, sed ipse soli absens est [He is not to be had for the sun, whereas the sun is waiting for him; possibly, the sun is objectively at his disposal]; sic omnis stultus, omnis iniquus, omnis impius, caecus est corde. Praesens est sapientia, sed cum caeco praesens est, oculis eius absens est: [. . .] Quid ergo faciat iste? Mundet [oculos] unde possit

---

52. *Quaestionem Evangeliorum libri duo* II 15; PL 35, p. 1339.
*[Two words illegible.]
53. *Tractatus in Joannis Evangelium* I 18; PL 35, p. 1388.
54. *Tractatus in Joannis Evangelium* I 19; PL 35, p. 1388.

videri Deus. [. . .] quia sordidus et saucios oculos haberet" [Just as a blind man stands in the sun, the sun is present to him, but he himself is absent to the sun (He is not to be had for the sun, whereas the sun is waiting for him; possibly, the sun is objectively at his disposal); so every fool, every unjust man, every impious man, is blind in his heart. Wisdom is present, but since it is present to a blind man, it is absent from his eyes: (. . .) So what should that man do? He is to purify (his eyes) so that God can be seen. (. . .) because he had sordid and wounded eyes].[55] Then that which corrupts (*pulvis, fumus* [dust, smoke]—sin) is removed by the physician so that you can see what is meant for your eyes. "Tolle inde ista omnia, et videbis sapientiam" [Take all of this away, and you will see wisdom].[56] (Matt. 5:8: for "blessed are the pure in heart," etc.)—How does this "purification of the eyes" proceed? Through faith. Acts of the Apostles 15:9: ". . . τῇ πίστει καθαρίσας τὰς καρδίας αὐτῶν" ["and put no difference between us and them, purifying their hearts by faith" (after he purified their hearts through faith). "Mundat cor fides Dei, mundum cor videt Deum" [Faith in God purifies the heart, the pure heart sees God].[57] Through what faith ("*quali fide*") is the heart purified? (The demons, too, fear God and have a kind of faith in him, that is, not the right kind. Acts of the Apostles). Answer: "*Fides quae per dilectionem operatur (Galat.* V 6 [πίστις δι᾽ ἀγάπης ἐνεργουμένη]) [. . .] sperat quod Deus pollicetur. Nihil ista definitione perpensius, nihil perfectius. Ergo tria sunt illa [fides, spes, caritas]" [*Faith which works through love* (Gal 5:6), (. . .) hopes for what God promises. There is no more perfect, more thought-out definition than that. So we have these three (faith, hope, love)].[58] "Comes est ergo fidei spes. Necessaria quippe spes est" [Therefore, hope is the companion of faith. Hope is indeed necessary].[59] As long as we do not see what we believe. So that we do not fall. (This is a Plotinian concept, in a good Christian re-functioning.) "Tolle fidem, perit quod credis [then what he believes will perish]; tolle charitatem, perit quod agis. Fidei enim pertinet ut credas [fides = fiducia = trust, as in Luther]; charitati [pertinet], ut agas" [Take away faith, and what you believe perishes (then what he believes will perish); take away love, and what you do perishes. For it belongs to faith that you may believe (faith = trust = trust, as in Luther); (it belongs) to love that you act].[60] "Et modo ipsa fides quid agit?" [And what does faith itself do?][61] All the testimonies from Scripture, all doctrines and the corresponding instructions, what do they do? Only that

55. Ibid.
56. Ibid.
57. *Sermones* LIII 10, 10; PL 38, p. 368.
58. *Sermones* LIII 10, 11; PL 38, p. 369.
59. Ibid.
60. Ibid.
61. *Sermones* LIII 11, 12; PL 38, p. 369.

we see "per speculum in aenigmate" [by a mirror in an enigma].[62] But merely because faith does only that, there is no reason that you, in turn, return "ad istam faciem tuam" [to that face of yours],[63] to your own "makings" (that is, to what you have made of God for yourself, as an object). "Faciem cordis cogita" [Think of the face of the heart].[64] (God in His objecthood [*in der Gegenständlichkeit*], as appropriated by the heart in its authentic life.)

"Coge cor tuum cogitare divina" [Force your heart to think about divine matters],[65] do not leave it alone. (To interpret this as subjectivism is misguided. We are dealing with the condition of access to God. God is not made; rather, the self gains the enactmental condition of the experience of God. In the concern for the selfly life, God is present. God as object in the sense of the *facies cordis* [face of the heart] operates in the authentic life of human beings.) Shut out all those "similar" bodily things that leap into the mind of the one thinking in this way. You cannot say (of God) "that is how he is," but only "*non est hoc*" ["this is not what he is"]. When will you be able to say: "that is what God is"? "Nec cum videbis: quia ineffabile est quod videbis" [Not when you will see him, because what you will see is ineffable].[66] "Cogitanti ergo tibi de Deo, occurrit aliqua fortasse in humana specie mira et amplissima magnitudo" [So when thinking about God, perhaps some vast and wonderful shape in vaguely human form occurs to you];[67] for example, God is compared to an enormous human being. However, when you are engaged in this effort, [*finisti alicubi*] "si finisti, Deus non est. Si non finisti, facies ubi est?" [(somewhere you have reached the end of it); if you have reached the end of it, it is not God. If you have not reached the end of it, where is the face?][68] "Quid agis, stulta et carnalis cogitatio?" [What are you doing, foolish and carnal thinking?][69] You have created monstrosities for yourself; and yet you have removed yourself further and further from God. Another makes God even larger by simply adding a yard.

An objection from Scripture is raised against this (*Sermo* 53, ch. 12 n. 13). This matter is important for Augustine's interpretation of Scripture.

From Isaiah, a contradicting passage is drawn upon: Isa. 66:1, where God is thought of as a giant human being. Heaven is my throne. Augustine responds to this: You did not read it to its end! Who measured the heaven with the palm of his hand?

62. Ibid.
63. Ibid.
64. Ibid.
65. Ibid.
66. Ibid.
67. Ibid., p. 370.
68. Ibid.
69. Ibid.

The thought of *mundare* [purifying], as a condition of access, is already present in the earlier philosophical writings of Augustine, a Platonic thought, in Plotinus connected to his conception of ascesis. The *mundare* is enacted through the *fides Christiana* [Christian faith] (not through demonic faith). *Fides* is an enactmental complex of trust and love; the posture of expectation must be present. Every cosmic-metaphysical reification of the concept of God, even as irrational concept, must be warded off. One has to appropriate the *facies cordis* [face of the heart] (inwardness) for oneself. God will be present in the inward human being when we will have understood what breadth, length, height, depth (*latitudo, longitudo, altitudo, profundum*) mean, and therewith, the sense of the infinity of God for the thought of the heart. Ponder within yourself when I say: "extension." Do not leap away with your imagination to the measurements of earthly extension. Understand everything "*in te*" [in yourself]. *Latitudo* = richness, wealth in good works; *longitudo* = persistence and perseverance; *altitudo* = expectation of that which is above you (*sursum cor* [the heart upwards]); *profundum* = God's grace. All this is not to be understood according to an objective symbolism, but rather referred back to the enactmental sense of inner life.

Symbolism of the cross: *latitudo:* where the hands are fixed; *longitudo:* the body that stands; *altitudo:* the expectation of [. . .]* G.; *profundum:* concealed—"*inde*" [from it] [. . .]*70

Dilectio [love]: If you count it, it is one (ἕν Plotinian [. . .]**), but if you consider it, it contains many moments. "Si Deus dilectio, quisquis diliget dilectionem, Deum diligit" [If God is love, whoever loves love, loves God].71

Every love includes a certain benevolence (*benevolentia*) for the one who is loved. (Sensuous love = *amor*. *Dilectio* relates to things of higher value.) We do not love the human being in the way the Lord asked Peter: Do you love me? But we also should not love the human being in the way gourmands talk when they say: I love wild game. The gourmand loves them only to kill

---

*[Three words illegible.]

70. "Non frustra ergo crucem elegit, ubi te huic mundo crucifigeret. Nam latitudo est in cruce transversum lignum, ubi figuntur manus: propter bonorum operum significationem. Longitudo est in ea parte ligni, quae ab ipso transverso ad terram tendit. Ibi enim corpus crucifigitur, et quodam modo stat: et ipsa statio perseverantiam significat. Altitudo autem in illo ligno est, quod ab eodem transverso supernorum exspectatio. Ubi profundum, nisi in ea parte quae terrae dixifa est. Occulta est enim gratia, et in abdito latet. Non videtur, sed inde eminet quod videtur" [Thus, it is not for nothing that he chose the cross on which to crucify you to this world. The breadth of the cross is given by the horizontal beam, where his hands are fixed: thus signifying good works. Length is given by that part of the vertical beam which extends from the crossbeam to the ground. That is where his body is crucified, and, so to speak, stands: and this standing signifies perseverance. Height is given by that part of the vertical beam which sticks up above the crossbeam to the head, so that it signifies expectation of the things that are above. Where do we have depth but in the part which is fixed in the ground. For grace is hidden, and remains concealed. It cannot be seen, but from it rises up what can be seen]. (*Sermones* LIII 15, 16; PL 38, p. 371 f.)

**[One word illegible.]

71. *Tractatus in Epistolam Ioannis ad Parthos* IX 10; PL 35, p. 2052.

them. So he loves them such that they are not (*non esse*). One may not love human beings in this way, assigning them into one's own aims. Friendship, however, is something like *benevolentia* after all, a gift of our love. But what if there were nothing of our love that we could give? Since one loves, the pure benevolence as such suffices. We ought not and may not wish for miseries that enable us to do good deeds. Take away human misery and good deeds disappear! The work of mercy disappears, but the glowing of noble love remains. Originally (*per me ames* [?]) [you love through me], you love the human being in happiness, to whom you have nothing to give. Such love is pure and more noble if the other is noble; you elevate yourself, you attribute to yourself the achievement and you view the other to whom you give something as submissive to you.[72]

So wish for an equal to whom you cannot give anything in human affairs, so that he stands with you under the one to whom nothing at all can be given by humans. In this *optare* [wishing], you appropriate the possibility of genuine loving.

Authentic love has a basic tendency toward the *dilectum, ut sit* [being loved so that he may be]. Thus, love is the will toward the being of the loved one. (The content of the sense of being must correspond to the particular kind of the loved object.)

Love of oneself [*Eigenliebe*] has the tendency to secure one's own being, but in the wrong way: not as self-concern but as the calculation of the experiential complex in relation to one's self-world. Thus, "self-love" [*Selbstliebe*] is really self-hate. (Eliminate the secondary meaning of "hate"!)

Communal-worldly love has the sense of helping the loved other toward his existence, so that he comes to himself.

Genuine love of God has the sense of wishing to make God accessible to oneself as the one who exists in an absolute sense. This is the greater difficulty of life.

The problem of the phenomenological study of "emotional acts," placed in the framework of the schema of the complex and order of *value*-ranking, is nonsensical. The problem of love must be removed from the "axiological" realm. F. Brentano's so-called "phenomenological" analysis of acts runs exactly counter to the genuine tendency of phenomenology.

Objecthood of God. Deus lux, dilectio, summum bonum, incommutabilis substantia, summa pulchritudo [God the light, highest God, unchangeable substance, highest beauty].

In each of these determinations, different modes of access, and different modes of the point of departure and of the motive for the access, show themselves. Further, different modes *within* the access, within what is experienced

---

72. Cf. *Tractatus in Epistolam Ioannis ad Parthos* VIII 5; PL 35, p. 2038.

in the access to be explicated later. (The means of determination will be taken from different fields.) Finally, different modes of forming-out through the *means* of explication, which are at times self-illuminating—that is, they arise from a new point of departure in one's own experience—at other times, they keep within the traditional framework (sometimes entirely, sometimes in a modified form).—On the whole, however, the explication of the experience of God in Augustine is specifically "Greek" (in the sense in which our entire philosophy is still "Greek"). We have not arrived at a radical critical posing of the question and consideration of the origin (destruction).

This is especially true in reference to the determination of the objecthood of God from the modes of access. (Here, it is also questionable whether all modes of access themselves are original!) The modes of access have a connection in the current enactment, in the facticity of experience itself. An orientation toward the different attitudinal possibilities, faculties of reason, and the like, leads us astray, both in an ordering classification and in a "transcendental" formulation of the problem. One has to liberate oneself from this if one wishes to understand the problems of enactment. This "liberation" is not enacted all at once; rather, it is itself a task of gaining access as such.

For this problem, Augustine's treatment of the *tentationes* may serve as a guide. For the different directions of the *tentationes* are not gained by way of a classification according to the faculties of the soul, but in the factical enactment of (Christian) life. This becomes clear in progressing from the *concupiscientia carnis* [desires of the flesh] to the *ambitio saeculi* [secular ambition].

7. Intermediary Consideration of timor castus [chaste fear]
[Supplement following § 16]

As a complementary discussion, the phenomena of the *love of God* and the *fear of God* shall be treated in view of the *objecthood of God* that is rendered closer through them.

By falling into *tentatio,* one forsakes the possibility of a genuine love and of a pure fear of God: "vel [. . .] non amare te, nec caste timere te" [that men neither love You nor fear You chastely].[73] The *timor Dei* [fear of God] characterizes a decisive moment of the experiential complex in which God becomes an object [*gegenständlich wird*].

This is supposed to rid us of the misunderstanding that the real experience consists in a certain act—of a theoretical or non-theoretical kind—or in a connection of parts of such acts. Rather, the experience of God in Augustine's

73. *Confessiones* X 36, 59; PL 32, p. 804.

sense is not to be found in an isolated act or in a certain moment of such an act, but in an experiential complex of the *historical* facticity of one's own life. This facticity is what is authentically *original*. From it, isolated modes of comportment can be separated out and, in being torn loose from it, they can lead to an empty conception of religiosity and theology.

The tendency of *amare* [to love] is a concern for oneself, the genuine *amor sui* [self-love] is love of oneself. Exactly this leads us into temptation. For this reason, it is precisely here that serious trouble (*molestia*) arises. Since the individual is entirely on his own, the greatest danger emerges, the danger that he forms his possible communal world—before which he puts on airs—from out of himself. From this latter consideration, Augustine comes to the "*tremor cordis sui*" [trembling of his heart].[74] This is a phenomenon that is constitutive of the concern for oneself: the *genuine* timor [fear]. Slipping away from it is a self-removal from the "*caste timere te*" [chaste fearing of You], the *pure* fearing of God.

What now is the genuine "*timor castus*" [chaste fear] as opposed to the non-genuine "*timor servilis*" [servile fear]?

1. The *timere* in general and its possible motives.

2. Opposition: *timor castus—timor servilis*. (The How of the motivating affect.)

3. What sense does genuine fear have in connection with experiencing oneself? (That is, at once, in the basic experience of God.) How does God become an absolute object [*absolut gegenständlich*] in genuine fear? How is His objecthood determined on this basis?

(N.B. Our interpretation is still moving on a preliminary level: we do not yet have the authentic phenomenological concepts.)

Augustine begins with the concrete enactmental complex of fearing. He analyzes the *non timere* [not fearing] and its possible motives. He describes the mind of someone who claims to be without fear. In this, Augustine gains two motivational directions of not-fearing, and thus, the starting point of the division between *timor castus* [chaste fear] and *timor servilis* [servile fear]. He links *timere* with "*dolere*" [feeling pain] (*dolere* as a disposition of the mind, not pain but distress). In this, he begins with the *non dolere* or "*sanitas*" [health], of which different kinds are distinguished.

Enarrationes in Psalmos, ad Ps. 55, V. 4: *non timeo* [I do not fear]. Question as to the *causa* [cause]. The cause may be: 1. The *praesumptio, spes*, trust; 2. *duritia* (hardening): "multi enim nimia superbia nihil timent" [for many do not fear anything in excessive pride].[75]

---

74. "In his omnibus atque hujusmodi periculis et laboribus vides tremorem cordis mei" [In all these perils and travails, You see the trembling of my heart]. (*Confessiones* X 39, 64; PL 32, p. 806.)

75. *Enarrationes in Psalmos* LV 6; PL 35, p. 650.

"Aliud est sanitas corporis, aliud stupor corporis [dullness], aliud immortalitas corporis. Sanitas quidem perfecta, immortalitas est" [Something else is
the health of the body, and yet something else the stupor of the body [dull-
ness], and yet something else the immortality of the body. Indeed, perfect
health is immortality].[76] However, there is already health in this life, when we
are not sick. What does this show?

There are three *affectiones corporis* [conditions of the body]: (1) s*anitas*
[health], (2) *stupor* [stupor, dullness], (3) *immortalitas* [immortality].

1. "Sanitas aegritudinem non habet; sed tamen quando tangitur et moles-
tatur, dolet" [Health does not have sickness, but it is painful when one is being
touched and disturbed].[77]

2. "Stupor autem non dolet; amisit sensum doloris, tanto insensibilior,
quanto pejor" [But stupor feels no pain; it has lost the sense of pain; the more
insensitive, the worse it is].[78]

3. *Immortalitas:* it has no pain, since the possibility of *corruptio* [corrup-
tion, temptation] has been taken from it.[79]

Thus, with *stupor* and *immortalitas,* there is no pain, but this does not mean
that the *stupidus* [stupefied, dull person] is *immortalis* [immortal]. On the
contrary: the *dolere* of the healthy person is closer to immortality than is the
dull person's lack of pain: "vicinior est immortalitati sanitas dolentis, quam
stupor non sentientis" [the pain of the healthy one is closer to immortality
than is the stupor of the insensitive one].[80]

At times, arrogant people are seen as braver than Jesus who says: my soul
is sad until death. That cannot be. He who does not feel the pain because of
his insensitivity has not put on immortality but has taken off sensitivity ("non
immortalitate indutus, sed sensu exutus"[81]).

Do not keep your soul in a state without passion!—Genuine bravery requires the possibility of fear. The *delectari* [to be delighted] itself is eliminated
in the one who is hardened, although, in this hardening itself, there is still a
certain sense of *delectari.* Agreeableness with everybody is insensitivity, but
not true tranquility.

Having no fear in trusting something is what is genuine; the *fiducia* [trust],
as always-holding-on-to something (connection with *spes* [hope] and *amor*
(*caritas*) [love (charity, love)].

The interpretation of two textual passages that (seemingly) contradict each
other:

76. Ibid.
77. Ibid.
78. Ibid., p. 650 f.
79. Cf. ibid., p. 651.
80. Ibid.
81. Ibid.

1. 1 John 4:18: *"Timor non est in charitate"* [There is no fear in love]. (There is no fear in authentic love.)

2. Psalms 18, V. 10: *"Timor Domini castus, permanens in saeculum saeculi"* [The fear of the Lord is chaste, enduring forever and ever]. (An observation of the interpretation of Scripture follows: a comparison of two passages with the consonance—*consonantia*—of two flutes.)

The contradiction is resolved by the distinction between two kinds of fear: *timor castus* [chaste fear] and *non castus* [non-chaste fear]. "Si enim adhuc propter poenas times Deum, nondum amas quem sic times. Non bona desideras, sed mala caves" [For if you as yet fear God because of punishment, you do not love whom you thus fear. You do not desire the good things, but you are afraid of the evil ones].[82] *Timor* "non enim venit ex amore Dei, sed ex timore poenae" [This fear does not come from love of God, but from fear of punishment].[83]

But he who has begun to strive for the good for its own sake lives in *pure* fear. "Quis est timor castus? Ne amittas ipsa bona. Intendite. Aliud est timere Deum, ne mittat te in gehennam cum diabolo; aliud est timere Deum, ne resedat a te" [What is chaste fear? The fear that you lose the good things. Mark! It is one thing to fear God lest He cast you into hell with the devil, and another thing to fear God lest He forsake you].[84] This fear does not have the direction of keeping something or someone at bay, but of pulling something or someone toward oneself. *Timere separationem (est) amare veritatem* [Fearing separation (is) loving the truth]. In this fear, the soul feels the *majestas Dei* [majesty of God].

Pure fear is connected to trust. *Si times latronem* [If you fear the robber], you hope for somebody else's help, not for help from the one who threatens you most of all (the robber). But if you fear God this way, to where should you turn? *Vis ab illo fugere? Ad ipsum fuge! Vis fugere ab irato, fuge ad placatum! Placabis, si speras* [You want to flee? Flee to Him! You want to flee from wrath, flee toward reconciliation! You will reconcile if you have hope].[85]

---

82. *Tractatus in Epistolam Joannis ad Parthos* IX 5; PL 35, p. 2048. [Augustine reads *"timor castus"* instead of the *"timor sanctus"* of the Vulgata. Editor's note.] Cf. *Enarrationes in Psalmos* XVIII 10; PL 36, p. 155.
83. *Tractatus in Epistolam Joannis ad Parthos* IX 5; PL 35, p. 2049.
84. Ibid.
85. [Editor's note: This passage is probably based on the following passages.] "Si vis ab illo fugere, ad ipsum fuge. Ad ipsum fuge confitendo, non ab ipso latendo: latere enim non potes, sed confiteri potes" [If you want to flee from Him, flee to Him. Flee to him by confessing, not from Him by hiding: you cannot hide, but you can confess]. (*Tractatus in Epistolam Joannis ad Parthos* VI 3; PL 35, p. 2021.) "Ille corde tuo interior est. Quocumque ergo fugeris, ibi est. Teipsum quo fugies? Nonne quocumque fugeris, te sequeris? Quando autem et teipso interior est, non est quo fugias a Deo irato, nisi ad Deum placatum: prorsus non est quo fugias. Vis fugere ab ipso? Fuge ad ipsum" [He is more interior to you than your heart. Therefore, wherever you flee, He is there. Where do you flee from yourself? Do you not follow yourself wherever

The first fear (*timor servilis* [servile fear]), the "fear of the world" (from out of the surrounding world and the communal world), is the anxiousness that grips and overwhelms a person.—By contrast, *timor castus* [chaste fear] is the "selfly fear" that is motivated in authentic hope, in the trust that is enlivened from out of itself. This fear forms itself within myself from out of the relation in which I experience the world, in connection with the life's concern for authentic self-experience. *Nam si non times, aufert Deus, quid dedit* [For if you do not fear, God carries off what He gave]. Precisely in fear, I keep a *bonum* [good thing].

8. The Being of the Self
[Concluding Part of Lecture]

"*Vita*" (life) is no mere word, no formal concept, but a structural complex which Augustine himself saw—without, however, yet achieving sufficient conceptual clarity. Today, this clarity has still not been attained, because Descartes moved the study of the self as a basic phenomenon in a different, falling direction. Modern philosophy in its entirety has not been able to rid itself of this.

Descartes blurred [*verwässert*] Augustine's thoughts. Self-certainty and the self-possession in the sense of Augustine are entirely different from the Cartesian evidence of the "*cogito.*"

Cf. *De civitate Dei*, lib. XI, c. 26 ff. Following the dogma of the trinity, Augustine considers the human being. (Cf. the treatise *De trinitate.*)

We find in ourselves an image of the highest trinity, for:

1. *Sumus:* we *are* (*esse*).
2. We *know* about ourselves, as such (*nosse*).
3. We *love* the knowledge about our own being (*amare*).

These are the determinations of the authentic being of the self. "In his autem tribus [. . .] nulla nos falsitas veri similis turbat" [Moreover, in these three (statements) (. . .) we are not confused by any falsity masquerading as truth].[86] These are not objects; rather, without the stormy play of the imagination, that being which I know I love is most certain to me. Thus, it is certain: (1) that we love being, (2) that we love the *nosse* [knowing], (3) that we love the love itself in which we love (*ipso amor quo amamus* [the love itself that

---

you flee? So if He is more interior than you yourself, you cannot flee anywhere from an angry God except toward a reconciled God: it is precisely not where you may flee. Do you want to flee from Him? Flee toward Him]. (*Enarrationes in Psalmos* LXXIV 9; PL 36, p. 952 f.—Cf. *Enarrationes in Psalmos* XCIV 2; PL 37, p. 1217.)
   86. *De civitate Dei* XI, 26; loc. cit., p. 497.

we love]).—"Ibi esse nostrum non habebit mortem, ibi nosse nostrum non habebit errorem, ibi amare nostrum non habebit offensionem" [Then our being will not possess death, then our knowledge will not possess error, then our loving will have no obstacle].[87]

Although we have a self-certainty of our being, we are nonetheless uncertain as to how long we have to live (*quamdiu futurum sit* [how long the future may be]), whether our being will not let go at some point.

The self-certainty must be interpreted from out of factical being; it is possible only from out of faith.

Methodologically, it is important that one may not view this evidence in isolation, which would constitute a falling.

The evidence of the *cogito* is present, but it must find its foundation in the factical. For every science ultimately rests in factical existence.

<hr />

87. *De civitate Dei* XI, 28; loc. cit., p. 502.

THE PHILOSOPHICAL FOUNDATIONS OF MEDIEVAL MYSTICISM

[Outlines and Sketches for a Lecture, Not Held, 1918–1919]

The Philosophical Foundations of Medieval Mysticism[1]

The formulation is ambiguous. Phenomenological research into religious consciousness is the driving problem and method. This means: 1. (negatively) renunciation of constructive philosophy of religion, 2. (negatively) non-absorption in the purely historical as such, 3. tracing back to the genuinely clarified and genuinely originally seen phenomena to pure consciousness and its constitution. But herein lies the problem: gaining and understanding such phenomena in the first place *out of the historical*—this and its facticity in phenomenological primordial understanding.

In regard to this principal original tendency—and this is the only genuinely scientific one—the announced [project] involves a limitation in several respects, and indeed precisely when we become conscious of the ambiguities. First of all, turning to this, there arise:

A. The theme can be viewed purely according to the history of philosophy. "Philosophical foundations" means then: the metaphysical presuppositions, the epistemological views, the ethical doctrines, and above all the scientific aspect of the sphere of experience, the psychological positions of medieval mysticism. In this, the latter is understood as much as a form of experience as it is understood as (and especially) the theory and doctrine thereof—and at the same time as metaphysical interpretation and illumination on its basis. Pursuing these foundations in the history of philosophy leads us to Augustine, Neo-Platonism, Stoicism, Plato, and Aristotle. With this, "philosophical foundations" receives a different meaning, depending on how "mysticism" is to be understood.

The foreconception of mysticism can be clarified to a certain extent from the beginning, insofar as the differences are separated into entirely different regions: I. Experience ("life") [*Erlebnis* ("*Leben*")]; II. Theory of the experienced (mystical theology) and its theoretical metaphysical utilization (religious, mystical world-view); III. Theory of the experiencing itself; IV. What is tightly and in part necessarily bound up with I.: experiential guidance of experience itself, not to be confused with III.—which (taken genuinely) is what phenomenological understanding in its original return means, but which certainly may then no longer be characterized as "theory." Re. IV. The forms and shapes of practical guidance and realization and their teleology and structure, themselves experiential, not yet seen ("asceticism"). Why precisely IV. in mystical religiosity? Because here the religious world concentrates on the turbulence of the specific experience of the finding of God that secludes itself.

Question: In what direction and aim does our investigation regarding medieval mysticism proceed, if the primordial-scientific, phenomenological goal

1. Editor's note: this manuscript carries the date August 10, 1919.

genuinely guides us? *Which* aspects of mysticism, and *how* do they come into consideration? How is understanding guided and motivated? This means:

B. How must the theme be understood primordial-scientifically?[2]

This leads to problems of principle: regional division of worlds of experience (their completeness a spurious problem)—historical position in pure consciousness. Are all equally "primordially historical"? Genesis of the basic level also in the religious?

Experience and "concept." Our goal can never be to awaken religious life. That only [occurs] through such life itself.

Difficulty: only a religious person can understand religious life, for if it were otherwise, he would have no genuine reality. Certainly, but does this have any systematic or methodological disadvantages? It means only: "hands-off" for those who do not "feel" genuinely at home here. That holds everywhere.

On the other hand, experiences are brought into the sphere of absolute understandability precisely through primordial understanding. They are understood, and indeed genuinely so, and as such, *they* are *themselves* [experienced]—but not "themselves" in the sense of being unedited. "Opposition": "self" as edited and unedited. Above all, understandability does not mean "rationalization," dissolution of experience into its "logical components."

The phenomenological primordial understanding is so little prejudiced—not in the sense of neutral, rather originally absolute—that it carries within itself the possibilities of entering into the different worlds and forms of experience. It may not be thrown together with the specifically or regionally *theoretical.* In order [to arrive] at the *primordial-theoretical,* a new destruction of the situation [*Situationszerstörung*]—within the theoretical itself—is required—modification to original seeing [*Ursprungs-Sehen*].

To be carried out further, and likewise in order to illustrate the phenomenon of religious experience.

Understanding religious experiences, access to their forms of expression. How does a religious experience express itself? "Prayer" as expression (and individual starting point for return and entry). (The relational motif-reference of this entire problematic. Ultimately this holds true for the entire phenomenology.)

If we approach the religious life itself, genuinely and purely methodically: which fundamental strata, forms, turbulences are found there? How is this life constituted?

In this question of constitution one may not be misled by analogy with the theoretical and the constitution of the object of cognition, in the sense that one inquires only, raw and naked, into the religious thing or object. Rather,

---

2. And how is thus A to be taken into B in order to guarantee scientific authenticity?

one has to begin—purely and without prejudging the matter—with the fundamental turbulences and their motivational genesis: the fulfillments of an entirely originary [*originären*] "I can." "I"? (Here one must always pay attention to the levels and pre-forms and types of completion as well. These and the resulting of the result is itself always to be taken into the idea and essential motivation.)

Mysticism in the Middle Ages

Medieval mysticism as form of expression of religious experience. "Philosophical foundations" has several meanings. Intentionally without prejudging. It means:

The means for the formation of the expression.

Means for the ways of experience itself.

Means for the systematics ("conceptual" expression).

Medieval mysticism as form of expression: forms of expression of religious experience in general.—The problem of expression as such. (Cf. Spranger, *Volkelt-Festschrift*[3])—interpretive expression—justifying expression.—Problem of the fulfillment of experience in principal connection with it.

To extract the moments of constitution in medieval mysticism (phenomena of love of God in particular).

Understanding from out of the genuine aspect of consciousness (precisely to dismiss the Scholastic-Aristotelian, Platonic "explanations" and in part misinterpretations).

Reigning viewpoint: motivation, and consequently, also to research the doctrine of "causes."

Always to be separated in the investigation are: pure experience as such, the expression (the expressing elements), the "explanation" (interpretation), the employment.

The forms of experience are always only and *only* to be taken in their essence from out of their genuinely possible situations and situational circles. At issue is the concrete fullness precisely in the *eidos,* not isolated deduced concepts of genera.

Problem of the eidetic concretion, and that always at once with full fitting-into a *general* structure of experience and possibilities of modification.

"Time" therein, freed from its linear spatial conception, not as bare frame of construction, but as *motive.*

The experiential effects of "power," "grace," "wrath" of God.

---

3. Eduard Spranger, "Zur Theorie des Verstehens und zur geisteswissenschaftlichen Psychologie," in *Festschrift Johannes Volkelt zum 70. Geburtstag,* Munich 1918, pp. 337–403.

Constitution of religious objecthood: Is God constituted in prayer? Or is he already somehow religiously *pre-given* in *faith* ("love")? And prayer a special comportment toward God?

To what extent is there a possible multiplicity of constitutional types? Is there an essential connection between them?

Pay attention to the view that the Middle Ages had of emotional life. And indeed how? Released from the specific scholastic character.[4]

Mysticism (Directives)

A constituting moment: comportment toward the world (negative—repulsive?). To integrate the phenomenon and really localize it. To extract the problem as a fundamental one of constitution. (Therein to separate: I. the religious person in himself, II. the one coming around to religiosity. The latter type is derivative, and the ways of coming are to be understood only out of I.)

Return to the phenomenological aspects of the "world" and access to its constitution. The medieval image of the world may here not disturb the in-itself of phenomenal givenness, as long as only naturalistic and metaphysical explanations are taken not as a theoretical result *about,* but rather as *motivated* by, a particular *aspect of world.* This aspect itself is to be taken into account.

"Seclusion": its primordial motivation in the *religious,* also in the form of devotion to the world, also in Luther.[5]

What is the *positively constituting,* and out of what common ground are these "negative" and "positive" turbulences motivated? (Is this a genuine characterization at all?)

Seclusion: not a theoretical not-seeing, but an emotional one, in its primordial form precisely religious, and accordingly the ways and steps to it as "repulsion."

(Here, it also becomes questionable, whether the genuine is reached, with the bare seeing of God as the "positive" side of seclusion; whether the form of unification is not a different one. "Love.")

---

4. Cf. Wilhelm Dilthey, "Die Funktion der Anthropologie in der Kultur des 16. und 17. Jahrhunderts" [I.1 Fortbestand und Umbildungen der zwei Hauptformen der mittelalterlichen Anthropologie], in *Gesammelte Schriften,* vol. II, Leipzig and Berlin, 1914, pp. 418–422.

5. Cf. *Anfänge reformatorischer Bibelauslegung,* ed. Johannes Ficker, vol. 1: *Luthers Vorlesung über den Römerbrief 1515/16,* Leipzig, 1908, p. LXXXIII.

Construction (Starting Points)

The constitution of the experience of God (birth of God). The specific a priori of natural corruption (not capacity), humble letting-be [*Gelassenheit*], *gratia operans—gratia cooperans*. (To see everything in pure consciousness and to understand it as motivation.)

To understand the absolute originarily as religious, independent of any naturalistic-theoretical observation and "valuation" of being. It is precisely seen from out of the religious.

The motive of mysticism in absolute history as the preparation of *fides* [faith]. Realization of *humilitas* [humility] through seclusion. Mysticism gave Luther "a world of inner experience and also showed him the methodical way to win it and to expand it. For this reason, the motive of *humilitas* could also not by itself impede the happy, secure unfolding of *fiducia*. The *humilitas*, the *tribulatio*, comes to express itself as the personal certainty of salvation."[6]

The basic kinds of fulfillment of religious experiences, the motivating forms of constitution and formation of the fulfillment of given experiences: "revelation," "tradition," "congregation."

A part of the ontology of religion, major aim: phenomenology. Only a certain strongly methodical radius. No high-flying philosophy of religion. We stand at the beginning, or more precisely: we must go back to the genuine beginnings, and the world can calmly wait. For as a *religious person* I need no trace of the philosophy of religion. Life generates only life, but not the absolute intuition [*Schau*] as such; an entirely original material complex with its own laws.

Faith and Knowledge

The problem moves within a falsely one-sided *epistemologically* oriented sphere and is therefore no genuine problem at all, insofar as one has once seen the originary problem of the origin of worlds of experience. (A certain real kernel of legitimacy—which for a long time has still not been purely worked out, and which can be worked out only on the basis of the above— lies in the problem of theology as the "science of faith" in contrast to the other sciences.)

Sharply divorce the problem of theology and that of religiosity. In theology one must take care to note its constant dependency on philosophy and on the situation of the respective theoretical consciousness in general. Theology has

6. Ibid.

heretofore found no original theoretical basic posture that corresponds to the originality of its object.

On note 1, p. 67: Protestant faith and Catholic faith are *fundamentally differ-ent*. Noetically and noematically separated experiences. In Luther an *original* form of religiosity—one that is also not found in the mystics—breaks out.

The "holding-to-be-true" of Catholic faith is founded entirely otherwise than the *fiducia* of the reformers.

Phenomena which first come to be understood within the doctrine of the constitution of the religious world in general.

From there also the concept of "grace" differentiates itself, and with it, the entire "relationship" of grace and freedom, nature and grace; and the meaning of the phrase "gratia supponit naturam" [grace underlies nature]; the doctrine of the "iustificatio" and the conception of the sacrament.

In turn, the religious sense complexes are qualitatively entirely otherwise in primordial Christianity. The development of theology out of its various motives and its relationship to faith.

Irrationalism[7]

The chatter about mysticism as the "formless" is merely talk of fundamentally unscientific methods of conceptual or clever "oppositions." One reduces it to formulas, which is to say, says nothing substantial and cannot, in clinging to a word and a dogma. One intends what is correct: religious experience is not theoretical. But what does theoretical mean, and what does not theoretical mean?

In order to first of all reach this differentiation, I must *understand* from a higher point and without prejudice. The "concepts" of understanding, and all understanding in the genuinely philosophical sense, have not the slightest to do with rationalization.

What does it mean to "destroy" experience? What lies within this indicated "destruction" [*Zerstörung*] then, as soon as one becomes clear about its aim and its necessity? No substitution, no dissolution into concepts, no better explanation, not an active, likewise originary, *motivation* of the experience in question. As if now the philosophy of religion could after all encourage and enliven religion and the religious. But one can, after all, do only one thing: in the case of the inauthentic platitudes and constructive conceptuality, push aside into regional [?] districts of life, into a fabricated dimension of alleged philosophical "problems."

---

7. Editor's note: The ms. carries the date of August 14, 1919.

Historical Pre-givenness [Vorgegebenheit] *and the Finding of Essence*

"Pre-givenness" has precisely grown into essential constitution. The problem must be divided into different strata, and all inauthentic and *alleged* difficulties are to be excluded.

The question of whether non-religious persons understand the analysis as well is [to be distinguished] from the question of whether only religious persons can have a genuine "absolute" givenness. Further, whether that somehow limits the "essential validity" of the analysis, which, after all, is entirely independent of the number of those who recognize and understand.

From this, the entirely different question is [to be distinguished], in how far a completion of the essential determination can be reached through *one* historical formation or through several. Essence: essence-constituting determinateness, that is to say, essentially, belonging to the essential. And essence: totality as essential fullness and essential completion of the essential complex of what belongs to essence. And the corresponding constitutive correlates and modes of comportment and attitude.

[Religious Phenomena]

Problem: Silence as religious phenomenon (in connection with the problem of *irrationality*).

Worship: exuberant astonishment. All things and values to be differentiated from the nothing (non-being, non-value), their being emphasized, model [*Plastik*] of existentiality.

Phenomenology of *admiration* and *astonishment* [*Bewunderung und Verwunderung*] (admiration something "higher than").

Each Dasein is—as an emphasis (in relation to what?)—thus also a brightness [*Helligkeit*], grows up through particular illuminations [*Erhellungen*]—*concept of the primary brightness* [*Helle*]—primarily in the sense of an order of values. Irrationality and the problem of Being.

The Religious a priori

The problem has no place outside of transcendental philosophy. Within modern psychology of religion it is usually falsified and badly grounded. And the vivacity of the problem is in the least to be found in dogmatic, casuistic pseudo-philosophies, which pass themselves off as such philosophies of a particular system of religion (for instance Catholicism) and supposedly stand close to religion and the religious. Indeed, one ends up in the embarrassing predicament of having to be able to philosophically locate such a problem in the first place, since something like the philosophy of religion is unknown.

In the environment and sphere of realization of such systems, the capacity of experience in regard to the different regions of value in general and the religious in particular, stagnates—this being caused by a complete lack of original cultural consciousness. Apart from this, it is the fault a priori of the *structure of the system*—that itself did not grow out of an *organic* cultural deed—that the value-content of religion as such, content to be experienced in its sphere of meaning, must first find its way through contorted, inorganic, theoretically *entirely unclarified,* dogmatic principles and evidential procedures, only to finally dominate, darkly burden, and repress the subject with police force as an ecclesiastical-legal statute.

Still further: within itself, the system fully excludes an original, genuinely religious experience of value. Where one personality, who belongs to such a system, brings to the fore the elementary force of experience despite this, there the experience of value succeeds only to the effect that the system is eliminated for the sphere of experience and a new kind of context is sought. Because a genuine *sphere of experience and achievement,* which as such must *belong to the subject and must be of the subject,* is at issue, such sweeping to the side and transcending of the system becomes, *positively,* some kind of loosening up of the subject-sphere.

(Supplementary note: Already in the strongly natural-scientific, naturalistic theoretical metaphysics of being of Aristotle and its radical elimination and misrecognition of the problem of value in Plato, which is renewed in medieval Scholasticism, the predominance of the theoretical is already potentially present, so that Scholasticism, within the totality of the medieval Christian world of experience, severely endangered precisely the immediacy of religious life, and forgot religion in favor of theology and dogma. And already in the early days of Christianity, these dogmata exercised a theorizing, dogma-promoting influence on the institutions and statutes of church law. An appearance such as mysticism is to be understood as an elementary counter-movement.)

But the turn itself occurs always only within the limits of the respective cultural consciousness, so that it carries within itself its conditions and constitutive factors as aftereffects in themselves, due to which certainly a new kind of sphere may be discovered—albeit such that it does not master the new sphere with radically new means, but grasps and interprets it according to the principle of the genuine multiplicity of achievement. The loosening-up within the subject-sphere leads to a specific experience of the meaning and structure of the *subject of mysticism.*—Object-problem and the subject in Scholasticism. The emergence of a new motivational complex in the experiencing subject. As impetus to a mystical-theoretical superstructure. Means and aim of the rational mastering of this atheoretical sphere stem from cognitive psychology and object-metaphysics. The ethical "ought" as methodological form of the constitution of objects and correlative to subject-formation in mysticism. Central concept: "seclusion." Increase of inner vivacity. The structural character of the unity of object and subject. The specific irrationality of this mysticism.

Before this, short presentation of the view of the religious a priori in transcendental value philosophy (Windelband, Troeltsch).

"This *natural necessity of the norm-adverse* in the empirical functions of reason is the general fundamental fact from which critical philosophy in all its disciplines begins; it is, grasped in this generality, the problem of all problems, and likewise the touchstone of the philosophy of religion. This antinomial coexistence of norm and norm-adverse in the same consciousness is the primordial fact, which can be shown but never conceptualized: rather, out of this all problems of critical philosophy develop."[8]

The holy is to be determined only through the epitome of the logical, ethical, and aesthetic norms. They are holy as the value-contents of a *higher* reality of reason. "The holy is thus the normal consciousness of the true, good, and beautiful, *experienced as transcendental reality.*"[9] "*Religion is transcendent life.*"[10]

Irrationality in Meister Eckhart

The immediacy of religious experience, the uncontained vivacity of devotion to the holy, godly, does not issue forth the form from out of itself and the contemplation of the genuine performance-character; rather, it emerges as the culmination of a particular historically determined epistemological doctrine and psychology, a culmination which, however, as such results in the new and the correlate of the vivacity of experience.

One must get clear about this connection in order to really understand Eckhart's mysticism as such, and not fall into misinterpretations from the beginning. From here also first arises the concept of the specifically irrational in this mysticism.

The irrational is not what lies before all rationality as the fullness of multiplicity. The decisive moment is not that of a lacking overview, of theoretical indomitability, of sinking into fullness, but rather—because the object [*das Gegenständliche*] is approached in the essence or the form as the general or the universal, the value of objecthood [*Gegenständlichkeit*] increases with the

---

8. Wilhelm Windelband, "Das Heilige. Skizze zur Religionsphilosophie," in *Präludien,* Tübingen, 1914, vol. II, pp. 295–332, here, p. 302.
9. Ibid.
10. Ibid.

increase of the general—the ever-expanding exclusion of particularizations from the form, out of the magnified emptiness of the same.

Not the not-yet-determinable and not-yet-determined—rather, that which is essentially without determination in general is the primordial object, the absolute.

Corresponding to the fundamental principle that the same is recognized only through the same—that the same becomes object only *for* the same—the theory of the subject, the soul[11] develops; here also the process of undoing the multiplicity, of the rejection of the individual forces in their individuality and determinate directionality, the return to their ground, origin, and their root.

Elimination of all change, multiplicity, time. Absoluteness of object and subject in the sense of radical unity and as such unity of *both: I am it, and it is I.* From this the namelessness of God and ground of the soul. In this sphere, no opposition—and therefore the problem of the precedence of *intellectus* [intellect] or *voluntas* [will] no longer belong to this sphere, although Eckhart necessarily requires a designation and characterization of mystical experience.

An opinion that grasps the subject-correlate of the absolute as summation, as the totality of specific achievements and faculties, and correspondingly views the value of the holy as some kind of result of the true, good, and beautiful, is entirely misguided.

Eckhart's "fundamental conception"—"you can only know what you are,"[12] becomes conceivable only from out of specific concepts of cognition. Here cognition determines subject and object.

The problem of universals as unclarified problem of object suffused with a bad metaphysics of nature. Realism—nominalism.—Form of objectivity as general validity becomes the content and ontologically constitutive principle of the general universal ("universal").

For the actual problem, nothing results because one does not go further to the subject, which at least in nominalism lies along the way; attempts in Scotus and in particular in his doctrine of meaning.

Now, it is strange that in as extreme a realism as that of Eckhart, a progression to the subject is found. The motive is not a theoretical one, just as the return to the ground of the soul in general may not be grasped as a theoretical process. It remains atheoretical—only Eckhart seeks to grasp it rationally and thus places it into theoretical contexts.

---

11. And with that the problem of the subject in the distinguished sense.

12. Hermann Leser, "Das Religiöse Wahrheitsproblem im Lichte der deutschen Mystik," in *Zeitschrift für Philosophie und philosophische Kritik,* vol. 160 (1916), p. 23.—Editor's note: The citation continues: "Thus God only, when, and insofar as you are God."

The new motivational complex for the mystical-theoretical superstructure stems from living religiosity, the living subject.

Means and aim of rational mastery stem from cognitive psychology and a metaphysic of objects. Along with the generality-character of the form of essence, the value of objecthood as such increases. Objecthood in general is indeed an empty form, but as object itself, the primordial object κατ ἔχον, the absolute.

The process of progressive elimination of contents and differences, oppositions, has an essential relation to the ethical *telos*. Multiplicity disperses and unsettles life, the subject. From an ethical perspective, the vacillation is as such unworthy. In religious experience, what is most valuable is to me an object with a priori certainty. Thought theoretically, each possibility of what is unworthy, thus of the multiplicity, of opposition, of difference, must be held at distance from it. Absolute value coincides with absolute oppositionlessness, that is, lack of determination, which is to say coincides with the object [*dem Gegenständlichen*] only as the object.

Only as such is it present to the mystical subject. And for this objecthood, the mystical subject must not be itself a subject beyond opposition, *prior to* opposition. Only in this way does the mystical-theoretical meaning of the central concept of *seclusion* first become clear.

The here and now, space and time are the forms of the multiple and oppositional; they offer no place to the perpetual "now," to the supra-temporal. Sensuousness is therefore not the subject-correlate of the true objecthood, but neither is the understanding, as judging, pulling apart into the duality of subject and predicate.

Reason and will, knowledge and love, however, lead to the absolute. Controversy regarding the primacy of each of the two "faculties." Eckhart is not in favor of theoretical reason as juxtaposed to the will, but rather of the primacy of the soul's ground, which is, mystical-theoretically, ranked above both. In another regard, he sees precisely in free will, by virtue of its freedom and devotion to value, the "faculty" that is superior value.

The form of objecthood in general becomes an absolute object [*Gegenstand*]. The less the object [*Gegenständliche*] presents distracting content, stimulating a diverting and captivating apprehension, the more valuable and pure the objecthood itself becomes.

On Schleiermacher's Second Address "On the Essence of Religion"

Necessity of a phenomenological attitude toward the religious experience. "For it belongs to the still ever-developing opposition of contemporary times against the old, that one is never any longer [just] one, rather each is everything. And thus it occurs, as the educated peoples have opened up such a many-sided commerce amongst themselves, that their own particular character in the individual moments of life no longer surface unmixed, and such that in the sphere of human feeling such a wide-ranging and complete sociability is founded, that"[13] no performance proceeds and takes effect in isolation, but rather is "moved and pulled through by the obliging love and support of the others"[14] and thus it remains most difficult "to differentiate the reigning initiating force in this combination"[15]—that is, the essential meaning of the performance in its pure essence. "Thus now everyone can understand each activity of the mind [des Geistes] only insofar as he can, at the same time, find it and observe it within himself."[16]

The reigning intention: Religion (1) now a kind of thinking, faith, its own way of observing the world, *a theoretical formation;* (2) now a *way of acting,* its own lust and love, a special way of comporting oneself, and of moving inwardly, *a practical phenomenon.* Religion belongs to both sides.[17] (Most often, and also now, one appreciated the expressions, the documents of religion according to the profit they yielded for morals and metaphysics. So the cutting opposition of faith to morals and metaphysics, of piety against morality, is first to be shown.)

Thus religion renounces such pretensions and gives everything back what it lent there, or what was imposed upon it from there, so in order to "rightly reveal and situate with determination its original and own particular possession."[18] (Elimination of particular positings which carry within themselves an independent teleology; *within* phenomenology this particular ἐποχή is valid in order to purely isolate out the individual teleologies for themselves.)

"For what is your science of being striving, your science of nature, into which all that is everything real of your theoretical philosophy must still unite itself? To know, I think, the things in their own particular essence; to show the special relationships through which each thing is what it is; to determine each in its position in the whole, and to correctly differentiate it from all the rest; to place everything actual in its mutual conditioned necessity, and to demonstrate the unity of all appearances with their perpetual laws." The essence of religion is perceived without community with this knowledge, even if it ascends up to God as the highest order of the lawfulness of being. "For

---

13. Friedrich Schleiermacher, "Ueber die Religion. Reden an die gebildeten unter ihren Verächtern," in *F. Schleiermacher's sämmtliche Werke,* Division I, vol. I, Berlin, 1843, p. 173.
14. Ibid., p. 174.
15. Ibid.
16. Ibid.
17. Cf. ibid., p. 174.
18. Ibid., p. 183.

the measure of knowledge is not the measure of piety."[19] (Measure, that is, criterion of value). God placed in the sphere of knowledge, as the ground of the knowing and the known, is not the same as the pious way to have God and to know about him.

Reflection [Betrachtung] is essential to religion, not closed-off stupidity. *Reflection*—under this is grasped "the excitement of the mind retracted from everything externally effectual."[20] Sense and taste for the infinite = "life of the finite immediately in us, as it is in the infinite."[21]

Infinite being—with this it is impossible not to imply God. This particular meaning and the respective expression had been avoided, "because otherwise with the idea itself, a certain kind of representation would have easily emerged, and thus a decision would have been given or at least a critique would have been exercised, about the different ways to think God and world together and separately, which does not belong here at all."[22] Foreign teleology, and precisely the most dangerously confusing theoretical one, [is] eliminated. The point is "to get down into the innermost holiness of life,"[23] where the original relationship of feeling and intuition is to be found. "But I must refer you to yourselves, to the grasp of a living moment. You must understand, likewise, for your consciousness to, as it were, eavesdrop on, or at least to reconstitute, this state out of the living moment for yourselves. You should notice here the becoming of your consciousness, rather than somehow reflecting on a consciousness that has already become."[24]

The point is to uncover an original region of life and performance of consciousness (or feeling), in which religion alone realizes itself as a certain form of experience.[25] From there we can read off[26] the elements of religion which, with that, proves to belong neither to a foreign teleology nor to corresponding foreign noetic contexts, and not to be determined in its meaning through them. Religion is to be sharply differentiated from what belongs to it.[27]

Universe—fullness of reality—in uninterrupted flows and operations; all individuals as parts of the whole. Religion is the specifically religiously intentional, emotional reference of each content of experience to an infinite whole as fundamental meaning. *Devotion:* original streaming in of fullness, without restraint, letting oneself be excited. *To lead back* the respective ex-

19. Ibid., p. 184.
20. Ibid., p. 266 (Note [2] to p. 189).
21. Ibid.
22. Ibid., p. 267.
23. Ibid., p. 191.
24. Ibid.
25. Cf. ibid., pp. 191–196
26. Cf. ibid.
27. Cf. ibid., p. 268 (see note [4] to p. 196).

perience into the inner unity of life. Religious life is the constant renewal of this procedure. *To act* is then the repercussion of this feeling; only acting in its entirety, not each individual act, should be determined in this way.

Mysterious moment of unstructured unity of intuition and feeling, the one without the other being nothing. The noetic moment is itself constitutive for the noematic entire content of experience.

Because any thetic character at all, any claim about being, is lacking, because nothing is decided about something, the fullness of experience stands in a certain neutrality; no object takes precedence over any other. A specific infinity of religious experience is thus given.

History in its most authentic sense is the highest object of religion, religion begins and ends in it. Humanity is to be seen as a living community of individuals in which isolated existence is to be lost.

Do all *with* religion not *from* religion. Religion should accompany, like a holy music, all the doings of life.

Phenomenology of Religious Experience and of Religion

The typical forms and formations of religious life and of historical consciousness.

The independence of religious experience and its world is to be seen as an entirely originary intentionality with an entirely originary character of demands. Likewise originary are its specific worldliness and valuableness.

Historical fullness—more precisely the few great uniquenesses of living religion—is to be evaluated with the elements of meaning and experience of religious consciousness, and not according to extra-religious and especially not "scientific" standards. Only thus will religious life be maintained in its vivacity, and not be endangered by so-called scientific world-views.

Religion, just as any world of experience, can gain its form only in historical consciousness, and come to a totality—not universality—in the sense corresponding to each (value-region).

No real religion allows itself to be *captured* philosophically [Er*philosophieren*]; philosophy, moreover, can hardly offer a legitimate standard of criticism, insofar as it has grasped its true vocation (cf. historical consciousness).

One of the most meaningful, *founding* elements of meaning in religious experience is the *historical*. However, that which gives the specifically religious meaning is already found in experience. The religious world of experience is centralized in its originality—not in its theoretical-theological separateness—into one great unique historical form (personally affecting fullness of life). The constitutive character of the concepts of revelation and tradition in the essence of religion is connected to this.

Analysis of the not intellectualized phenomenon of faith (πίστις). The dogma-historical material and primordial Christian material is to be divided on that point, and to be assessed phenomenologically. The phenomenon of trust and that of the co-given specific meaning of "truth."

Weakening the thinking of the transcendental *a priori* in its theoretical nature through the integration of the idea of *atheoretical validity* is still a rationalization of the problem of religious experience and faith. A legitimate tendency lies here, but with wholly inappropriate means in the framework of a heterogeneous systematic (transcendentalism).

Over and against this, only phenomenology can offer rescue in philosophical need, but only if it remains pure in its radical moments of origin, if intuition is not theorized and the concept of essence is not rationalized according to the general idea of universal validity; it can offer rescue only if "essence" is assured of the living possibilities of change and fullness of meaning corresponding to the different conduct of value and experience.

The view that then the supra-historical sphere of essence as such—given in intuition—would be an immanent heightening of the respective experience itself, is to be energetically dismissed.

Such realizes itself only in the specifically philosophical form of experience, where the intuited itself takes on an indeed new, and entirely genuine, kind of world-character, corresponding to the subject-comportment.

The Absolute[28]

"The relation [*Stellung*] to God gives direction for our experiential comportment to him."[29] What does "relation to God" mean? Meaningfully and constitutedly, only to be formulated as a comportment of consciousness, not, for instance, ontically, as being next to, or "under," an (absolute) being.

Rather, the opposite holds: our experiential comportment to God—the primary one, because welling up within us by grace—gives direction to the specifically *religious* constitution of "God" as a "phenomenological object." (Reinach sees this also in a certain sense, but does not take it as a methodological principle of the phenomenology of religion.) Therefore, the determinations of sense of this—that is, of the "absolute"—are to be discovered only in the specific structures of the constituting experience; and they are to be demonstrated [to have] the initially constituting moment of meaning with the

28. Editor's note: the manuscript carries the date June 1918. It follows the notation: cf. the corresponding m[anuscript] of Reinach.

29. Adolph Reinach, *Sämtliche Werke. Textkritische Ausgabe in 2 Bänden,* ed. by Karl Schuhmann and Barry Smith, vol. I. *Werke,* Munich/Hamden/Vienna, 1989, p. 607.

character of having been experienced for the logical-ontological element—
closed off [?] to being—of no-longer-increasability.

The "weight of experience" and the sphere of the contents of experience
[are] different indeed, but in which functional connection?

Perception of reality [*Wirklichkeitsnehmung*] "lies immanently contained in
the meaning of experience itself."[30]

Validity and cognitive meaning of religious experiences *genuine*—and still
today a problem—entirely new kind of sphere, where mere analogizing with
the aesthetic realm of values or with the taking of values in general does not
suffice, if it does not, from the beginning, take us in the wrong direction. Here
alone is the cure: radical analysis.

Critique of the "fundamental concepts of metaphysics." The absolute—deter-
minable only in the respective sphere of experience. Inside the respective
sphere, it receives its full concretion only in the way that it shows itself in a
historicity [Historizität]; and accordingly the analysis must *incessantly* show—
moving only within it—the *"historical"* as determinative element and always
otherwise directed and effective element of coloration, as well as element of
the living consciousness in general that gives primordial meaning and structure.

The living unity of sense of living being, found in the sense-structure of
consciousness as "historical" per se, determines also [?] somehow—even if
there again beginning entirely originarily (in the manner of a structure)—the
specific worldliness of the sphere of experience concerned as a religious one.

Conceptual material, such as "absolute," "highest standard," "standard in
general," taken from rationalistic metaphysics, separated from its constructive
method, is not only inappropriate to a genuine sphere of experience—insofar
as it may not be brought in from above, methodologically or unmethodolog-
ically, in an a priori moment, insofar as it further unexpectedly leads to a
constructive dialectic, or at least allows it to lead—even in returning to the
experience of *such* (imported) conceptual content. Above all, this conceptual
material has such a neutral, faded content, uncharacterized by the sphere of
experience, that it is shown in serious investigation as not at all original—
that is to say, as not being a conglomerate of sense-elements that originarily
arise from a sphere of experience. The critique of such "fundamental concepts
of metaphysics" would have to show precisely the arbitrary, historically coincidental compositeness and collusion of its sense-elements, above all the
disastrous influence of the concept of nature and its many-faceted elements;
such is also the case with the entire operating with the concept of infinity in

30. Ibid., p. 610.

Reinach, e.g., in the opposition of "leading into the infinite" and "containing infinity within itself."[31]

Reinach speaks of "innerly motivated transitions"[32] in the experience of different absolutenesses (formal ones—can be experienced at all!—and fulfilled ones) as opposed to any logical-theoretical development of their separation. Here again is seen the same methodological dualism, which, however, allows the basic direction toward the experiential to shine through. Phenomenon of motivation is here also significant in principle, as it is for the constitution of historical consciousness in general.

Reinach's differentiation between "explicit knowledge and knowledge immanent in experience" is valuable.[33] "The perception of reality is entirely otherwise in the feeling of shelter in God. Logically speaking, such perception would be the presupposition for that. But no one would draw the logical conclusion. Rather, it lies immanently contained in the sense of the experience. We must distinguish two things here: on the one hand, the knowledge of being sheltered, and then, on the other, the knowledge of the existence of God—that is to say, an immediately and a mediately immanent knowledge. Only a mediate knowledge dwells within the experiences of gratefulness and love; as modes of taking a position, they are in a certain sense derivative experiences.[34]

"I experience an absolute dependency on God. Insofar as I myself am participatory in this experienced relationship, this state of affairs does not stand before me—rather I myself experience myself in this relationship, a relationship then which, naturally, cannot become an object to me. In this way, if I perceive an object, the corresponding relation of perception and object is not an object to me. Then, however, a difference immediately follows: to me, in perception, the knowledge 'I perceive' emerges with reflection on perception. [Whereas] in the experience of dependency I *find* [author's emphasis] myself dependent, without a reflection being necessary—a reflection which could, after all, only lead to the knowledge that I feel myself dependent."[35]

These brief suggestions are very significant, even if the analysis has yet to begin here.

"The absolute dependency, the absolute being-sheltered, is not a 'fact.' "[36]

Reinach also sees at once the problem of validity. It will be necessary to

---

31. The citation completed by the editor: "What characterizes godly love as opposed to worldly love in such a way that the one leads to the infinite, while the other contains infinity within itself?" (Ibid., p. 606.)

32. Ibid., p. 607.

33. Ibid., p. 610.

34. Ibid.

35. Ibid., p. 611.

36. Ibid.

show that it cannot be disturbed from out of purely cognitive skepticisms, as long as what is specifically originary in the respective experiences, and above all the structure of primordial sense of historical consciousness, have been clarified.

Hegel's Original, Earliest Position on Religion—and Consequences

Decisive influence of Kant, who from the beginning excludes an immediate relation to the holy, one founded on an original experiential relation. *Morality* is the guiding purpose, and so religion is degraded to a means. Meaning of the acts of Jesus: "to raise religion and virtue to morality."[37]

This fundamental approach to religion *as a means* is decisive for the entire further spiritual [*geistige*] development of Hegel—and is to be followed and critically presented in this direction. Further, it is to be seen to what extent the problem of the historical is thereby pushed onto a very determinate [direction], and first becomes a philosophical problem in full originality—in unbounded form.

Problems

The *experience of being* in its typical form within particular periods of the history of ideas [*Geistesgeschichte*] and within different worlds of experience (Lyrical poetry, art in general, science etc.; e.g., *Verhaeren* and *Werfel*).

Today it is, for instance, not characterized in connection or in summation, but teleologically, value-taking, as having the character of an act.

Concept of *life-worlds,* their principal structure determined through historical consciousness in general, their specific structure determined through what—the essential possibilities of their connections and complications.

Faith

This title ranges over a multiplicity of modalities, which are not equal in the sense of species of a genus; rather, among which *one* is distinguished from the rest: primordial *doxa,* toward which the others are referred back *in a certain way.* (Correlatively, the modalities of being.)

If the distantiation of modalities of faith from the primordial *doxa* and

---

37. Citation after Wilhelm Dilthey, "Die Jugendgeschichte Hegels," in *Abhandlungen der Preupischen Akademie der Wissenschaften,* Berlin, 1905, p. 26.

accordingly the referral-back in each modality is a different one, such that a simple juxtaposition of species is excluded, then precisely the respective meaning of this distantiation and interpretation-back is central. That means: which moment of meaning in the primordial *doxa* is modified, and how is it modified? How—that means also: with what kind and extension of the modification to the plain entire content of the primordial *doxa*.

Piety—Faith

"In calm (*shébá*) waiting you will find salvation, your strength consists of quiet trust" (I, Moses 30, 15 [Gen. 30:15]).

Cf. the article "Faith," in *Die Religion in Geschichte und Gegenwart [Religion in History and the Present]*, vol. 2, especially III, where the analysis [is], however, most inadequate, and IV. "Glaube und Geschichte." Faith according to Troeltsch: "The cognitive moment of piety"[38] (N.B.: faith in Luther).

Faith is a "unique religious, mythical-symbolical, and practical way of thinking and knowledge, one that proceeds from historical-personal expression, which believes in myth for the sake of the practical religious force conveyed by it, and which knows how to express, to communicate, and to objectivate these forces only through myth."[39]

Structure and type and "lawfulness" of the life of faith. Cf. *Realenzyklopädie der Protestantischen Theologie,* "Faith," vol. 6, 3rd edition.

On Schleiermacher, "Christian Faith" ["Der christliche Glaube"*]—and Phenomenology of Religion in General*

Schleiermacher's characterization of "piety" as a "determinateness of feeling or of immediate self-consciousness."[40] (Historical consciousness—Steffen's description of feeling: "the immediate presence of an entirely undivided existence."[41])

This "authentic immediate self-consciousness, however, is not idea, but rather feeling in the authentic sense, is in no way always only accompanying,"[42] neither "something confused . . . nor something ineffectual."[43]

---

38. E. Troeltsch, "Glaube: III. Dogmatisch. IV. Glaube und Geschichte," in *Die Religion in Geschichte und Gegenwart,* ed. by F. M. Schiele and L. Zscharnack, vol. 2, column 1438.
39. Ibid., column 1440.
40. Friedrich Schleiermacher, *Der christliche Glaube,* 2nd edition, Berlin, 1830, p. 7.
41. Cited in ibid., p. 15.
42. Ibid.
43. Ibid., p. 15.

The *constitutive form* of the somehow determined (immediate) self-consciousness circumscribes the sense of *personal existence* and integrates itself into the primordial constituting element of historical consciousness as such.

What forms the moment of sense of the specific uniformity, unity, and continuity of personal consciousness?

The "having-been-affected-from-somewhere" of consciousness is possible only on the basis of the essential *openness to values* and *primary love of meaning* of the personally existing being. What can be affected is not an empty page, no empty "I," no point-like self, but rather only a personal being fulfilled and essentially longing for fulfillment, which has such a structure which makes possible for it being-fulfilled by certain goods of the life-world and, in being-fulfilled, makes possible further growth and becoming-felt. ("Feeling dependent" is already too close to theoretical objectification, to an exit from oneself and an ascertaining of a relationship of this objectified self to another.)

"Dependency as such": this interpretive meaning is too raw, it objectifies too much in the direction of theory of being—specifically that of the reality of nature.

Rather, the primordial relationship must be interpreted as oscillating from soul to absolute spirit and the reverse—but such that it shows a structure in which the possibilities for fulfillment (according to the structure) are inherent in the most multifarious way.

"The changing determinateness of our self" means: our living consciousness is a constant following and interweaving of situations. Even thus all is still too much characterized according to the theory of nature. The connections are rather such that they develop from out of the basic structure of consciousness. For this structure, the concept of foundation, strongly utilized by Husserl, is an extraordinary step forward into the true connections. Situations can follow one another purely on the basis of the contents of consciousness and their immanent connections, or *motivated* by certain gradations and vivacities of the specific act-characters.

The "situations" are all the more "purely" immediate (corresponding to the specific objectity [*Objektität*]), specifically more clear and certain, the earlier the respective experience attains an originary, independent fulfillment of a moment of the stream of consciousness, a living, rooted being-historical.

Consciousness is *historical* always only in the *fulfillment* of the moment— never in the mere reflection-of-the-pure-"I".

The pure "I" is the primordial constituting element, *the* form of the possibility of being-affected and of being-fulfilled at all. It is not a value-free matter, but also not a good (value-emphasized object). Primarily, it is the primordial form of openness for the valuable in general, and with that it is perpetually noble, an absolute distinction in the course of the a priori of forms.

The Holy [332–333]   251

Being-able-to-posit-oneself and having-become-from-nowhere-else are in no way its essence. Its ownmost primordial ground is at once and authentically a perpetual vocation and calling as absolute constituent of spirit and life in general. It, too, is of another, namely *called* by another, whether become [so] or however, is entirely secondary (*anima naturaliter religiosa* [the soul is by nature religious]).

Having-become-from-elsewhere is, therefore, no characterization of the "I"—as opposed to the consciousness of fulfilled moment. The pure "I" is rather the possibility (not logical, but vocational) of the being-historical of a fulfilled consciousness.

Fulfillment and being-fulfilled cannot, however, be interpreted phenomenologically as having-become [*Gewordensein*], not at all with regard to being [*seinsmäßig*]. That such exists at all belongs to the essence and to the "possibility" of living consciousness. Only in this way does the concept of *intentionality* gain its a priori interpretation as the primordial element of consciousness, and in it, any possible "not-having-posited-oneself-so" is first of all *grounded.*

The Holy
(Preparations for the review of Rudolph Otto, *Das Heilige* [*The Holy*], 1917)

Principal problems demand initially, if not solution, at least to be named and outlined.

1. *Problem of historical consciousness* (consciousness of personal existence and fulfilled originary sphere of life, and continuous reigning form of constitution therefrom in reference to the other imposing worlds).

2. *Problem of the irrational.* (Cf. Ms.)[44]

The irrational is still considered as a counter-projection [*Gegenwurf*] or limit, but never observed in its originariness and own proper constitution; from there always again the concession of some or other righteous people of reason and the "critique of reason."[45] We have no true insight yet into living consciousness and its original worlds, which [are] entirely originary but still have a common, although many-leveled enrootedness in the basic meaning of a genuinely personal existence. (The imposition of the irrational onto the rational must be avoided and fought against.)

The religious world of experience does not need to secure its self-certainty

44. Editor's note: More precise notation not given.
45. Cf. Natorp in his Memorial Address to Cohen: Paul Natorp, *Hermann Cohens philosophische Leistung unter dem Gesichtspunkte des Systems,* Berlin, 1918, p. 28.

in measuring itself against cultural "lawfulnesses" and ideas. In order to allow full insight into this, the *phenomenon-in-principle* of the self-sufficing of what originarily gives itself as certain must be set out and presented in its every marked-out dominance of consciousness.

Basic remarks about 1 and 2: the holy may not be made into a problem as theoretical—also not an irrational theoretical—noema, but rather as correlate of the act-character of "faith," which itself is to be interpreted only from out of the fundamentally essential experiential context of historical consciousness. That does not mean the explanation of the "holy" as a "category of evaluation." Rather, what is primary and essential to it is the constitution of an originary objectity.

The "noumenous"—the "special element" in the holy *minus* the ethical and rational moments. On what is the attachment of the latter to the holy grounded? And does this attachment belong somehow to the originary structure of the noumenous?

In principle, a debate over category and form and their function is necessary.

Distinguish between: the pure holy and the constituted holy worlds and objects.

Windelband ("Das Heilige"[46]) shows insight into almost the same fullness of religious phenomena, if, however, in strongly rational formulation, but he shows above all that the principle of the formulation of the problem in general is decisive and the division of the groups of problems and the *methodological* approaches are dependent upon that.

On the Sermones Bernardi in canticum canticorum (Serm. III.)

1. "Hodie legimus in libro experientiae."[47] [Today, we read in the book of experience.] Today we want to move apprehendingly (descriptively) in the field of personal experience.

Turning back to one's own sphere of experience and paying attention to the manifestations of one's own consciousness. A strong, implicitly formulated consciousness of the exclusive, principal value and right of one's own religious experience.

Religious longing for experience and giving effort toward the presence of Jesus is possible as genuine only as growing out of a basic experience. Such experiences not freely and deliberately at one's disposal in the observance of the rules of church law. "Knowledge" about these experiences and their essence arises only in actual having-experienced. Such an experience is only

---

46. In *Präludien II,* pp. 295–332.
47. S. Bernardi, *Serm. in cant. III,* 1, PL 183, p. 794.

truly effective in a closed complex of experience (stream of experience)—not transferable, cannot be elicited, through description. ("Est fons signatus, cui non communicat alienus."[48]) [It is the signified source that another does not communicate.]

The constitution of the noetic religious experiential context is a "historical" one (*qui bibit, ad hunc sitiat*) [he who drinks, may be thirsty for this]. The basic experience is therefore not only temporally primary (this is perhaps not required for it at all), but primary in the sense of *founding*. Direction of sense and form of such founding are essentially "historical," whereby the latter word should indicate not yet something final, but certainly *self-enduring* and primary. Thus we may not even link up with the founding relations of theoretical acts; rather we must begin with primary origins (which necessarily demands insight into the universal radicality of phenomenologically intuitive description and its lack of presuppositions; but precisely because of this plainness of attitudinal form, it itself is *the* problem, to the phenomenologist, in the whole of the constitutions).

Which[49] is the basic phenomenon in the total field of historical knowing and forming? How are the aim and meaning of its specific object-constitution to be won?

The constitutive elements of memory and their functional value in the objectification-process of historical understanding.

The originary constitution of the value characters and their function and meaning for the "historical" is connected to this. The moment of distinction, of precedence, of the increased, of the not at all purely theoretical, indifferently objective [*Gegenständlichen*]—and with that the noetic moment of originary relationality to the aforementioned noematic moments—indicate a specific condition of religious primordial experiences.

Immanent essential connections of gradation: "Nolo repente fieri summus; paulatim proficere volo."[50] [I do not wish the highest thing to be made all of a sudden; I wish to accomplish it little by little.] "Citius placas eum [Deum], si mensuram tuam servaveris, et alteriora te non quaesieris."[51] [You do not reconcile Him [God] if you have kept your measure, and have not searched for the other of you.] (The "higher than you," the superior should not be pulled down toward oneself, nor rigidly in its manner be excl [. . .],* rather the experiential realities of the religious should grow continuously from out of him; he should let the immanent connections take effect in him.)

The phenomenon of (inner) concentration and its motivations and tenden-

---

48. Ibid.
49. Editor's note: The manuscript carries the date of September 10, 1918.
50. *Serm. in cant. III*, 4, PL 183, p. 795.
51. Ibid.
*[Two syllables illegible.]

cies (special phenomenon: mystical silence, keeping silent, the problem of the relation to the "I").

Basic tendency of life: more-life. Already from out of this, the meditative meaning-motivated activity (nothing of the character of having-become—receptivity as originary activity of the religious world).

("Loneliness" a phenomenon of the personal historical existence as such.)

Phenomenon of the constituting process of the presence of God [is] an originary one. The "levels of prayer"—to be studied preliminarily: concentration, meditation, prayer of calmness.

Analysis, that is to say hermeneutics, works in the historical "I." Life as religious is already there. It is not as if a neutral material consciousness were being analyzed, but rather is to be detected in all the specific determination of meaning. Problem: The intuitive eidetic is, as *hermeneutical,* never neutral-theoretical; rather it itself has the *oscillations* of the genuine life-world only "eidetically" (not [. . .]* eidetic).

The stream of consciousness is already a religious one, at least in motivation and tendency. (Thus for instance St. Theresa sees, *as* a mystic, phenomenologically, [without] seeing eidetically and the specifically religious eidetic.)

The soul is "somehow" the place for God and the godly (cf. Eckhart, the place [*die stat*]), *the dwelling-place of God, primordial motivation.* Can be judged as to its worth only according to that. Cf. *Seelenburg* [*Castle of the Soul*] IV, 6 (Citation-entering into the castle of the soul).

"We bear in mind at least only seldom which great goods can be in this soul, or who dwells therein, or what value, what dignity it has."[52]

"Whoever does not believe such a thing [such as the dwelling of God in the soul—the religious and holy in general], he will also experience nothing of it; for the Lord is very pleased if one does not posit for him a standard and an aim in his works."[53]

"For that, which I want to present, is very difficult and dark, where no experience is there."[54]

Demand: Always see the innermost and the whole of the castle, not the mere sequence and adjacency of rooms—see totally and with understanding.[55]

---

*[A word illegible.]

52. *Die sämmtlichen Schriften der heiligen Theresia von Jesu,* ed. Gallus Schwab, vol. IV, *Die Seelen-Burg,* Sulzbach, 1832, p. 4.

53. Ibid., p. 6.

54. Ibid., p. 9.

55. Cf. ibid., p. 13f.

Afterword of the Editors of the Lecture Course Winter Semester 1920–21

Martin Heidegger held the lecture course "Introduction to the Phenomenology of Religion" as a private lecturer in the winter semester 1920–1921 at the University of Freiburg. According to the schedule of courses, it was held Tuesdays and Fridays from noon to one o'clock. It began on October 29, 1920; the last class was held on February 25, 1921. This is what it says in the dating of the postscripts.

The manuscript of the lecture course is lost. Even an announcement by the manager of the *Nachlass* in several wide-circulating newspapers brought no hint of its location. Yet there are five sets of notations, which allow for the approximate reconstruction of the train of thought and articulation of the lecture course. Three of these notations (Oskar Becker, Helene Weiß, Franz-Josef Brecht) are found in the German Literary Archives of Marbach; two are kept in the Husserl Archive of Leuven. From the total notations it is clear that Heidegger's lecture course falls into two distinctly differentiated parts, which are separated by a caesura at the end of the lecture on November 30, 1920. In Oskar Becker's notations, which employ a separate pagination for each of the two parts, the end of the first part is marked by the following sentence: "Owing to uncalled-for objections [*Einwänden Unberufener*], broken off on the 30th of November, 1920." A query addressed to the archive of the University of Freiburg could find no explanation of the sort of objections. Presumably through these Heidegger saw himself forced to proceed abruptly from the extensive "Methodological Introduction" to the "Phenomenological Explication of Concrete Religious Phenomena"—thus the title of the second part of the lecture course according to Becker. Becker's quite legible notation probably derives from stenographical notes which were immediately transcribed after each lecture. Even if he at times significantly simplified Heidegger's sentences, and, as a rule, shortened them as well as providing his own structure, his notations can serve, in regard to the first part of the lecture course, as a foundation for the preparation of the text. Becker's notes on the first part of the lecture course are complete; in the second part are missing the lectures given on December 10th, and those from the 10th to the 20th of February.

The notations of Helene Weiß and Franz-Josef Brecht, dated throughout, are dependent upon one another for many long passages, and in others literally identical. In Helene Weiß's handwriting there are three different versions [*Konvolute*]: the relatively legible, paginated text of notations itself; additions to this text; as well as a partial copy of Brecht's notes. Compared to Becker's notations there is here a sort of terminologically simplified, considerably shorter version of the lecture course. This is also true of the notes taken by

Brecht, in which some paragraphs without doubt originate from other unidentifiable note-takers. To these sources, we can add the notations of Franz Neumann of the Husserl Archive of Leuven, which was available to the editors in a transcription of unknown handwriting. They were made readily available to us by Professor S. Ijsseling and Mr. S. Spileers. The version contains only the first part of the lecture course, but it offers additional materials that were taken into account for the constitution of the text. The as yet untranscribed notations by Fritz Kaufmann in an old stenography, which are also in Leuven, could not be enlisted.

The preparation of the text required, first of all, the complete transcription of the Marbach notations through the editors. The reconstruction of the train of thought, which was carried out on the basis of an ascertained chronology of the particular lectures, made it possible to bring the available text material into a coherent order. For the first part of the lecture course, Becker's notations served as the guiding text. The preparation of the second part was more complicated in that Becker's notations lose precision and are also incomplete. Thus, the appropriate passages had to be reconstructed out of the other sets of notes. Every statement that was not redundant was considered.

In regard to authenticity, the text, prepared in this manner, cannot be compared to editions based on original manuscripts. The editors are aware of the problems regarding this sort of "secondarily authentic" constitution of texts.

In addition to the notations, there are Heidegger's handwritten notes from the context of the lecture course. We are dealing with single pages in a folder found in the German Literary Archive of Marbach. The handwriting is microscopically small and extraordinarily difficult to decipher. Because the pages are immediately related to the work of the lecture course and, in the absence of the originally handwritten lecture, are the only remaining original documents pertaining to the lecture course, they are reproduced in the appendices.

The punctuation has been updated carefully according to today's accepted rules. Titles originate from the editors in using Becker's table of contents as an orientation. The organization of sections and paragraphs was conducted likewise by the editors. In contrast to this, all the titles in the appendices are those of Heidegger himself. The wording of the various notations was in general maintained, but in integrating them into the body of the text they were occasionally modified with care. Square brackets [] in the quotations of the appendix indicate Heidegger's additions, while square brackets in footnotes indicate remarks of the editor. Instances of a missing passage are marked with ellipses [. . .] and stars [*], and questionable interpretations are marked with question marks [?]. Abbreviations were left alone if what they indicate was at all in doubt.

The lecture course "Introduction to the Phenomenology of Religion," held in the winter semester of 1920–21, is especially important for the understanding of Heidegger's early thought. Although there have been references to this lecture for decades in the scholarly literature, there reigned a general unclarity with regard to the available textual basis as well as the precise train of thought. The present edition should rectify this lack as much as possible. The position and status of the lecture course within Heidegger's oeuvre are determined by its object: nowhere else has the uniqueness of the philosophical fore-conception [*Vorgriff*] been established as decisively in contrast to the scientific method, or are religious questions taken up with such extension and exegetical exactitude. Heidegger combines a critique of contemporary philosophy of religion (Troeltsch) with fundamental considerations of how factical life experience may be grasped in its historicity. The expansive discussion of the methodological fundamental concept of the "formal indication" constitutes the background against which the earliest witnesses to primordial Christianity undergo an intensive phenomenological analysis. In the framework of an "enactment-historical" explication Heidegger interprets selected passages from the letter to the Galatians as well as both letters to the Thessalonians. Heidegger works out in this manner the basic determinations of primordial Christian religiosity out of the phenomenon of the Pauline gospel. According to these determinations, we can recognize the enactmental character of factical life as such.

Since 1918, Heidegger's closeness to Edmund Husserl, both personal and in terms of philosophical content, determines the fact that these analyses stand under the sign of a "phenomenology of religion." Husserl had entrusted the more specific working out of this phenomenology to his student, who, however, already worked on his own conception of phenomenology on the basis of the notion of factical life experience. In this way, the constant confrontation with the Christian tradition constitutes the background against which Heidegger will develop his "hermeneutics of facticity." For the winter semester 1919–1920 he had announced a lecture course on medieval mysticism which he did not then give (cf. part III of this volume). The lecture courses published here from Winter Semester 1920–21 and from Summer Semester 1921 indicate the high point, and at the same time the end, of his studies in the phenomenology of religion.

The editors thank the manager of Heidegger's *Nachlass,* Dr. Hermann Heidegger, for entrusting us with this edition of the lecture course. It is also necessary to thank Prof. Friedrich Wilhelm von Hermann and Dr. Heidegger for help with deciphering passages which were difficult to make out. We gratefully thank Dr. Hartmut Tietjen for countless instruction regarding formal and textual composition of the lecture course, for transcription of notes and sketches of the lectures (Appendix) that were very difficult to read and for reading through for corrections; we thank Jutta Heidegger, Torsten Steiger, and Dr. Mark Michalski for their generous assistance in working out the corrections.

Frankfurt/Main, August 1995   Matthias Jung
                                                              Thomas Regehly

Afterword of the Editor of the Lecture Course Summer
Semester 1921 and of the Outlines and Sketches 1918–19

The bibliographical main title of volume 60 is taken from a school binder in which Heidegger had bound his 1918–19 studies of the phenomenology of religion. On the second page is found the original title: "Phenomenology of Religious Consciousness." Later the word "consciousness" is crossed out by Heidegger and replaced with the word "life." This earlier title is also found in his letter of May 1, 1919, to Elisabeth Blochmann: "My own work is very concentrated, basic and concrete: basic problems of the phenomenolog[ical] method, becoming free from the last shackles of acquired positions—constant new progress toward the real origins, preparations for the phenomenology of religious consciousness—firmly geared up for intensive, high-quality academic effectiveness, constant learning in the company of Husserl" (*Martin Heidegger–Elisabeth Blochmann, Letters 1918–1969,* edited by Joachim W. Storck, Marbach on the Neckar, 1989, p. 16). That Heidegger speaks of "preparations" in respect to his studies of the phenomenology of religion probably refers to the announcement of Heidegger's planned lecture course of Winter Semester 1919–1920, "The Philosophical Foundations of Medieval Mysticism." But beyond that it seems to indicate in general a longer-standing project, for, next to the basic problems, the phenomenology of religion is the only concrete problem that Heidegger seems to "approach" at this time.

*

The original text of the Summer Semester 1921 three-hour lecture "Augustine and Neo-Platonism" consists of nineteen handwritten pages in folio format. Along the left side Heidegger wrote the progressive text, on the right side he left room for notes, insertions, citations, supplements, as well as explanations of the translations. In the interpreting part of the lecture manuscript are found fifteen to twenty—on one page even thirty—marginal notes per page: many of them not only underneath one another, but also in outlined bundles next to each other, often again with further insertions and supplements, and, accordingly, most of the time with a loss of grammatical congruence. The high number of these associative notes probably has to be explained by reference to the oscillation between the progress of the interpretation and a deepening reading. Except with the insertions, the marginal notes are without clear reference to the continuous text. These references could be established only by attending to the relations of content and by considering the spatial nearness (parallel lines, position of the text) to the paragraphs Heidegger made. In order to make the differentiation between the text itself and the marginal notes clear to the reader, the notes were consistently rendered in round brackets and pushed to the end of the respective paragraph. Inside the round brackets, the single notes were separated by dashes. The order of the notes was again measured by the context of thought and the spatial nearness. In those cases in which additions and insertions afforded no integration into the text at all or impeded the interpretive flow, footnotes were introduced. If Heidegger himself used round brackets, these were in all cases changed to parentheses. Square brackets were used above all for Heidegger's explications inside citations; in a few, easily recognizable cases [they were used] also for conjectures of the editor. The editor completed the punctuation, which was often given only sparingly in the manuscript. Passages in the manuscript which could not be deciphered (missing passages) are marked in the text with square-bracketed ellipses, and, in addition, the missing numbers of words or syllables are indicated in starred footnotes. Questionable readings are indicated with question marks in square brackets.

For the transcription of the original handwritten manuscript, a copy by Dr. Hartmut Tietjen was available to me. Also helpful were the handwritten notations of Oskar Becker, Fritz Schalk, and Karl Löwith. All of these writings were repeatedly collated.

All titles were given by the editor. Most of the time they are phrases out of the interpreted text or prominent formulations in the lecture manuscript.

Regarding Appendix I: Some supplements indicated through cross-references that Heidegger must already have made a large number of sketches—above all on the problem of *tentatio*. These were found in a collection that Heidegger apparently put together again in preparation for his seminar "Augustine, Confessions XI (on time)" (WS 1930–31). Because they represent a central theme of the lecture course and with reasonable certainty also belong to the preparations for the lecture, which the notations also make clear, they are presented in print in this volume. All of these notes and sketches have been transcribed for the first time. The location for all of the employed citations was established; the citation follows the edition of Migne.

Regarding Appendix II: Since Heidegger went beyond his prepared text several times during the lecture course, I adopted a number of supplementary notes from Oskar Becker's extensive notations. For the "overview of the phenomena" there was, in the aforementioned fascicle, a scanty blueprint on a small piece of paper. It holds the same for all of these supplements as it does for the lecture course notations and sketches: for all citations, the source-locations had to be established.

On the third part of the volume: The already mentioned fascicle, "Phenomenology of Religious Life," consists of twenty-two sheets. For the transcription I had available a copy, probably from Fritz Heidegger.

The sheets begin with the first notes on the never-held lecture course "The

Philosophical Foundations of Medieval Mysticism." Heidegger had announced such a lecture course for Winter Semester 1919–1920. The manuscript that was left behind makes it known that he began working it out on August 10, 1919, and on August 14 attempted a continuation and then broke it off. On August 30, 1919, Heidegger requested from the Department of Liberal Arts a change in the lecture course: "In setting up the plans, the undersigned had counted on a longer autumn break. In the current conditions, however, a working-through of the material—one that meets stringent demands—for the announced lecture course "The Philosophical Foundations of Medieval Mysticism" is impossible. The undersigned requests therefore permission, instead of the aforementioned lecture course, to change the lecture course otherwise announced as a one-hour course on "Selected Problems of Pure Phenomenology" into a two-hour course under the title: "Fundamental Problems of Phenomenology," Tuesdays and Fridays from 4–5 o'clock (for beginners) with additional colloquium Tuesday from 6–7:30." (University Archive of Freiburg, documents on "Philosophical Seminars," call no. B 1/3348).

The non-chronological ordering of the sheets, which in this printing is maintained, may be understood in that the further notes have been assigned to the planned lecture course. Work on mysticism had indeed already been announced in the concluding chapter of the *Habilitationsschrift*.

In regard to the study of the absolute inspired by a philosophy of religion fragment by Adolf Reinach, it is to be mentioned that Heidegger cited the manuscript of this fragment. It is possible that the manuscript was made accessible to Heidegger by Husserl. The manuscript was partly published in 1921 in the introduction to the Collected Works of Reinach by Hedwig Conrad Martius. A complete verification of the citations was first made possible through the critical edition by Karl Schuhmann.

∗

The phenomenological interpretation of the three *tentationes* is the focus of the interpretation of the tenth book of the *Confessions*. Heidegger worked out here what he would later carry out in *Sein und Zeit [Being and Time]* as the existential analytic of fallenness.

Discussion of the "falling of a purely self-worldly directed significance into the surrounding-worldly significance, and, within it, in the faded strata of the mostly secondarily carried along" (*Phänomenologie der Anschauung und des Ausdrucks [Phenomenology of Intuition and Expression]*, ed. by author, GA volume 59, p. 84; cf. p. 37) is already found in the lecture course of Summer Semester 1920. But this "falling" remains comparatively external as opposed to the inner temptation of life itself and thus does not yet reach the full phenomenon of fallenness.

The question of historical development of Heidegger's intentions regarding a phenomenological interpretation of *tentatio* in Augustine leads back to the lecture course from Winter Semester 1919–1920, in which Heidegger once briefly mentions that Christianity is the deepest historical paradigm for a particular possibility of factical life, namely for "transposing the principal points of factical life and of the lifeworld in the self-world and in the world of inner experience" (*Grundprobleme der Phänomenologie [Basic Problems of Phenomenology]*, ed. by Hans-Helmuth Gander, GA volume 58, p. X). And a little later Heidegger continues, "Only to these newly emerging basic motives of a new position of the self-world is it comprehensible why we encounter in Augustine something like his *Confessions* and *City of God. Crede, ut intelligas* [Have faith, so that you understand]: live your self vivaciously—and knowledge is first erected on the basis of this experience, your last and fullest experience of self. Augustine saw in '*inquietum cor nostrum*' [our unsettled heart] the great unstoppable distress of life" (ibid., p. 62).

That Heidegger in no way gave up his interest in Augustine after turning to Aristotle—a seminar on "De Anima" in the same semester and the lecture courses in the following semesters—as is occasionally asserted, is shown by a remark from the first Marburg lecture (Winter Semester 1923–24). The latter shows that to him all of these problems which he already indicated in this lecture course on Augustine—for instance the ambiguous tendency of Augustine toward axiologization—still occupied him, and indeed as much in the material problematic as in regard to their historical effects: "It also clear that just as ἀληθής fell to *verum* [the true] and *certum* [the certain], the ἀγαθόν has undergone up to the present a process of decay [*Verfall*], to the point where it becomes determined as value. I will draw out the most important points about these connections in the Augustine lecture course, and indeed in the analysis of the Augustinian concepts of *summum bonum, fides, timor castus, gaudium, peccatum, delectatio* [the highest good, faith, chaste fear, joy, sin, delight]. In Augustine are centered various possibilities of the kind whose efficacy extends to the Middle Ages and modernity." (*Einführung in die phänomenologische Forschung [Introduction to Phenomenological Research]*, ed. by F.-W. von Hermann, GA volume 17, p. X.)

*

During the work on this edition, I have often remembered the maxim of Hotho, editor of Hegel's aesthetic. It had been his endeavor, he says in the preface, to give the lectures a "bookly character and context."

In order to achieve this goal, much support was needed. I am very grateful to Dr. Hermann Heidegger, who worked on especially stubborn problems of deciphering, which only he was able to solve. Likewise, I thank Prof. Dr.

Friedrich-Wilhelm von Hermann for his additional collation of the extended supplemental material, and that means as well gratitude for many improvements. The same goes for Dr. Hartmut Tietjen, who looked through the proofs at various stages, and to whom fell the task of final editor of the entire volume—a task that includes considering everything together. I am also thankful to Mrs. Jutta Heidegger for her collaboration with the reading for corrections, as well as Dr. Mark Michalski, who double-checked all Latin and Greek citations. And finally a special thanks goes to Dr. Andreas Preussner and Mr. Georg Scherer for their all-encompassing assistance that was never restricted to the "letter."

Cologne, August 1995 Claudius Strube

Glossary of Key Terms

Ansatz: starting point
Bedeutsamkeit: significance
Bedeutung: meaning
Bekümmerung, bekümmern; *curare*: concern, to concern oneself; to be concerned
Berufung, Beruf: calling; vocation
Betrachtung: study
Betrachtungen: studies, considerations
Bezugssinn: relational sense
cupiditas: lust, avarice
concupiscentia, Begierlichkeit: desire (lust)
Dasein: existence; Dasein
delectatio: delight
Einstellung; Einstellung- . . . ; einstellungsmäßig: attitude, attitudinal . . . ; attitudinal
Erfahrung; Erlebnis: experience
Erkenntnis; Erkenntnis . . . , erkenntnismäßig: knowledge; cognitive
Evangelium: gospel; evangelism
frui: enjoyment
Gegenstand: object; thing [if contrasted with *Objekt*]
Gegenständlichkeit: objecthood
gegenständlich werden: becoming an object
Gegenwärtigung: presentation (to myself)
Geschäftigkeit: bustling activity
Gewesensein: having-been
Grund . . . : basic, fundamental
Haltung: posture
illecebra: allurement
Kenntnisnahme: taking-cognizance-of
Mitwelt, mitweltlich: communal world, communal-worldly
Not: anguish
Objektivität: objectivity
Objektität: objectity
sachhaltig, Sach . . . : material
Sachlage: situation of the material
selbstlich: selfly
Sinn: sense; meaning
Sinnzusammenhang: complex of sense; sense-complex
Umwelt, umweltlich: surrounding world, surrounding-worldly
Urchristentum: primordial Christianity
Verfall, Abfall, verfallen: falling, to fall (into)
Vergegenwärtigung: representation (to myself)
Verlockungen: lures
Verkündigung: proclamation
Vollzug; vollzugsmäßig: enactment; enactmental, in the manner of enactment
Vollzugssinn: sense of enactment
vollzugsgeschichtlich: in historical enactment; enactment-historical
Vollzugszusammenhang: complex of enactment; enactmental complex
Vorstellung, vorstellungsmäßig: idea, ideational
voluptas: pleasure

Vorgriff: foreconception
Zerstreuung: dispersion
Zusammenhang: complex; connection; context
Zwiespältigkeit: conflicted nature, conflict